In his authoritative Introduction, Mr. Peel discusses the social history of Spencer's provincial background, the cross-currents of nineteenth-century thought, and the philosophical aspects of Spencer's ethics. He examines the interconnections between Spencer's biological, philosophical, and sociological concerns, and his former and continuing influence as a sociologist.

The editor stresses both the relevance of Spencer's concepts for the contemporary advance of theories of modernization, and the need for caution among those who would retrace his steps. We have inherited a great deal from Herbert Spencer, Mr. Peel concludes, but in facing the heritage of sociology we must be prepared "to reject it as well as to revive and develop it." Consideration of Spencer's important writings on social evolution is basic to either decision.

J. D. Y. PEEL graduated from Balliol College, Oxford, with first class honors, and received his Ph.D. from the London School of Economics, where he is lecturer in sociology. He has taught at Nottingham University, and is the author of *Aladura: A Religious Movement among the Yoruba* and *Herbert Spencer: The Evolution of a Sociologist.*

Herbert Spencer

ON SOCIAL EVOLUTION

THE HERITAGE OF SOCIOLOGY

A Series Edited by Morris Janowitz

Herbert Spencer

ON SOCIAL EVOLUTION

Selected Writings

Edited and with an Introduction by

J. D. Y. PEEL

THE UNIVERSITY OF CHICAGO PRESS

CHICAGO AND LONDON

THE UNIVERSITY OF CHICAGO PRESS, CHICAGO 60637
THE UNIVERSITY OF CHICAGO PRESS, LTD., LONDON

Printed in the United States of America
ISBN: 0–226–76891 (clothbound); 0–226–76892–9 (paperbound)
Library of Congress Catalog Card Number: 76–172616

Contents

IV. EVOLUTION IN GENERAL

V. THE ANALYSIS OF INSTUTITIONS

VI. THE END OF THE CENTURY

Introduction

Herbert Spencer (1820–1903) was the first, and probably remains the greatest, person to have written sociology, so-called, in the English language. He is also, despite the recent revival of interest in him, the most neglected of the classical sociologists. The chief difficulty for the selector of Spencer is that he was not just a sociologist but only came to sociology as wider ethical and philosophical concerns prompted him. His sociology, it is essential to remember, is contained within a universal system of knowledge; and Spencer judged the unity of this System of Synthetic Philosophy to be of great importance. A degree of misrepresentation is therefore inevitable in severing the sociology from the metaphysics, ethics, psychology, and biology. The two chief purposes of this introduction, however, are to place the sociology within the whole and to relate it to the unique social and intellectual context which produced it. It is not yet possible for us properly to determine the place of Spencer within the tradition of European social and ethical thought that led to modern sociology.

The question of how we might benefit from a rereading of Spencer is inseparable from our conceptions of what sociology is and ought to be. The oldest and also the most enduring debate within the subject concerns how far sociology can be one of the sciences. Spencer's voice is prominent among those who maintain that sociology can truly be, in all essentials, a science of society as there are sciences of nature. This may be held to be the orthodox view among sociologists, despite a ragged but continuous note of dissent. A revival of interest in Spencer, however, presents difficulties for such a view. Either sociology has been ludicrously unsuccessful at being a science like other sciences, or there are important ways in which such claims are forever unsubstantiable. For since the natural sciences aim at the gradual, cumulative improvement of their understanding of nature, a sign of their success is that, though there may have been greater geniuses in the past, today's run-of-the-mill scientists have a far better understanding. Whatever may be the point of rereading Boyle, Newton, or Lavoisier, it is not the contemporary advance of their subjects. Hence A. N. Whitehead's admonition that "sciences which hesitate to forget their founders are lost"; hence too the widespread belief among sociologists (that is yet so belied by their practice) that the history of sociology is quite another thing from, and perhaps utterly irrelevant to, the ongoing creation of sociological theory.[1]

But perhaps the present situation—the still dubious status of sociology's achievements qua science, and sociologists' continual preoccupation with their founding fathers in a manner that resembles contemporary philosophers' relations with Plato and Hume—should not be deplored as the outcome of sociologists' delinquencies at all. A logical distinction may be maintained between the history of sociology and sociological theory, but nonetheless their connections are significant for both. A possible connection but, as it seems to me, one of the less important, is that there may be truths important for contemporary theory that we have forgotten and can relearn from the classics. If this were so, it would imply that something had gone badly wrong indeed with the development of sociology. In the case of Spencer, the most that can be claimed in this respect is that we have rediscovered for ourselves the importance of topics such as social change which engaged him and subsequently fell into relative neglect; and that we are fortifying ourselves in this rediscovery by proclaiming the importance of such early theorists of social evolution as Spencer.

1 Cf. R. K. Merton, *Social Theory and Social Structure*, rev. ed. (Glencoe, Ill.: Free Press, 1957), p. 4. This judgment is qualified somewhat in his more recent "On the History and Systematics of Sociological Theory," in *On Theoretical Sociology* (New York: Free Press, 1967).

The relevance of the past for ongoing theory in sociology is due to the necessarily close relationship between the sociologist and his own age. This has two aspects:

1. Sociologists aspire to produce a theory that is universal in scope, and hope that collectively they will build up such a theory. However, their theoretical constructions betray the fact that they are dominated by the social forms of their own age. It is thus a major task of each generation of sociologists to free itself from its initial dependence on models and theories which express prior social realities. (Our notions of "class" are a prime example of this.) Sociological argument, when it is not between contemporaries but is of the "debate with the ghost of X" type, is to be seen less as the replacement of one image of social reality by an intrinsically superior one, than as an attempt to establish a new image of a new reality. For our subject matter, society, changes as well as, if not more than, our theories. Hence we need to study our founding fathers critically against their contexts, precisely in order to bring out the uniqueness of our situation.

2. The stance of the sociologist vis-à-vis his data (and correspondingly the social functions of his work) is problematic and needs constantly to be reconsidered. Whereas a natural scientist may have any of a wide variety of motives for studying nature, these are not relevant to the formation of good theory, which is in the end simply theory that is isomorphic to the phenomenon studied. The discoverable laws of nature are what they are independently of what he or anyone else may think about them; they are not to be changed but rather obeyed if the physical world is to be manipulated to human ends. (For science continues to have social functions.) In the case of social sciences, however, we cannot begin to speak of laws in quite the same sense—as existing whatever we do and think about them—for our actions *are* the laws in operation. Consequently the ideas of the theorist cannot be wholly distinguished from the subject matter of his theories. The content of the theories is determined not just by the character of the social facts but by the purposes of the theorist: Is he studying in order to change or to preserve, or to understand others' beliefs which he finds puzzling, or to criticize by pointing out dis-

crepancies between ideals and practice? Do his categories reflect his own moral decisions and priorities or mirror his social allegiances? Since contemporary society is the primary subject matter of sociology, the same social context furnishes both the theorist's purposes and his theme.

At this point, if the argument convinces, people tend to replace questions about validity by questions about commitment; as one New Left writer has put it, the question "How can I know that I am right?" is more easily reformulated as, "What purposes shall I pursue?"[2] But it is *not* the same question, and it would be premature to abandon the question of validity. We may need to start from purposes, but study should enable us to reflect critically upon them and the categories implied by them. The dialectic that this gives rise to is the essence of sociological argument. The adequate critique of our present purposes and theories involves contrasting them with former purposes and theories, especially since most of our theoretical baggage is inherited. The history of sociology is thus integral to the explicit formulation of purposes and theories in each generation. We must at least take pause from the fact that while evolution has been revived in a strikingly Spencerian form, Spencer's social purposes, which were integral to his conception, and peculiarly the offspring of his age, cannot command our support.

Before examining the substance of Spencer's thought in the light of his own social context, it may be helpful to present an overview of the chief elements of his system which will merit our attention. First there is that aspect which was immediately and permanently absorbed into the sociological tradition, so much so that we forget that we owe it to Spencer: the notions of structure, function, system, and equilibrium, which, though derived from his organic analogy, have become part of our basic terminology. Second there is his conceptualization of change, especially his theory that evolutionary change consists fundamentally of a process of differentiation. This is a pregnant idea whose implications and limitations have hardly been properly explored. Third,

2 Thus N. Harris, *Beliefs in Society* (London: Watts, 1968), p. 253.

there are the typologies he created to define the differences between societies: militancy and industrialism; simple, compound, and doubly compound societies. Fourth, there are the mechanisms he puts forward to explain the process: adaptation to the environment in a Lamarckian manner both by men as individuals and by institutions, and, to a lesser extent, adaptation through Darwinian natural selection. Fifth, there are the moral assumptions and inferences that Spencer associates with the system: political liberalism of a thoroughgoing variety, broadly utilitarian ethics, etc. Sixth, there are the methodological principles which pervade the whole: methodological individualism, positivism, rejection of history, particular conceptions of nature and of science. As they are put forward in Spencer's writings, these various elements form a very coherent unity. But it is the relations between them which are of most relevance to our contemporary interests.

The Cultural Origins

Spencer was certainly a great original, but he also belongs firmly to a tradition which produced the three most significant works of pre-sociology: Smith's *Wealth of Nations*, Millar's *Distinction of Ranks* and Ferguson's *History of Civil Society*. But in Spencer's case it is better to regard the tradition as one of distinctive social experience rather than merely as a line of intellectual descent. It was the urban, provincial, and Dissenting experience of the Industrial Revolution.

Derby, Spencer's birthplace, was an old county town which in the half-century before his birth had developed into a middle-sized industrial center.[3] His father, a private school teacher of modest means, was attached to the Wesleyan Methodist body, though he was rationalist in temper and an attender at Quaker meetings; and except for his uncle Thomas, an Evangelical parson with a rural

3 On this background cf. R. S. Fitton and A. P. Wadsworth, *The Strutts and the Arkwrights 1758–1830* (Manchester University Press, 1958); also treated at length with detailed reference to Spencer in J. D. Y. Peel, *Herbert Spencer: the Evolution of a Sociologist* (London: Heinemann, 1971).

parish near Bath, Herbert's relatives were Methodists or Dissenters. Within the town the Spencers belonged to the radical section of the Liberals, whose leaders were the Strutts, wealthy Unitarian manufacturers equally responsible for the industrial transformation of society and for the gradual reordering of its cultural and political life. So it was appropriate that the young Herbert should, on finishing his full-time education with his uncle Thomas (who was a close associate of Cobden, Bright, and other leaders of nationwide middle-class radicalism), both become a railway engineer, on and off from 1837 to 1848, and involve himself in radical politics. He was involved in three movements in particular, with overlapping memberships: the Anti-Corn Law League, under Cobden, with its demand that in Britain the common interests of the "industrial classes" should take precedence over what was presented as the selfish "class legislation" of the landed aristocracy; the Complete Suffrage Union (whose Derby secretary Spencer was), led by the Birmingham Quaker Joseph Sturge, which aimed unsuccessfully at a joint program with the moderate Chartists; and the Anti-State Church Association, specifically a Dissenting pressure group led by Edward Miall of Leicester, editor of *The Nonconformist* (motto: "The Dissidence of Dissent"), which published Spencer's first significant work—the radically laissez-faire *Proper Sphere of Government* (1842). The common thread was the opposition of radical provincial opinion to the traditional state, dominated by the aristocracy and an alien church. The 1840s were, however, the last period in which a significant middle-class leadership preferred to make common cause with their working-class fellow townsmen against the aristocratic state, rather than to be absorbed into the established system of deference in order to defend property. Spencer's later cantankerous refusal to accept any official honors was a survival of that provincial independence which Cobden reluctantly admitted was beginning to disappear by 1850.

The tradition of provincial radicalism goes back to the mid-eighteenth century. Joseph Priestley is the critical figure, remembered now more for his experimental chemistry than for his Unitarian theology or political philosophy. He developed the political theory of Dissent into a radical critique of established English society, and argued for the utilitarian principle, laissez-faire, the superiority of voluntary association, and the demand for competence rather than hereditary status or aristocratic clientage to determine social position. A close connection with Spencer can be established. For Spencer's father and the leading radicals of Derby were, from the 1780s to the 1830s, members of the Derby Philosophical Society, founded by Charles Darwin's grandfather Erasmus when he moved to Derby in 1783, and modeled on the famous Lunar Society of Birmingham, to which Priestley with other leading Midlands manufacturers, natural philosophers, and Dissenters belonged.[4] When Priestley's house was sacked in the Birmingham riots of 1791, and when he left England for Pennsylvania in 1794, the repercussions were felt in Derby. The ideals of the radicals, led by those "right true Jacobins," the Strutts, survived the repressive war years to reappear, enormously strengthened, in the 1830s and 1840s. The young Spencer's principles were essentially those of Priestley, and he shared with the Dissenter the ideal of a society with which he could fully identify, on different lines from the established social order yet already emergent from it.

Spencer is thus an outstanding exception to the thesis persuasively developed by R. A. Nisbet that the origins of sociology are to be sought in the line of conservative thought, beginning with Maistre and Bonald, that rejected the ideals of the Enlightenment and the French Revolution.[5] It is even argued that perhaps sociology as such has an intrinsic vested interest in certain "conservative" tenets: that society's fundamental problem is that of social order, and that society has some sort of moral or logical priority over the individual. Yet Spencer's closest affinities are with those outrunners of the Enlightenment—Priestley, Paine, and Godwin—and with the Scottish moralists; and like them he

4 R. S. Schofield, *The Lunar Society of Birmingham* (Oxford University Press, 1963), and E. Robinson, "The Derby Philosophical Society," *Annals of Science* 9 (1953).

5 R. A. Nisbet, *The Sociological Tradition* (London: Heinemann, 1967).

was more concerned with progress than with order, which indeed seemed to him less and less of a problem, and with the conditions of the individual's emancipation from social repression.

Now a curious feature of Enlightenment thought (which we think of as being, par excellence, a French creation) is that though it may have been most coherently and self-consciously expressed by Frenchmen, it was most rooted in widespread social experience in Britain. (The same was to be the case with proletarian socialism, as Marx observed). From Montesquieu through to Saint-Simon and Marx, emergent and actual social practice in England tended to be a model for the social blueprints which were drawn up before, during, and after the Revolution in France. Hence, sociology's British roots tend to derive, not from the vision of a conservative past or a revolutionary future in which the features of existing society were negated, but from concepts and judgments which stood in a close, often almost mimetic relationship to the present as experienced and perceived. The interpretation of the Industrial Revolution in its widest sense, in provincial radical circles whose ideals were those of the Enlightenment, provided the most basic materials from which Spencer elaborated his sociology.

The view of human nature expressed in these circles found confirmation in the facts of social change. The fundamental axiom of Enlightenment philosophy, sharply in contrast with that of the conservatives, was that men were essentially good and that their potential virtue was fast becoming actual—as fast, that is, as the demolition of traditional and corrupting institutions would allow: the traditional state, the established church, closed guilds and corporations, rigid systems of social deference. In the eighteenth century the ancient doctrine of man's Original Sin (and hence his need for institutions, particularly the state, to restrain him and make society possible) was effectively challenged for the first time; and its corollary was that philosophers might realistically enjoin mankind to be perfect. What had been in France a clearly antireligious ideology was in England clothed by Unitarians and others in the dress of a semisecularized Christianity. The Evangelical Revival (in itself a thoroughly anti-Enlightenment movement) could be used to strengthen the position. It was presented by Spencer and others as having contributed to man's perfectibility and the dispensability of institutions by having created internalized controls that rendered the external ones superfluous. (One should add that, though Spencer's outlook was always quite rationalist, the structure of his personality was stamped by his evangelical background). Against the coercive regulation of the traditional state they set the natural and spontaneous systems of cooperation formed by men in the course of fulfilling their desires for material satisfaction, art, company, religion, knowledge, love, and friendship. The distinction between state and society (perhaps the most basic prerequisite of sociology) became ever more salient. Paine's words sum up the general view: "Society and Government are different in themselves and have different origins. Society is produced by our wants and government by our wickedness. Society is in every state a blessing; government even in its best state but a necessary evil."[6]

Paine and Priestley were citizens of the French Republic; but their views could not be much more than aspiration in a country where Napoleon completed Louis XIV's work of state centralization. But the facts of English history seemed to indicate their progressive realization. Despite the importance of such factors as the English monarchy's earlier homogenization of the country, the stimulus to development of London's growth, the aristocracy's promotion of rationalized agriculture and hence investment surpluses, and, ultimately, the state's judicial containment of social protest, the "take-off," when it came, occurred away from the centers of power, in unincorporated towns and largely among semi-enfranchised groups like the Dissenters, and created novel forms of organization. It was unanticipated by the political elite, whose institutions were challenged and then transformed or swept away by it. In a very real sense it was shown that the motor of change

6 *Common Sense,* cited by W. Godwin, *Political Justice,* 2nd ed. (London, 1796), p. 125.

did lie outside the polity; and the polity itself was seen as a reflexion of new *social* relationships, whether as a superfluity or as a necessary instrument.

This was the situation which challenged social theorists in Britain (who were themselves mostly of the rising, innovating groups). It gave rise to a conflicting variety of more general theories of society, and theories about the nature of thought itself. A common view was that thought, at least general thought and political philosophy, is fairly epiphenomenal to social change—a view not perhaps congenial to philosophers, yet now widely voiced for the first time. The only exception is scientific ideas, particularly those of technological application; the Birmingham Lunar Society knew itself to be in the forefront of change. Thought itself is often viewed pragmatically, as borne up on the wings of social practice, or called into being by social requirements. In an age when events truly did outstrip the power of anyone to envisage them totally, it was fitting for Ferguson to write that "nations stumble upon establishments, which are indeed the result of human action, but not the execution of any human design."[7] Social progress derives, not from the conscious plans of society's rulers, but from innate principles of growth. Hence the powerful appeal of organic metaphors, casual enough in, say, Ferguson ("the seeds of every form are lodged in human nature; they spring up and ripen with the season"), but worked out in great detail by Spencer. Comte provides us with the sharpest contrast. Developing Saint-Simon's model for imitative industrialization and preoccupied with the breakdown of social order, he restores the primacy of the polity and makes philosophy the motor of social change. In England such positions were only taken reluctantly and under Comtean influence, as with J. S. Mill, until they were generally adopted much later in the nineteenth century, by which time Spencer was coming to seem an anachronism.

The real motor of change, if neither politics nor general ideas, was variously conceived. Four items may be distinguished,

7 *An Essay on the History of Civil Society* (Edinburgh University Press, 1966), pp. 122–23.

sometimes running into one another and sometimes contradictory —but all more akin to economic than to political behavior: namely, character, public opinion, the economic structure of society, and technology. Some saw individual character, as it developed, as the chief determinant ("the aggregate of men's instincts and sentiments," as Spencer put it). In its most cultural form, character was seen as public opinion, often conceived on the lines of demand in economics. George Eliot's novel *Felix Holt* contains a wonderfully Spencerian passage in which the hero, a radical Nonconformist watchmaker, acclaims public opinion as "the greatest power under heaven" and "the steam to work the engines [of political change]."[8] But the most striking exploration came from a Liberal Member of Parliament, W. A. Mackinnon, whose *Rise, Progress, and Present State of Public Opinion* (1828) explored the determinants of public opinion to find them in economic development and the growth of a middle class. Likewise, Richard Cobden, whose Anti-Corn League was an empirical exercise in the antipolitics of opinion and blatantly a middle-class movement, merely generalized from his own experience when he wrote that "what brings great changes of policy is the spontaneous shifting and readjustment of interests, not the rediscovery of new principles."[9] For we come at last to concepts of analysis—class and economic determinism—which have too long been associated exclusively with Marx, despite Marx's open acknowledgment of his indebtedness for them to spokesmen of the English bourgeoisie.

The new word *class* (in the sense of "social stratum") began to come into fairly general use by the 1790s, and implied a new social theory, or rather that the character of social divisions was changing.[10] Compared with its rivals *order*, *rank*, and *estate*, it

8 *Felix Holt: The Radical*, chap. 30.

9 J. Morley, *The Life of Richard Cobden*, 13th ed. (London: Fisher Unwin, 1906), p. 406.

10 Cf. S. Ossowski, *Class Structure in the Social Consciousness* (London: Routledge and Kegan Paul, 1963); A. Briggs, "The Language of Class in Nineteenth Century England," in A. Briggs and J. Saville, eds., *Democracy and the Labour Movement* (London: Macmillan, 1960); and H. J. Perkin, *The Origins of Modern English Society 1780–1880* (London: Routledge and Kegan Paul, 1969), pp. 21–32.

stressed mobility rather than stability of social position, and achievement over ascription. On these points Mill's essay *The Spirit of the Age* (1831) suggests that the ideals of middle-class Dissent, above all the "career open to the talents," were becoming social reality. Class implied economic determinism in the sense that wealth increasingly determined power, rather than the reverse as in the semibureaucracy of the aristocratic state with its "placemen" and sinecures—the "Old Corruption." With the Scottish moralists, as of course with Marx, economic determinism became a key for the interpretation of universal history; and a hostile review of Comte in the *Economist* (the influential liberal journal of which Spencer became a sub-editor) declared that "unerring natural laws determine [the distribution of wealth] . . . [and hence] all the subordinate phenomena of society."[11] Finally class came to imply a society horizontally divided according to interest, rather than one united by vertical bonds of deference running up from "the lower orders" and "the middling ranks" to "those of better station." It was the manufacturers who produced for an impersonal market, and not the professionals who were personal clients to the aristocracy, who were able to break deference and assert a distinctively middle-class consciousness. Only by the 1840s had the concept *class*, originally a middle-class instrument against the aristocracy, become an indicator of the widening gulf between the radical working-class Chartists and their erstwhile political allies. Yet this division was more marked in London and Lancashire than in Spencer's native habitat, the towns of the Midlands.

The Creation of the Evolutionary Synthesis

Spencer moved to London in 1848, his post with the *Economist* giving him an adequate income, time to pursue his chosen career of writing, and opportunities of meeting the leaders of intellectual and cultural opinion in the capital. Yet his first book, *Social Statics*, is very much a justification of the ideals of provincial, Dissenting radicals of the 1840s. It is hardly a book of

11 The *Economist*, 10 Dec. 1853, p. 1386.

sociology, for the sociological ideas of the radical culture are presupposed rather than argued for or developed, and there is very little analysis of contemporary or any other society. In 1850 Spencer did not know much more about Comte than that he disagreed with him; and he disclaimed as titles both "sociology" and "social science," which tended to mean Owenite or socialist plans for the reorganization of society. The book is remote from that anxious concern with the gap between what Disraeli called "the two nations" which gave rise to the remarkable crop of "industrial novels" in the late 1840s. It is equally remote from the collection of statistics about topics like crime, poverty, housing conditions, drunkenness, sanitation, and mortality from which developed the distinguished tradition of empirical social science, which in Britain has often been a substitute for genuine sociology.

Instead, *Social Statics: or the Conditions essential to Human Happiness specified, and the First of them Developed* was a work of moral philosophy, and a naïve one at that (see chapter 1, this volume). Its first part sets out to show, by means of abstract argument, what the "Divine Will" (for this is the only one of Spencer's works that is deist) is for mankind. In a friendly critique of Benthamism, Spencer asserts that the greatest happiness is best secured by allowing every man the maximum liberty to exercise his faculties consistent with the possession of a like liberty by everyone else (see chapter 3, this volume). He demonstrates the implications of this principle in various fields, the result being an extreme Priestleian laissez-faire, with the state reduced to an absolute minimum. The name "social statics" (which owes nothing to Comte's use of it for a division of his sociology) refers to the fact that the perfect system of morality thus outlined will only be possible in the future when a "social state" is attained and men are naturally adjusted so that their desires do not conflict. Two intellectual affinities are manifest here: first, with Thomas Hodgskin, the radical individualist and Ricardian socialist, Spencer's superior at the *Economist*, who had already defined the task of moral science as the delineation of a system of unrealized *perfect* morality; and second, with William Godwin, who in *Political Justice* (1792) described a "social state" in which government ("that brute engine which has been the only perennial cause of the vices of mankind") would wither away and mankind would become capable of free and voluntary cooperation. We happen to know that Godwin's book, which provoked Malthus' attempted refutation, was read and admired in radical circles in Derby.

But the work becomes sociologically interesting because of a secondary argument that Spencer used. He criticized the typical Enlightenment theories of "human nature" on the grounds that human nature was evidently highly variable; hence, the ideal could not be inferred from the existent forms of it but must be an unrealized perfection. But by making the variable existing forms of human nature into stages of mankind's long-term "adaptation to the social state," he could both reconcile unity with variety (which had been Bentham's major problem) and underpin the abstractly demonstrated perfect morality with quasi-sociological evidence that it was coming to pass (see chapter 2, this volume). Spencer pictures human history as one long process of mankind's "adaptation" to the requisites of perfect social life, when all men could be free because all would be altruistic. But things bad in themselves, such as the coercive state, are not wholly bad because they both express an imperfect nature and help to socialize it. Spencer is thus able to explain phenomena that earlier radical moralists had merely condemned. It is clearly implied, however, that the perfect morality is soon to be realized: in England, at least, coercive institutions have done their work, and advanced spirits are both displaying a developed altruism (e.g. Quaker humanitarianism, pacifism, hostility to capital punishment, penal reform) and demanding ever greater popular liberties (free trade, a free press, abolition of the state church and of censorship, universal suffrage). In an industrial nation these things—closer to the perfect morality—are actually fitter. Above all, the state, "begotten by necessity out of evil," will virtually disappear. Progress is therefore not "an accident, but a beneficent necessity," and the demonstration of an ethical system has come to require the proof of its historical inevitability (see chapter 4 this volume). Ethics is made to depend on sociology; and the sociology is essentially concerned with change.

Yet much of the evidence for the alleged process of adaptation to the social state derives not from sociological but from biological reasoning. Civilization (meaning a process rather than a state) is "all of a piece with the development of the embryo or the unfolding of a flower"; the necessity of adaptation is proved by its universal occurrence in nature. How did Spencer come to biologize the Enlightenment's faith in progress? Belief in the uniformity of natural processes he derived from his father. And we may suspect that, when Lyell's *Principles of Geology* convinced him of the truth of Lamarckian evolution, he was recalled to the evolutionary beliefs of the "Darwinians" of Derby (as the members of the Philosophical Society were known, after their founder). Evolution in a popular, teleological form had been put about by the anonymous *Vestiges of the Natural History of Creation* (1843), and Spencer's was one voice among many to express evolutionary ideas in the 1850s.[12] Curiously, the biologists were the most sceptical—particularly T. H. Huxley, whom Spencer first met in 1852 and with whom he maintained a long and fruitful friendship. After *Social Statics* Spencer turned to develop his ideas on biological evolution, reading new biological work extensively (especially Milne-Edwards on animal morphology and von Baer on embryology) and attending scientific lectures in London. The effect was chiefly to draw out and develop ideas already contained in *Social Statics.*

An important series of essays followed. "A Theory of Population" (1852) put forward the view that population pressure, far from being the obstacle to human perfectibility, is its only guarantee, since it alone forces organisms to be fit to survive and encourages more elaborate forms of cooperation—a truly Godwinian revenge on Malthus (see chapter 5, this volume). As will be seen, Spencer was further than he and others have thought from anticipating the theory of natural selection, for his notion of adaptation was Lamarckian. This essay was followed by "The Social Orga-

12 Cf. C. C. Gillispie, *Genesis and Geology* (Harvard University Press, 1951), and G. Himmelfarb, *Darwin and the Darwinian Revolution* (London: Chatto and Windus, 1959).

nism" (1854), putting forward both the static comparison of societies and organism in terms of the division of labor (reintroduced to the social sciences from Milne-Edwards's biology), and their common development through differentiation (as proposed by von Baer) (see chapter 7, this volume). We also find a theme endlessly reiterated elsewhere: the condemnation of statist intervention in social process on the grounds that it interferes with "natural" processes of "growth." Finally, in "Progress: its Law and Cause" (1857), Spencer attempts to show how progress in all spheres—sociology, biology, psychology, and astronomy—conforms to an identical pattern consisting of a transformation from a chaotic homogeneity to an ordered heterogeneity, which proceeds from one fundamental principle: the tendency of a single cause to produce multiple effects (see chapter 6, this volume). In 1858 he issued the prospectus for what was to be the great obsession of the remainder of his long life—the System of Synthetic Philosophy, a compendium of knowledge demonstrating the universality of evolution in all spheres and culminating in ethics. *The Principles of Psychology* he had already written (1855), but it was to reappear, at twice its length, within the system; and the opening volume of metaphysics, *First Principles*, was issued in 1862 (see chapter 8, this volume).

The sociological bearings of this tour de force are not at once clear. It is utterly independent of Darwin's *Origin of Species* (1859) and offers, not an application of it, but something quite different: not a simple mechanism to explain how species evolve, but both a description and explanation of the pattern of the evolving cosmos, in whole and in parts. Natural selection, though accepted, was a late and superfluous element in a system that was essentially Lamarckian.[13] The Lamarckian principle that acquired characteristics may be transmitted to descendants (which Spencer

13 Spencer is more often misunderstood on his treatment of struggle and natural selection than on any other topic (e.g. P. Abrams, *Origins of British Sociology* [University of Chicago Press, 1968], pp. 67–68; Harris, *Rise of Anthropological Theory* [London: Routledge and Kegan Paul, 1969], pp. 105–6, 120, 125). On his view of the role of struggle in evolution, see below, chap. 17.

was still stubbornly defending in the 1890s when nearly all biologists had renounced it) was crucial because it alone permitted a plausible unity to be claimed between the subject matters of sociology and natural science. Although natural selection might be applied to some social phenomena by Bagehot in *Physics and Politics* and by many "social Darwinists," the dominant cultural mode is one by which learned or acquired traits are passed on, as Spencer had maintained in the "Theory of Population." Because of his Lamarckism, Spencer is even able to talk about the Americanization of Irish immigrants and their descendants in a chapter on inheritance in the *Principles of Biology*.[14] The fundamental thing was to insist on the overriding unity of organic and superorganic processes, and hence on the unity of science. Why was this?

Though Spencer emphatically rejected the label, there is one sense in which he was, like Comte, a positivist. He wanted a rational foundation for ethics at a time when their traditional religious base no longer commanded adequate support, and he did in fact call his work the "secularization" of ethics. The crisis of authority was far less acute than it had seemed to Comte in France, but Spencer tackled it in a similar way. Positivism asserted two things which are today, properly, understood to be incompatible: that sociology should yield ethical principles and that it should be rigorously scientific. By contrast, some modern positivists have insisted on the literal meaninglessness of moral language. But for Comte and Spencer the appeal of science was that it had *authority*, that it could and did *compel* assent, which was just where existing systems of ethics failed. As science was the knowledge of nature, an authoritative analysis of the moral realm was only possible if its subject matter were shown to be part of nature; and this was Spencer's fundamental assertion about society. The "laws" which he sought to discover were, contradictorily, both invariate statements of relationships between phenomena, holding willy-nilly, and injunctions to men to act in particular ways. Evolution circumvented the dangerous inconclusiveness of moral argument by pur-

14 See *Principles of Biology* 1:248.

porting to show how morality was guaranteed by a necessary, scientifically demonstrated process of change. Organic processes were given a moral cachet: the moral principles were read into nature.

In *First Principles*, coming out during the debate between science and religion that followed Darwin's bombshell, Spencer was distinctly conciliatory to religion, though he restricted its proper scope to that of reminding mankind that there was an Unknowable entity behind all the phenomena of science (see chapter 20, this volume). And well he might be, for his own system was essentially a naturalistic theodicy whose enormous appeal was that it integrated and placed within a single framework a confusing welter of experience. Jack London's autobiographical novel *Martin Eden* best illustrates this aspect of Spencer. Spencer's message that, despite appearances, order existed and change was necessarily progress (a view he later revised) must have been like balm to a generation which had undergone an unprecedented explosion both of their social world and of their vision of nature. Nonetheless, Christian providence lay behind Spencer's evolutionary progress and predestination behind his smiling secular necessity.

Analytical and Methodological Principles

For some years after *First Principles* Spencer was occupied with other things than sociology, except for the occasional article lamenting the trend toward "collectivism" in social and public affairs. But after completing the revision of the *Psychology* (1872) he decided, on the prompting of E. L. Youmans, his chief promoter in America (where he was now beginning to make a tremendous impression), to bring out a general volume defining the nature of this novel subject. Then he would proceed with the *Principles of Sociology*. First coming out in serial form in 1872–73, *The Study of Sociology* was and remains one of the most important statements on the methods and the social bearings of sociology.

As the opening chapter, "Our need of it," makes clear, Spencer intended to affect practice (see chapter 9, this volume). He wished to reduce faith in the power of governments by showing how impossible it is to foretell the remoter consequences of human actions. At times, especially when mocking the scientific ignorance of politicians educated in the classics, he seems to hold out hope for a future in which a fuller knowledge of sociology will permit rational public planning and positive legislation. But he also uses the organic model of society to suggest that the positive acts of politicians will be either harmful or superfluous. He "naturalizes" society and suggests it is governed by immanent principles of growth, valid independently of the wills of men, which should never, and ultimately *can* never, be disrupted by interventionary actions. Society is not a machine or the manufacture of human purposes. In another aspect the organic anology is the parent of functionalism (and that involving a theory of social change too), in that it bids the sociologist look on society as an interdependent system of specialized parts, acting together to bring about society's adaptation to the environment.

Hence, the organic analogy commits Spencer to a holistic vision of the social system, rather in the manner of Comte, from whom he took the term *consensus* (meaning the coordination of subsystems rather than the normative compliance of individuals). But unlike Comte he also adopted the methodological principle that the whole, or aggregate, was to be explained in terms of the character of its units. Both Comte and Spencer believed that methodological individualism implied political liberalism:[15] "Society exists for the benefit of its members. The claims of the body politic are nothing in themselves, and become something only insofar as they embody the claims of its component individuals." In practice, however, he departed from this methodology; for although he always maintained that society evolved only as fast as the character of individuals, in becoming more social and

15 Further on this topic see S. Lukes, "Methodological Individualism," *British Journal of Sociology* 19 (1968); E. Gellner, "Holism and Individualism in History and Sociology," in P. Gardiner, ed., *Theories of History* (Glencoe, Ill.: Free Press, 1959); and W. H. Dray, "Holism and Individualism in History and Social Science," in *The Encyclopedia of Philosophy*, ed. P. Edwards, 1967.

altruistic, permitted it to, he also allowed for a reciprocal influence of institutions on character, and even for situational constraints (such as population pressure or the presence of hostile alien societies). His statement that "the individual citizen [is] imbedded in the social organism as one of its units, moulded by its influence and aiding reciprocally to remould it," is unexceptionable—but says very little. A tendency is clear, however: to see change as arising from relatively unmanipulable, steadily evolving factors, from culture and personality (to use modern terms) rather than from structural constraints or incentives. It enables him to make an ideological point against socialists, who wanted by "alchemy" to get noble actions out of ignoble natures. "Forms of government are valuable only when they are products of national character. No cunningly devised political arrangements will of themselves do anything."

It is certainly true that organic imagery was mostly used in the nineteenth century by conservatives and by radicals who criticized liberal capitalist society in terms of an idealized "organic community" of the past—figures like Ruskin or William Morris.[16] But the image itself does not dictate what may be inferred from it; hence perhaps its evergreen appeal. The conservatives, who tended to be those who wanted a strong and active state, made two simple inferences. First, as highly developed organisms have large brains, so complex societies need strong governments (and Spencer was often "refuted" on this ground). Second, a vague parallel was drawn between the functional unity of a living body and the supposed integration of traditional society in contrast to the dissensus and competition of industrial society. Spencer merely drew out different aspects of the analogue: growth, as against manufacture, to the support of laissez-faire, and integration seen in terms of the division of labor. Hence, if all societies were organisms, industrial society was the most so since its specialized parts were more subtly interdependent.

Unlike most other users of the analogy, Spencer also itemizes

16 On "organic" see R. Williams, *Culture and Society 1780–1950* (Harmondsworth: Penguin Books, 1961), pp. 256–57.

the respects in which a society is not like an organism; and at times he treats the analogy as logically dispensable, being merely an expository device or a psychological stimulus. Elsewhere, especially in tracing out—sometimes to absurd lengths— the parallels between the sustaining, distributing, and regulating systems of organisms and societies, he seems to be asserting that the two are, virtually, different species of the same category. But his final and most subtle position is to assert an identity only at the most abstract level, having stripped off all superficial features; and here he anticipates modern systems theory in seeing organisms and societies as systems or structures of dependent functions, reciprocally acting to preserve an equilibrium with the environment (see chapter 14, this volume, and *Autobiography* 2:433–34). We are, of course, enormously indebted to Spencer for much of our basic language here. It is necessary to note two concepts which Spencer employed somewhat differently: (1) lacking the functional concept of role, he tended to see "structure" in a rather mechanical and literal fashion, rather after the manner of formal anatomy; (2) he used "equilibrium" to refer, not only to an instantaneous condition of the system, but to the long-term process of the adjustment of man and society to "the social state" and thus as almost synonymous with evolution itself.

Particularly in its emphasis on the fact of society's growth, the organic analogy was not just an ideological prop, nor the sum of a number of instructive parallels between society and organism, but something that followed directly from sociology's status as a science, which is *The Study of Sociology's* chief assertion. Probably Spencer was not wholly aware that he subscribed to a theory of nature as old as the Greeks and the earliest of sociology's forefathers, Thucydides: knowledge or science can only be had of what is constant and unchanging; hence the knowable "nature" of anything is an essence or reality beneath the phenomena; change is either random and unknowable, or the development of the fixed existing potential (otherwise the *telos*). The irony is that Spencer considered his own theory of evolution to be nonteleological compared with, say, that of Erasmus Darwin or the *Vestiges*. But in fact the *telos* of human history is "the social state," to which mankind is *necessarily* adapting itself; but its necessity is either unjustifiable, or depends, as it were, on a "pull" exerted by the social state—a function become a pseudo-cause. In *Social Statics* Spencer almost seems to see the social state as a fulfillment of a preexisting disposition; and he continually asserts an identity between processes in which the outcome is predetermined (like an embryo's maturation) and those in which it is not (like socialization or social evolution). The more the latter could be assimilated to the former, the more certain and necessary would their outcomes be.

There were a number of advantages in this concept of nature. Since it was something unrealized and apart from the phenomena, it could be used as a moral standard, to discipline the phenomena. Spencer's criticisms of the work of historians is instructive here (see chapter 10, this volume). History as practiced is accused of dealing with trivia, such as the doings of kings and great men; it is reproached for failing to plumb basic social forces and structures, for upholding sentimental concepts of free will and indeterminacy, for encouraging false sociological notions, for being associated with reactionary social strata. In his youth he argued that history was superfluous if one already possessed a "true theory of humanity" and meaningless if one did not; and, fundamentally, this remained his belief even when he admitted that history provided materials for the construction of sociology's laws. For sociology was really what Ferguson had called "the *natural* history of society," whose aim was to produce the "natural sequence among social actions" and the "order among those structural and functional changes which societies pass through." Spencer believes not only that social behavior is law-governed (as one may show by citing statistical regularities) but that there is one organic law of social evolution. As an empirical generalization this law should emerge from the facts and explain them—and, let it be said, Spencer's generalizations *do* unite many observations. But there are exceptions to it, and Spencer tells those who use these as counterevidence to the law, that the facts must be divided into "essential" and "incidental." The "incidental" facts are those which cannot be generalized and do not therefore relate to the knowable "nature" of society! Hence, the law is not in fact empirical, since any possible counterevidence can be dismissed; it is a moral norm *for* history, derived from processes elsewhere in nature and only requiring illustration with appropriate historical facts. Historical change is in fact highly discontinuous; but, since Spencer sees natural change as gradual, uniform and incremental (as in Lyell's *Principles of Geology*), his law of social evolution must be less a generalization or explanation of actual historical process than a guide to its interpretation. Contemporary sociology, one is sad to say, is often no more indebted to Spencer than in its continued estrangement from history.

Spencer's argument for what sociology must be qua science connects with what he considered its proper social function. It was not to be an instrument to further the attainment of social goals (for that would have implied that progress was contingent on fallible human decisions rather than governed by its own inner necessity). Instead, "a true theory of social progress is not a cause of movement, but simply oil to the movement—serves simply to remove friction," that is, to reconcile man to the inevitable process of evolution. *The Study of Sociology* is passionately committed to this view of sociology's function, and contains several chapters of tirade against rival sociological orientations as "bias" (see chapter 12, this volume). Spencer was reluctant to admit that different societal models express, not just different views as to what exists, but different decisions—which still need to be made—as to what sort of role in social process we wish the activity of theorizing about society to have. He believed that he could rule out of court all other viewpoints by representing his own as objective, grounded in the nature of things. In dealing with the thought of primitives or other misguided people, Spencer observes understandingly that their absurd notions do make sense if they are seen from their holders' standpoints;[17] but he believes that the subjectivity of thought, equated with bias, is both dispensable and gradually disappearing until it will be nothing other than the mirror of nature. He does this by means of a scheme of

17 Cf. *Principles of Sociology* 1: 137, 441.

development to guarantee that in the end the real, rational, essential, potential, and natural (which all come to mean the same thing) condition of man in society will necessarily come about. Only when such schemes fell into disrepute at the end of the century was it possible, in the work of Weber, for proper consideration to be given to the intricate relationship between sociology and the purposes which prompt it.

Institutions and Social Change

For Spencer's detailed analysis of social institutions we must turn to what is perhaps the most significant of his works, *The Principles of Sociology* (1876–97), whose eight parts, after describing the general character of social evolution and its primitive base line, go on to treat in turn domestic, ceremonial, political, ecclesiastical, professional, and industrial institutions. From 1874 there began to appear a series of folio-size volumes, the *Descriptive Sociology*, compiled by others under Spencer's direction. Each one contained vast columns of classified social structures and functions about the "English," "Mexicans, Central Americans, Chibchas and Peruvians," "Lowest races, Negrito races and Malayo-Polynesian races," etc., facts for inductions which would coincide with the deductions from the general principles. This very novel venture was financed at a personal loss by Spencer himself (who by this time was at last making a reasonable living from book sales, especially in the U.S.A.) and was continued after his death under the terms of his will. Later the rigid format was abandoned; but at least one notable book, Reuben Levy's *The Social Structure of Islam*, began its career in the series. For all its massive size the *Principles of Sociology* is incomplete, for Spencer never was able to attempt the volumes on evolution in art, language, and thought —what we would call culture—which he had envisaged at the outset in 1858.

The Principles of Sociology tends to disappoint, despite its learning (the list of references to books of history and travel is prodigious) and its many good discussions of particular topics. Much of it is a mechanical citation of facts to confirm well-established principles like differentiation with too little discussion of the anomalies (for which the blanket excuse is a "law of rhythm"). Then, too, a great deal of space is devoted to primitive peoples, and the treatment of modern institutions suffers from their being subordinated to evolutionary trends of such length and geological gradualness that only their very general features, or those aspects that either exemplify or conspicuously fail to fit what Spencer considers the chief trends, are discussed. One misses the historical analysis of unique situations in the light of general categories that one may find in Marx, who was no less attached to his own suprahistorical scheme. Yet, as we shall see, Spencer's conceptualization of the total span of change is an extrapolation of a common view of the English Industrial Revolution.

There are two general processes of social evolutionary change which Spencer initially felt were uniquely compatible with one another. First, differentiation and growing complexity, as in the division of labor. This is used particularly in the discussion of professional and industrial institutions. The root causes are the greater adaptive merits of specialization and, beyond this, the general tendency to heterogeneity in nature. A further process, put forward in *Political Institutions* for relatively primitive societies, is the process of aggregation, as smaller, simpler units are united (largely through war) to form larger, more complex ones, giving rise to political differentiation (see chapter 15, this volume). But the resultant classification of simple, compound and doubly compound societies is hardly used. The second process is the trend from militancy to industrialism, the necessary consequence of the gradual socialization of man's character (see chapter 16, this volume). These two processes should be intimately connected since altruism both makes possible and is encouraged by the subtle interdependence of highly differentiated societies. But the methodological individualism which is supposed to underlie the militant/industrial trend is broken by the fact that Spencer wants militancy to be, not merely a phase which human societies move out of, but one which they must go through since it fulfills positive functions in the evolutionary scheme. Whereas the noncoercive cooperation of industrialism is an expression of the altruistic character, the coercion of militancy is imposed on unsocial primitives in order to socialize them as well as being an expression of the warlike character.

In two ways we may see the mark of his own society on Spencer's thought here. First, he was employing a distinction used, not only by Saint-Simon as we all know, but by the Scottish moralists and by many spokesmen of middle-class radicalism: Paine, Cobden, Mackinnon, Ure, Smiles, Harriet Martineau, J. S. Mill, and Buckle. They saw war and trade as fundamentally inimical, and the aristocratic state, with its sinecures, paternalism, established church, and all the remnants of feudalism, as wholly incompatible with the pacific industrial society of which they were the chief creators. "Militant/industrial" was a way of characterizing the whole social transition; and Spencer, true to his uniformitarian principles, extrapolated the dichotomy to the whole course of social evolution. Primitive man differed from nineteenth-century man in the same way as immediately preindustrial man, only much more so. Second, we may note that the portrayal of the savage character—unsociable, improvident, unutilitarian, unpredictable—has an extraordinary similarity to the way factory owners saw the last remnants of preindustrial man in England, the first generation of factory workers, still unused to the rhythms and constraints of industrial life. And when Spencer talks about the role of religion in socializing the unruly primitive, he is really paraphrasing what many have said about the evangelical movement in England.

Reluctantly, one feels, since it so disrupted evolutionary continuity, Spencer came to regard differentiation and the militant/industrial trend as cross-cutting rather than coincident; and the latter as a typology rather than the description of a trend. For the ethnographies threw up plenty of primitives who were mild and sociable (the "industrial" character); and there were highly industrial societies, like Bismarck's Germany, which made nonsense of the classification. But as types (not very ideal ones) militancy and industrialism are contrasted at every point. "The militant type is one in which the army is the nation mobilized, and which, therefore, acquires a structure common to army and nation." Directed toward the outside, it requires that individual interests be subordinated to the collectivity's; as a form of cooperation it relies on coercion, and its structure is a hierarchical system of ranks; it is marked by status, not contract (Maine's terminology is readily adopted), and needs to be supported by symbols and ritual; power has precedence over wealth; such societies are conservative rather than spontaneously innovatory, for the satisfaction of individual needs is held well in check. In industrial societies, however, the form of cooperation rests on voluntary association to satisfy individual's needs; its functions are chiefly internal; the collectivity is subordinated to the interests of individuals; it is a system of specialized roles rather than hierarchical ranks, and these do not need the support of irrational means like ritual; and constant innovation is the norm. Most actual societies are mixed, but there is a systematic affinity within the features of each type and a systematic opposition between the two, and still, overall, there is a tendency for industrialism to succeed militancy. Only in one place, and there obscurely and tantalizingly, does Spencer admit that there may be a third type of society, designed neither for production nor for war but for enjoyment and self-expression.[18]

Before criticizing these two types, let us note that there is something of a genuine fundamental contrast between them: we see a version of them in Apter's "mobilization" and "reconciliation" systems for developing polities, or in Dahrendorf's distinction between plan and market rationality.[19] They also represent the contrast between political and economic modes of seeing a social system, and between institutions and social networks. Strangely, one might think, for a sociologist, Spencer disliked institutions. Not only did he show himself personally a persistent critic of all established and constituted bodies, but he believed them to be essentially transitory and dispensable. Volumes 4, 5, and 6 of the *Principles* treat ceremonial, political, and ecclesiastical institutions as plants which flourish in their season and then,

18 Cf. *Principles of Sociology* 2: 595–96.

19 Cf. D. E. Apter, *The Politics of Modernization* (University of Chicago Press, 1965); R. Dahrendorf, *Essays in the Theory of Society* (London: Routledge and Kegan Paul, 1968), chap. 8.

having conferred their fruits on mankind, wither away (see chapters 18, 19, and 21, this volume). Spencer very largely anticipated Durkheim's functional theory of religion, but unlike Durkheim he did not look to find in religion any constant and universal features of society (see chapters 20 and 21, this volume). He saw nothing constant in human society except the unrealized "social state" to which it was tending, a wholly antiinstitutional utopia, a sort of meeting place for hippies in whom self-control has become so internalized that doing one's own thing does not lead to chaos. The linchpin of modern sociology is a theory of social control based equally on Durkheim's analysis of institutions and Freud's account of the internalization of social norms, external and internal controls constantly supporting one another. Spencer identified both these processes but separated them in time as successive phases of evolution: first the tough external constraints of militancy, then the unfelt internal controls of socialized man. In Victorian England there were many people who illustrated this—Spencer himself, George Eliot, Huxley, Leslie Stephen, Bradlaugh, and others, who rejected Evangelicalism but knew that morally they were its products. Spencer was able both to present progress as the individual's liberation, in the manner of the Enlightenment, and to give a positive explanation of the restraining institutions that were being left behind.

Spencer's treatment of contemporary industrial society could have been more realistic if he had fully recognized militancy and industrialism as ideal types rather than generalized descriptions of reality. He might then have been able to analyze certain societies as combining features of both to a high degree, rather than necessarily becoming more of the one as they became less of the other. This is very clear in his treatment of status/power and role/function. There is a real element of truth in the view that, in the early Industrial Revolution at least, when the new language of class came into being, status in a vertical system of ranks yielded to function or role in the division of labor as the leading element of social structure; and that wealth (property) came to determine political power, rather than the reverse. But these were matters of degree, not, as Spencer seems to have thought, evidence of a permanent transition between fundamentally opposed poles. He ignored what became clearer when the scale of industry was bigger and alliances were formed between business capital and the landed aristocracy—that power and status are coordinates of wealth and function, and that industrialism does not mean the abolition of power relationships. Spencer's understanding of class is greatly inferior to Marx's. He uses the word quite inconsistently —sometimes to refer specifically to the power element in, say, the aristocracy's control of the polity or the manufacturer's control of his employee's work life, and sometimes with no connotation of power whatever, as when he speaks of whole industries (cotton, wool, steelworking etc.) as classes, competing for capital as bodily organs compete for blood. It is a failure of theory on Spencer's part more than a failure of insight, for his scattered and uncoordinated remarks about industrial society are often acute, for example on the effects of the divorce of ownership and control in industries like the railways (see chapter 22, this volume) or on the alienating character of factory work (see chapter 23, this volume). (Here, indeed there is a most striking similarity to the Marxian concept of alienation). But he sees these not as entirely new forms of power and status, engendered by industry, but as survivals or revivals of old forms of militancy. (The theory behind Veblen's description of conspicuous consumption—that it is a survival of the warlike past—is purely Spencerian.) Spencer was never more critical of industry than in his late years, when its scale had greatly increased. He continued to dismiss socialism but held out impossible hopes for a system of cooperation in which, there being no differentials of power, the free contracting of equals might be a reality.

One might sum this up by saying that modern bureaucracy, where function and rank are directly related, was a social fact that Spencer could not embrace in his theory. It is significant that the classical discussion of it, Weber's, came from a country where an elite with strong military and bureaucratic traditions directed an industrial revolution to achieve state goals, and kept in subservience both its bourgeois and its proletarians. Dahrendorf echoes Spencer in saying that German industrialization failed "to upset a traditional outlook in which the whole is placed above the part, the state above the citizen, or a rigidly controlled society above the lively diversity of the market, the state above society."[20] And nearly all subsequent industrializations have shown how "tradition" may not only give way to "modernity," but determine and envelop it. It is possible that Spencer might have gone some way to tackling new forms of industrialism if he had developed his neglected notion of integration, which was to accompany differentiation. But the integration he refers to is the growing internal cohesion of each differentiated part, not any higher integration or control of the whole system. So strongly was the manner of England's breakthrough stamped on his imagination that he could not see this as a serious problem; for it was in principle solved through the growing internal control within each individual character, and through the diffuse and spontaneous controls exercised by the market.

The Decline of Spencer's Reputation

Spencer found little enough to please him in the last thirty years of his life. He was increasingly afflicted by a neurotic nervous condition which had first struck him when he was thirty-five. Insomniac, he found it hard to concentrate on his work except in short violent bursts, and at times social intercourse and intellectual argument so overwrought him that he had to give them up. He had never married (though he did have an unsuccessful affair in 1852–53 with Marian Evans, yet to become George Eliot), and in his bachelor lodgings in London or Brighton he began to feel very lonely, especially as Huxley and other friends died. His once busy social life became very attenuated, and the wave of admiration from afar (Andrew Carnegie, the new rulers of Japan [see chapter 24, this volume], enthusiastic Indians and Arabs) hardly compensated. His greatest solace was to visit the large family of Richard Potter (a businessman whom he had known since 1844),

20 R. Dahrendorf, *Society and Democracy in Germany* (London: Weidenfield and Nicolson, 1968), pp. 33–64.

whose daughter Beatrice (later Webb) was his especial confidant and intended by Spencer as his literary executor.

Worst of all, he began to sense or fear that his evolutionary system, the great obsession of his life, was bankrupt. "I have finished the task I have lived for," he said on completing *The Principles of Sociology* in 1897. But already damaging criticisms had been made. His Lamarckian biology was dismissed; the quasi-physical support for progress in *First Principles* seemed ludicrously irrelevant as well as dubious—entropy had displaced differentiation; and new trends in psychology and philosophy went far beyond him. As for his sociology, new social developments were tending in the opposite direction to that which he had desired and predicted. In his essays *The Man versus the State* (1884) he fulminated against "collectivism" or the growth of state intervention in social life, in welfare measures, education, social services, imposed professional standards, labor relations. He interpreted this as a shift back to militancy and saw as another aspect of the same process the swelling tide of imperialism (see chapter 25, this volume). Many others connected imperialism and the rise of labor: Joseph Chamberlain, the Birmingham manufacturer turned politician, who advocated imperial protection as well as positive welfare policies at both state and municipal levels, or the Webbs, who joined Fabian socialism and imperialism with a lively admiration for the Germany of Prince Bismarck. Spencer's last serious political act was to try to get up an Anti-Aggression League in 1881–82, and during the Spanish-American war of 1898 he spoke with utter pessimism of "an era of social cannibalism in which the strong nations are devouring the weaker." He believed that "there is a bad time coming, and civilized mankind will morally be uncivilized before civilization can again advance."

In this climate Spencer's theories seemed more irrelevant than wrong. Those who wanted the state to make up the deficiencies of liberal capitalism found a much more congenial philosophy in the Hegelianism of T. H. Green and Bosanquet—"old world nonsense . . . incredible dogmas . . . unthinkable propositions," it seemed to Spencer. His conception of sociology was not just unhelpful for those who, like Beatrice Webb or Charles Booth, wanted to bend empirical social science to social policy; it acted to wholly undermine the validity of meliorism. In America Lester Ward even looked to Comte to counterbalance the harsh laissez-faire of Spencer and his disciple Sumner. The only area where Spencer's theories were akin to the spirit of the age was in the Social Darwinist justification of imperialism. But despite his reputation as a generalizer of natural selection, Spencer's conception of struggle was different from that of most Social Darwinists; and he continued to oppose the sanctification of colonial wars, although he had given war a great role in the past formation of society (see chapter 17, this volume). In Italy and Germany there were even weird syntheses of Spencer and Marx to form nationalist socialisms. Spencer, one knows, would not have welcomed the First World War with the alacrity shown by both Weber and Durkheim.

Modern sociology (at least in the very influential perspective of Parsons's *The Structure of Social Action*) began with the rejection, in the 1890s, by Weber, Durkheim, and Pareto, of "positivism," whose chief representative was Spencer. That there was a decisive wave of innovation is clear enough. But it is hard to see it as a simple step of progress in scientific theory. For it involved not just a better approach to old problems but the tackling of new ones, posed by the character of late nineteenth-century society. Power and order, which had been unproblematic for the older liberal sociology, now bulked large again in theory. Politics was no longer reduced to economics; concepts like elite and bureaucracy challenged class; order was recognized as a constant problem for society and sociology. The chief reason for these new emphases was that, in countries industrializing under their political elites or experiencing acute disharmonies at the public level, power and order in society become major preoccupations. And where nations become, as it were, ships to be steered in particular directions by their political elites through the use of power (just what liberal sociology had asserted to be impossible or undesirable), ideas recover their importance as variables in social change. Weber's "debate with the ghost of Karl Marx" about the role of ideas in social change is as much a refutation of Spencer; and Lenin's development of Marxism (with its stress on the role of political power and the critical function of the revolutionary elite's ideas) makes very similar points. The case of Weber shows how the potency of ideas is related to a new conception of the function of sociology itself. Spencer, as we have seen, regarded both ideas in general and sociology as of minor importance and the chief role of evolutionary sociology as being to reconcile man to inevitable processes. When evolution's credibility collapsed, it also lost its major function, since mature industrial society no longer needed the kind of assurance it gave; and it was unable to fulfill a new function—showing how social policies might be effected. It was with precisely this in mind that Weber put forward his plea for a sociology that could only be useful through being value-free. Values themselves would no longer seem to be necessary because grounded in the evolutionary process, but must be taken as the contingent starting points for social investigation. Sociology, and social thought in general, recovered their proper integral and interventionary role in social change. Nothing, I think, so separates us from Spencer as our different view concerning what sociology's role is.

But Spencer made his mark on sociology even where he was rejected and forgotten. The social anthropologists, recoiling from conjectural history, yet drew the basic vocabulary of functionalism from him; his influence on Durkheim and Radcliffe-Brown is clear enough. Boas, in America, rejected Spencer and Tylor more decisively because of their blurring of race and culture—a unity which was only finally and effectively sundered when biology utterly abandoned belief in the inheritance of acquired characteristics. But Spencer's influence remained very strong in the U.S.A. Though he was always an outsider to the British intellectual establishment, in America he dominated university courses in philosophy and the social sciences for over twenty years after his rapturous reception by Fiske and others in the 1860s. The beginnings of the first notable native American school of philosophy, pragmatism—closely involved with sociology right up to the time of C. Wright Mills—lie in a critical development rather than a rejection of Spencer. For all that the pragmatists, especially William James, set themselves against what was rigid and mechanistic in

Spencer's system (as all systems must ultimately prove to be), they tended to reiterate Spencerian themes: functional justifications of religion, the dissolution of logic into psychology, the rejection of absolute standards of truth, operationalist definitions, the elevation of practice over theory.[21] As late as the 1920s and 1930s, when Spencer's social philosophy was indeed discarded, his educational ideals were promoted afresh by Dewey, and his classification of societies by Veblen. The chief difficulty is to decide where Spencer's influence is directly felt, and where it is merely a case of spontaneous affinity within a common social and cultural tradition. Two elements of Spencer's sociology were never abandoned at all and constantly recur in American sociology to this day: a penchant for economistic models of social structure (e.g. Homans, Blau) and methodological individualism, usually in the form of the view that culture, mediated by personality, is the crucial or critical determinant of social arrangements (e.g. Lipset, Verba, Pye). Here Spencer's influence is masked by overt references to Pareto and the constantly reinterpreted Weber.

Neo-Evolutionism and Development

But we must also speak of a positive revival, within the last decade or so, of interest in Spencer and of Spencerian lines of argument.[22] There are several strands to this revival. First, a number of leading American anthropologists, notably L. H. White, J. H. Steward, Sahlins, and Service, have not only used an evolutionary scale as a means of classifying and ordering cultures (chiefly on the basis of energy production) but have seen the chief theoretical task of anthropology as the plotting of the paths by which cultures "evolve"—i.e., become differentiated, acquire

21 Cf. P. P. Weiner, *Evolution and the Founders of Pragmatism* (Harvard University Press, 1949).

22 Apart from works cited below, see especially S. N. Eisenstadt, ed., *Readings in Social Evolution and Development* (Oxford: Pergamon Press, 1970), and R. M. Marsh, *Comparative Sociology* (New York: Harcourt, Brace and World, 1967), both containing extensive references; also H. R. Barringer, G. I. Blanksten, and R. W. Mack, *Social Change in Developing Areas: A Reinterpretation of Evolution* (Cambridge, Mass.: Schankman, 1966).

greater adaptive and manipulative power over their environment. Here the chief focus of debate is the question of how "unilinear" or "multilinear" the path of evolution has been, and Spencer and the classical evolutionists, while their historical contribution is acknowledged, are taken less as an inspiration that as an example of the errors of unilinearism.

A second strand, emerging later and more consciously Spencerian, is the work of a number of the greatest theorists of development, especially those working in the Parsonian tradition: Smelser, Eisenstadt, Bellah and others. Neo-evolution is the joint consequence of attempts to integrate a growing corpus of monographic material on social change in developing countries, and Parsons's own continuing preoccupation with the immanent development of his theory. The central concept here is differentiation, refloated by Smelser in his remarkable *Social Change in the Industrial Revolution* (1959). The notion of stages or levels of development, which is less Spencerian than Marxian or Tylorian, is also prominent—perhaps deriving support from its use in W. W. Rostow's influential *The Stages of Economic Growth.* There is moreover an attempt, by Parsons in particular, to reestablish the links between sociological and biological evolution; hence the view that what evolution confers is a "generalized adaptive capacity," and the analogy between genes and cultural symbols.[23] This of course is genuinely Spencerian but also goes back to a more specifically American source—the influence of Cannon and L. J. Henderson, establishing a common language for talking about living, inorganic, and social systems. Much of what Parsons has to say is "general systems theory" with a strong dynamic application.

This deliberate neo-evolutionism (usefully synthesized with an enormous range of empirical studies by R. M. Marsh in his *Comparative Sociology*) finds a widespread resonance among sociologists of development because it chimes with a number of assumptions which seem inescapable or are implicitly followed. Dichot-

23 "Evolutionary Universals in Society," *American Sociological Review* 29 (1964); and *Societies: Comparative and Evolutionary Perspectives* (Englewood Cliffs, N.J.: Prentice-Hall, 1966).

omous typologies, often variants or amplifications of the nineteenth-century ones, are a necessary instrument when comparing two categories of objects, such as the various institutions of the developed and the underdeveloped countries; and since understanding involves comparison, they are part of the stock-in-trade of every empirical sociologist. Where the aim of analysis is not merely to understand but to facilitate the attainment of modernity, the dichotomy at once suggests a historical path to be sought in the pasts of developed nations and engineered in the futures of underdeveloped ones. The notion of stages of "growth" (as a "natural" historical path should be known) is easily added at this point; while the idea of there being different actual pathways (e.g., those of liberal capitalism, communism, nationalist autocracy as in Japan) is an easy concession to the vagaries of historical circumstance which does not conceal the fact that the traditional origin and the modern terminus are conceived similarly, and hence the overall significance of the various paths remains the same. The logical need for comparison encourages the use of numerical measures of different dimensions (either "natural" ones like G.N.P. or amounts of energy produced, or contrived ones like indices of differentiation or political mobilization), and this reinforces a tendency to see secular social change as Spencer saw it: a long uniformitarian sequence of incremental changes. Even those who would reject such a gradualist model for one emphasizing discontinuity, as some Marxists do, find it hard to escape the evolutionist schema at a fundamental level; and it can be plausibly argued that Marx's view of development was not so vastly different from that of contemporary developmentalists.[24] But if it is understandable enough that evolution should be so revised, what is the role of Spencer in this? It is hard to speak of Spencer exercising a direct influence on contemporary theory, such as Weber exercised on American sociology through the mediation of Parsons, Bendix, and others from the 1930s through the 1950s. Smelser's use of differentiation, or Etzioni's of "epigenesis" (cf. Spencer on the compounding of political units), do not seem to

24 See the persuasive argument by S. Avineri, "Marx and Modernization," *Review of Politics* 31 (1969).

rest on an *application* of Spencer;[25] and even Parsons, who is more conscious of his intellectual forbears, seems to stress the novelties and improvements of his own approach rather than the respects in which he is directly indebted to Spencer. But as I have shown elsewhere and as Nisbet has also argued,[26] the differences are more apparent than real; the core of neo-evolutionism is thoroughly Spencerian.

How appropriate is the evolutionary model for the sociology of development? The aim of the sociology of development is not just to explain what has happened, or to predict what is going to happen. Both of these are involved, but its central aim is to intervene in the historical process, to analyze particularities, and to create theory in order that what men desire for their societies should be brought about. Hence, a major tenet of Spencer's evolutionism—that the desirable is also inevitable—is utterly repudiated, and any theory of social change today must admit a large element of sheer contingency about the future. If any sort of necessary pattern of societal evolution is proclaimed, our first objection must be a logical one: either its "necessity" is spurious, or it has no relevance to the sociology of development, which assumes that the future is *not* determined prior to our actions. For if a particular pattern of evolution were necessary, then an interventionary sociology of development (which still seems to be accepted by Bellah, Eisenstadt, and other empirical students of development) would be quite pointless.

But even if necessity is denied, a theory of evolution may still

25 N. J. Smelser, *Social Change in the Industrial Revolution* (London: Routledge and Kegan Paul, 1959); A. Etzioni, "The Epigenesis of Political Communities at the International Level," *American Journal of Sociology* 68 (1963). Smelser has subsequently discussed Spencer's theories directly in his "Towards a General Theory of Social Change," in *Essays in Sociological Explanation* (Englewood Cliffs, N.J.: Prentice-Hall, 1968).

26 J. D. Y. Peel, "Spencer and the Neo Evolutionists," *Sociology* 3 (1969); R. A. Nisbet, *Social Change and History: Aspects of the Western Theory of Development* (New York: Oxford University Press, 1969); and Nisbet, "Developmentalism: A Critical Analysis," in J. C. McKinney and E. A. Tiryakian, eds. *Theoretical Sociology* (New York: Appleton Century Crofts, 1970).

be worth our attention as an account of how change has in fact occurred, with respect to the majority of cases so far examined. And here we must admit that in a general, rough-and-ready way there is a lot of truth in current evolutionary conceptions of social change. As Spencer, Parsons, and Eisenstadt insist, development does largely consist of the differentiation of institutions, functions, and roles. Marsh has found a clear, if by no means universal, positive correlation between differentiation (as measured by constructed indices) and other aspects of modernity. It is also true that the more developed nations produce more energy than, and differ systematically in a whole range of interconnected ways from, underdeveloped ones: they are more secularized, their populations are more integrated and politically mobilized, there is more homogeneity between centre and periphery within the national unit, they are more bureaucratized, their transactions are more impersonal, and so forth. Much the same is implied by many nineteenth-century continua, though these are perhaps less empirical truths expressed in evolutionary theory than tautologies which follow from the meanings of the words "modern" and "non-modern."

As development studies progress, and as history provides us with new material, the original unilinearity of evolution is loosened. And just as Spencer came to compare evolution to a branching tree, so the moderns emphasize the variety of paths that may take nations to modernity and the wide variability which exists at all stages. Vestiges of unilinearity still exist however in the stages, Parsons's "evolutionary universals," and the implied continuum between traditional and modern (especially in studies with a psychological focus, like those of D. Lerner and Inkeles).[27] But the degree of emphasis on either side is crucial; and only insofar as the emphasis is on the universal, unilinear elements is the theory specifically evolutionary. Where the variations are not just ac-

27 A. Inkeles, "Making Men Modern," *American Journal of Sociology* 75 (1969); D. Lerner, *The Passing of Traditional Society* (Glencoe, Free Press, 1958); and "Towards a Communications Theory of Modernization," in L. W. Pye, ed., *Communications and Political Development* (Princeton University Press, 1963). Cf. also the well-known studies of E. E. Hagen and D. C. McClelland.

knowledged but become the chief object of study, as they do in the work of Gerschenkron and Barrington Moore,[28] we have comparative history rather than evolution. Perhaps the acid test of intention is to see whether a particular case is of interest because it fits a general evolutionary scheme or not, or whether the evolutionary scheme is used to pinpoint the significance of unique and particular circumstances. Parsons and Spencer are clearly both concerned with the former. Insofar as we choose the latter, we abandon evolution in any very specific sense.

When we consider evolutionary theories in their detail and substance, there is little that is not vacuous that cannot be challenged in its application to particular instances. That evolution produces a higher "generalized adaptive capacity" is a statement so vague that it is barely possible to refute it. Occasionally it gives rise to clear counterinstances. For example, the traditional social system of the Ibo was far less specialized and centralized, with a less developed technology, than that of the Hausa. The Hausa should, on the theory, be more "adaptive" to further changes.[29] In fact, in modern Nigeria the Hausa have proved far more conservative and resistant to modernizing influences. The factors which have made for their adaptiveness seem to be independent of specific "evolutionary" considerations. Differentiation is a much more substantial notion, and, as we have seen, the development of society can be roughly characterized in these terms. But it often fails to apply in detail. Industrialization often involves a selective dedifferentiation of particular sectors of society, as Charles Tilly has shown;[30] and in certain contexts the maintenance or the creation of nondifferentiated institutions has been a key to

28 A. Gerschenkron, *Economic Backwardness in Historical Perspective* (Harvard University Press, 1962); B. Moore, *The Social Origins of Dictatorship and Democracy* (London: Allen Lane, The Penguin Press, 1966).

29 Cf. R. A. Levine *Dreams and Deeds: Achievement Motivation in Nigeria* (University of Chicago Press, 1966), comparing Ibo, Yoruba, and Hausa; and S. Ottenberg, "Ibo Receptivity to Change," in W. R. Bascom and M. J. Herskovits, eds., *Continuity and Change in African Cultures* (University of Chicago Press, 1959).

30 "Clio and Minerva," in McKinney and Tirykian, *Theoretical Sociology*.

planned development (e.g., in Soviet Russia or Japan at critical stages of their industrialization). It is still generally true that development is associated with differentiation; but it does not follow that differentiation is necessary for development in all particular cases. Hitherto we have had little success in establishing just why and where differentiation does apply. Spencer had a theory to explain differentiation (which does in fact fit the case of cotton production in Britain as treated by Smelser); but despite its general inadequacy (e.g., in explaining relations between party and bureaucracy, or religion and politics, during industrialization) it has not been much improved on by anyone.[31] There is always the option when things go wrong for the theory (e.g., when dedifferentiation occurs, or industrialization does not bring democratic institutions with it) of regarding these as cases of regression or anti-evolution. This is logical enough, but it is achieved at the cost of making evolutionary propositions tautologous and of turning a statistical norm of what has typically happened into a moral norm for future developments. This latter is thoroughly Spencerian! In the end we must choose whether it is more illuminating to regard fascism, for example, as the concomitant of a particular path to development (with B. Moore) or merely as a regression or aberration (with Eisenstadt, and Nettl and Robertson).[32]

Modernity, or the condition to which developing countries evolve, is seen as a bunch of characteristics, associated with one another and universally felt to be morally superior to their antithesis. There is more than an echo of nineteenth-century optimism and sheer ethnocentrism in the typical evolutionist's belief (1) that the moral and political features of "modernity," such as democracy and respect for the individual, necessarily follow from

31 This despite the claims of Smelser, *Essays in Sociological Explanation*, pp. 351–52, or the discussion of P. Nettl and R. Robertson in *Modernization and the International System of Societies* (London: Faber, 1968), pp. 46 ff.

32 Moore, *Social Origins of Dictatorship and Democracy*, pp. 447–51; Eisenstadt, *Modernization: Protest and Change* (Englewood Cliffs, N.J.: Prentice-Hall, 1966), p. 133; and Nettl and Robertson, *Modernization*, p. 48.

its economic features, and (2) that the political system of the U.S.S.R. is less "evolved" than that of the U.S.A. (proved by its association with lower per capita income, higher proportion of farmworkers, less differentiated economy), but will develop in the right direction.[33] This "convergence thesis" now commands less support than it did. Veblen, the last of the classical evolutionists, was its clearest proponent in *Imperial Germany and the Industrial Revolution*.[34] Well aware of the success for industrialization of Germany's peculiar combination of the archaic and the up-to-date, he still asserted an "unavoidable habituation" between industrialism and democracy. Fascism was still in the future. Beliefs about the inevitable links between industrialism and democracy can in any case only be justified by a theory which tells us why, and under what specific circumstances, they *are* necessarily linked. Such a theory would draw its evidences from past occurrences but would be logically independent of any evolutionary scheme. It remains a weakness of evolutionary theorists, but a remediable one, that they tend to sit back satisfied when the correlation of variables and the establishment of typical sequences has been done. But this is only the first step to *explaining* anything about the course of history.

The evolutionary view of development essentially consists of the comparison of a number of distinct units—national histories—in the light of some overall conception of progress by stages or along a continuum. But this simple schema cannot be sustained in the face of the fact that both the starting points ("tradition") and the targets ("modernity") are constantly shifting. The mere fact that any sort of "modern" state of society is more differentiated, or displays higher income levels or greater political centralization, than any state that we would be prepared to call "traditional," cannot obscure the enormous differences in the paths that modernization means for different countries. The differences are com-

33 As an example, G. L. Buck and A. L. Jackson, "Social Evolution and Structural Functional Analysis: An Empirical Test," *American Sociological Review* 32 (1968).

34 *Imperial Germany and the Industrial Revolution* (New York: Kelley, 1915), pp. 228–29.

pounded of (1) variations in the "starting-points" (compare England in 1500 or 1750, Japan in 1868, Mexico in 1910, Indonesia or Malawi or Iraq today); (2) variations in what is aspired to (compare Great Britain in 1850 with Japan or U.S.A. or U.S.S.R. today, let alone what any of these might be in the future); (3) variations in the global conditions within which modernization takes place. These differences are not just unidimensional (i.e., in how "backward" or "advanced" a nation is). We may indeed be able to construct a scale of differentiation, as Marsh has done, including all tribal peoples and all nations too; but we cannot use it to infer that any people has an advantage over another because it is thus more "advanced." Development is not a linear (whether uni- or multi-) race like that at all, as the Hausa/Ibo comparison introduced above, shows clearly. As countries industrialize, and consequently involve other countries in a network of economic, political, and cultural relations, the task of development is made quite different, if not more difficult, for all the others that are still undeveloped. The effects of colonialism and the tightening net of international relations do not simply affect the internal character of each country; they change the context of development so that it becomes a supranational problem, where the mere attempt to replicate the past courses of industrial nations is wholly inadequate.[35] Here there is considerable force in some of the criticisms made of orthodox sociology of development by Marxist writers like A. G. Frank,[36] despite their attachment to their own archaic models.

Perhaps the ultimate reason why sociologists are so prone to evolution is that it represents the only plausible candidate (except for its Marxist variant) for something they think they ought to have: a "theory of social change." The work of sociology is seen as a collective labor to build up over time ever more perfect theories about various aspects of society, and the rationale of

35 Sociologists as informed and subtle as Eisenstadt and Smelser are clearly aware of these facts, but the appeal of a theoretical model which pulls the other way is too strong for them.

36 See his *Capitalism and Underdevelopment in Latin America* (New York: Monthly Review Press, 1967).

empirical research is that it is needed to "test" and "refine" these theories. But this is to put the cart before the horse. Theories are needed in order to explain facts, rather than facts (or empirical studies) in order to create theories. (This distinction may seem logically immaterial, but it is psychologically very important.) In the matter of development, sociologists tend to think that there is a process and a mechanism of development, general and universal, which it is the task of theory (1) to discover (as if they were "there") and (2) to apply in particular cases, albeit with suitable adjustments made for local but superficial peculiarities. This really is a sociological shibboleth or, to put it more kindly, a Holy Grail. The Holy Grail did not exist, though the quest for it undoubtedly had beneficial consequences. And evolutionary theory has indeed given rise to a number of suggestive schemata, such as the notions of differentiation or stages of development, but little more.

But beyond this the most the neo-evolutionists can possibly show is that in the past certain characteristic sequences of change (to which there are still a great many (exceptions) have been found. Yet these processes are not somehow self-explanatory: they demand explanation themselves; and there is nothing particularly "evolutionary" about the explanations which are offered in the field of development. As with all historical and sociological explanations they merely refer to the association of particular causes and effects: that communism or parliamentary democracy is the outcome of specified relations in the preindustrial period between landlords and peasants, or that the type of investment institution varies with the scale of the appropriate industry and the urgency of pressures to develop, or that the difficulties of developing business in two contrasted Javanese towns is due to the absence of one of two prerequisites of modern businesses, a rational economic ethos and adequate motives for cooperation.[37] Even with Parsons's own "evolutionary universals" what there is of explanation consists of some straightforward functional propositions to the effect

37 Thus B. Moore, *Social Origins,* Gerschenkron, *Economic Backwardness,* and C. Geertz, *Peddlers and Princes* (University of Chicago Press, 1966), three works which in different ways provide us with real explanatory theory about actual phenomena.

that, for example, a market economy is a necessary cause of industrialization.

Evolutionism's quest for general processes tends to represent development as an immanent, ongoing, natural, unproblematic process, seemingly divorced from the variety of specific contingencies which have given rise to it in every case. Hence it appears proper to consider the actual histories of underdeveloped countries as "breakdowns" of development,[38] as if they were abnormal growths rather than merely social situations which may be modified by historical actors, just like any other social situation. What is needed is a comparative sociological history which may indicate what the costs, constraints, and prerequisites of the attainment of particular goals are likely to be. The historically specific situation is where analysis must begin and end. Spencer's contempt for history and his dismissal of the particular, conjoined with his view of the inability of theory to modify social change, constitute a dire warning to those about to follow in his footsteps. Let him not be forgotten! His was a singular achievement; but let us also be prepared to face the heritage of sociology to reject it as well as to revive and develop it. Historical self-knowledge is necessary for both.

Note about the Selection

I should, in conclusion, say a few words about the selection which follows. It represents only a tiny portion of Spencer's sociological writings, let alone his work on other subjects. I have opened the selection with some excerpts from the semisociological *Social Statics,* since the moral preoccupations expressed there were so much the framework for the subsequent sociology. It seemed important, in order to give an impression of the growth of his ideas (an organic metaphor seems doubly appropriate), to include sizable portions of what Spencer wrote between *Social Statics* and the mature statement in the *Principles of Sociology;* and to conclude with some brief items illustrating his response to the changed

38 Thus Eisenstadt in *Modernization: Protest and Change*, passim.

conditions of the end of the century. The order of the selections is principally thematic but also in large measure chronological: *Social Statics,* approaches to the evolutionary synthesis, the methodological declarations of *The Study of Sociology,* the finished evolutionary scheme, and the institutional analysis of the *Principles.*

The items are chosen not to present Spencer in the most flattering and up-to-date light, but to indicate all the major elements of his system as it really was: a coherent attempt to answer intellectual problems posed by a mid-nineteenth-century context. One cannot represent Spencer by a dozen self-contained essays illustrating his main contributions; one must excise and chop up items, sometimes whole chapters and sometimes single paragraphs, from massive works planned as architectonic wholes. I can only hope the result does not seem too disjointed, though it must sacrifice the magnificent cumulative sweep of his demonstrations.

My chief regret is that the limits of space have prevented the inclusion of more from Spencer's splendid occasional articles on social and political topics—cantankerous to the point of obsession, indignant and testy, well written (quite different from the leaden measures of the *Principles*) in a vigorous sardonic prose, full of odd testimonies and snippets of curious fact. Some of these, polemics on behalf of laissez-faire, may be found, along with *The Man v. the State* (which I have also left out entirely), in the recent selection edited by D. G. MacRae.

J. D. Y. Peel

I. Social Statics

1

THE SEARCH FOR AN ETHICAL CODE

"GIVE US A GUIDE," cry men to the philosopher. "We would escape from these miseries in which we are entangled. A better state is ever present to our imaginations, and we yearn after it; but all our efforts to realize it are fruitless. We are weary of perpetual failures; tell us by what rule we may attain our desire."

"Whatever is expedient is right," is one of the last of the many replies to this appeal.

"True," rejoin some of the applicants. "With the Deity *right* and *expedient* are doubtless convertible terms. For us, however, there remains the question—which is the antecedent, and which is the consequent? Granting your assumption that *right* is the unknown quantity and *expediency* the known one, your formula may be serviceable. But we deny your premises; a painful experience has proved the two to be equally indeterminate. Nay, we begin to suspect that the *right* is the more easily ascertained of the two; and that your maxim would be better if transposed into—whatever is right is expedient."

"Let your rule be, the greatest happiness to the greatest number," interposes another authority.

"That, like the other, is no rule at all," it is replied; "but rather an enunciation of the problem to be solved. It is your 'greatest happiness' of which we have been so long and so fruitlessly in search; albeit we never gave it a name. You tell us nothing new;

From *Social Statics* (London: John Chapman, 1851), pp. 1–3, 31–34.

you merely give words to our want. What you call an answer, is simply our own question turned the right side up. If this is your philosophy it is surely empty, for it merely echoes the interrogation."

"Have a little patience," returns the moralist, "and I will give you my opinion as to the mode of securing this greatest happiness to the greatest number."

"There again," exclaim the objectors, "you mistake our requirement. We want something else than opinions. We have had enough of them. Every futile scheme for the general good has been based on opinion; and we have no guarantee that your plan will not add one to the list of failures. Have you discovered a means of forming an infallible judgment? If not, you are, for aught we can perceive, as much in the dark as ourselves. True, you have obtained a clearer view of the end to be arrived at; but concerning the route leading to it, your offer of an *opinion* proves that you know nothing more certain than we do. We demur to your maxim because it is not what we wanted—a guide; because it dictates no sure mode of securing the desideratum; because it puts no veto upon a mistaken policy; because it permits all actions—bad, as readily as good—provided only the actors *believe* them conducive to the prescribed end. Your doctrines of 'expediency' or 'utility' or 'general good' or 'greatest happiness to the greatest number' afford not a solitary command of a particular character. Let but rulers think, or profess to think, that their measures will benefit the community, and your philosophy stands mute in the presence of the most egregious folly, or the blackest misconduct. This will not do for us. We seek a system that can return a definite answer when we ask—'Is this act good?' and not like yours, reply—'Yes, if it will benefit you.' If you can show us such an one—if you can give us an axiom from which we may develop successive propositions until we have with mathematical certainty solved all our difficulties—we will thank you. If not, we must go elsewhere."

In his defence, our philosopher submits that such expectations are unreasonable. He doubts the possibility of a strictly scientific morality. Moreover he maintains that his system is sufficient for all practical purposes. He has definitely pointed out the goal to be attained. He has surveyed the tract lying between us and it. He believes he has discovered the best route. And finally he has volunteered as pioneer. Having done this, he claims to have performed all that can be expected of him, and deprecates the opposition of these critics as factious, and their objections as frivolous. Let us examine this position somewhat more closely.

Assuming it to be in other respects satisfactory, a rule, principle, or axiom, is valuable only in so far as the words in which it is expressed have a definite meaning. The terms used must be universally accepted in the same sense, otherwise the proposition will be liable to such various constructions, as to lose all claim to the title—a rule. We must therefore take it for granted that when he announced "the greatest happiness to the greatest number" as the canon of social morality, its originator supposed mankind to be unanimous in their definition of "greatest happiness."

This was a most unfortunate assumption, for no fact is more palpable than that the standard of happiness is infinitely variable. . . .

It seems at first sight a very rational way of testing any proposed rule of conduct to ask—How will it work? Taking men as we know them, and institutions as they are, what will result from carrying such a theory into practice? This very common-sense style of inquiry is that by which most opinions on morals and politics are formed. People consider of any system, whether it seems feasible, whether it will square with this or the other social arrangement, whether it fits what they see of human nature. They have got certain notions of what man *is*, and what society *must be*; and their verdict on any ethical doctrine depends upon its accordance or discordance with these.

Such a mode of settling moral questions, is clearly open to all the criticisms so fatal to the expediency-philosophy. Incapacity for guiding ourselves in detail by making estimates of consequences, implies incapacity for judging of first principles by that method. But passing over this, there is yet another reason for rejecting an inquiry so pursued as worthless; namely, that it assumes the character of mankind to be constant. If moral systems are adopted or condemned, because of their consistency or inconsistency, with what we know of men and things, then it is taken for granted that men and things will ever be as they are. It would be absurd to measure with a variable standard. If existing humanity is the gauge by which truth must be determined, then must that gauge—existing humanity—be fixed.

Now that it is not fixed, might have been thought sufficiently obvious without any proving—so obvious indeed as to make proof look ridiculous. But, unfortunately, those whose prejudices make them think otherwise are too numerous to be passed by. Their scepticism needs to be met by facts; and, wearisome though it may be to the philosophic reader, there is no alternative but to go into these.

And first, let us pause a moment to consider the antecedent improbability of this alleged constancy in human nature. It is a trite enough remark that change is the law of all things: true equally of a single object, and of the universe. Nature in its infinite complexity is ever growing to a new development. Each successive result becomes the parent of an additional influence, destined in some degree to modify all future results. No fresh thread enters into the texture of that endless web, woven in "the roaring loom of Time" but what more or less alters the pattern. It has been so from the beginning. As we turn over the leaves of the earth's primeval history—as we interpret the hieroglyphics in which are recorded the events of the unknown past, we find this same ever-beginning, never-ceasing change. We see it alike in the organic and the inorganic—in the decompositions and recombinations of matter, and in the constantly-varying forms of animal and vegetable life. Old formations are worn down; new ones are deposited. Forests and bogs become coal basins; and the now igneous rock was once sedimentary. With an altering atmosphere, and a decreasing temperature, land and sea perpetually bring forth fresh races of insects, plants, and animals. All things are metamorphosed; infusorial shells into chalk and flint, sand into stone, stone into gravel. Strata got contorted; seas fill up; lands are alternately upheaved and sunk. Where once rolled a fathomless ocean, now tower the snow-covered peaks of a wide-spread, richly-clothed country, teeming with existence; and where a vast continent once stretched, there remain but a few lonely coral islets to mark the graves of its submerged mountains. Thus also it is with systems, as well as with worlds. Orbits vary in their forms, axes in their inclinations, suns in their brightness. Fixed only in name, the stars are incessantly changing their relationships to each other. New ones from time to time suddenly appear, increase and wane; whilst the members of each nebula—suns, planets, and their satellites, sweep for ever onwards into unexplored infinity.

Strange indeed would it be, if, in the midst of this universal mutation, man alone were constant, unchangeable. But it is not so. He also obeys the laws of indefinite variation. His circumstances are ever altering; and he is ever adapting himself to them. Between the naked houseless savage, and the Shakespeares and Newtons of a civilized state, lie unnumbered degrees of difference. The contrasts of races in form, colour, and feature, are not greater than the contrasts in their moral and intellectual qualities. That superiority of sight which enables a Bushman to see further with the naked eye than a European with a telescope, is fully paralleled by the European's more perfect intellectual vision. The Calmuck in delicacy of smell, and the red Indian in acuteness of hearing, do not excel the white man more than the white man excels them in moral susceptibility. Every age, every nation, every climate, exhibits a modified form of humanity; and in all times, and amongst all peoples, a greater or less amount of change is going on.

There cannot indeed be a more astounding instance of the tenacity with which men will cling to an opinion in spite of an overwhelming mass of adverse evidence, than is shown in this prevalent belief that human nature is uniform. One would have thought it impossible to use eyes or ears without learning that mankind vary indefinitely, in instincts, in morals, in opinions, in tastes, in rationality, in everything.

2

THE EVANESCENCE OF EVIL

ALL EVIL results from the non-adaptation of constitution to conditions. This is true of everything that lives. Does a shrub dwindle in poor soil, or become sickly when deprived of light, or die outright if removed to a cold climate? it is because the harmony between its organization and its circumstances has been destroyed. These experiences of the farmyard and the menagerie which show that pain, disease, and death, are entailed upon animals by certain kinds of treatment, may all be generalised under the same law. Every suffering incident to the human body, from a headache up to a fatal illness—from a burn or a sprain, to accidental loss of life, is similarly traceable to the having placed that body in a situation for which its powers did not fit it. Nor is the expression confined in its application to physical evil; it comprehends moral evil also. Is the kindhearted man distressed by the sight of misery? is the bachelor unhappy because his means will not permit him to marry? does the mother mourn over her lost child? does the emigrant lament leaving his fatherland? are some made uncomfortable by having to pass their lives in distasteful occupations, and others from having no occupation at all? the explanation is still the same. No matter what the special nature of the evil, it is invariably referable to the one generic cause—want of congruity between the faculties and their spheres of action.

Equally true is it that evil perpetually tends to disappear. In virtue of an essential principle of life, this non-adaptation of

---

From *Social Statics* (London: John Chapman, 1851), pp. 59–65.

an organism to its conditions is ever being rectified; and modification of one or both, continues until the adaptation is complete. Whatever possesses vitality, from the elementary cell up to man himself, inclusive, obeys this law. . . .

Man exhibits just the same adaptability. He alters in colour according to temperature—lives here upon rice, and there upon whale oil—gets larger digestive organs if he habitually eats innutritious food—acquires the power of long fasting if his mode of life is irregular, and loses it when the supply of food is certain—becomes fleet and agile in the wilderness and inert in the city—attains acute vision, hearing, and scent, when his habits of life call for them, and gets these senses blunted when they are less needful. That such changes are towards fitness for surrounding circumstances no one can question. When he sees that the dweller in marshes lives in an atmosphere which is certain death to a stranger—when he sees that the Hindoo can lie down and sleep under a tropical sun, whilst his white master with closed blinds, and water sprinklings, and punkah, can hardly get a doze—when he sees that the Greenlander and the Neapolitan subsist comfortably on their respective foods—blubber and macaroni, but would be made miserable by an interchange of them—when he sees that in other cases there is still this fitness to diet, to climate, and to modes of life, even the most sceptical must admit that some law of adaptation is at work. Nay, indeed, if he interprets facts aright, he will find that the action of such a law, is traceable down to the minutest ramifications of individual experience. In the drunkard who needs an increasing quantity of spirits to intoxicate him, and in the opium eater, who has to keep taking a larger dose to produce the usual effect, he may mark how the system gradually acquires power to resist what is noxious. Those who smoke, who take snuff, or who habitually use medicines, can furnish like illustrations. Nor in fact, is there any permanent change of bodily state or capability, which is not to be accounted for on the same principle.

This universal law of physical modification, is the law of mental modification also. The multitudinous differences of capacity and disposition that have in course of time grown up between the Indian, African, Mongolian and Caucasian races, and between the various subdivisions of them, must all be ascribed to the acquirement in each case of fitness for surrounding circumstances. Those strong contrasts between the characters of nations and of times awhile since exemplified admit of no other conceivable explanation. Why all this divergence from the one common original type? If adaptation of constitution to conditions is not the cause, what is the cause?

There are none, however, who can with anything like consistency combat this doctrine; for all use arguments that presuppose its truth. Even those to whose prejudices the theory of man's indefinite adaptability is most opposed, are continually betraying their involuntary belief in it. They do this when they attribute differences of national character to differences in social customs and arrangements: and again when they comment on the force of habit: and again when they discuss the probable influence of a proposed measure upon public morality: and again when they recommend practice as a means of acquiring increased aptitude: and again when they describe certain pursuits as elevating and others as degrading: and again when they talk of getting used to anything: and again when they advocate certain systems of mental discipline—when they teach that virtuous conduct eventually becomes pleasurable, and when they warn against the power of a long-encouraged vice.

In fact, if we consider the question closely, no other arrangement of things can be imagined. For we must adopt one of three propositions. We must either affirm that the human being is wholly unaltered by the influences that are brought to bear upon him—his circumstances as we call them; or that he perpetually tends to become more and more *un*fitted to those circumstances; or that he tends to become fitted to them. If the first is true, then all schemes of education, of government, of social reform—all instrumentalities by which it is proposed to act upon man, are utterly useless, seeing that he cannot be acted upon at all. If the second is true, then the way to make a man virtuous is to accustom him to vicious practices, and *vice versâ*. Both of which propositions being absurd, we are compelled to admit the remaining one.

Keeping in mind then the two facts, that all evil results from the non-adaptation of constitution to conditions; and that where this non-adaptation exists it is continually being diminished by the changing of constitution and suit conditions, we shall be prepared for comprehending the present position of the human race.

By the increase of population the state of existence we call social has been necessitated. Men living in this state suffer under numerous evils. By the hypothesis it follows that their characters are not completely adapted to such a state.

In what respect are they not so adapted? what is the special qualification which the social state requires?

It requires that each individual shall have such desires only, as may be fully satisfied without trenching upon the ability of other individuals to obtain like satisfaction. If the desires of each are not thus limited, then either all must have certain of their desires ungratified; or some must get gratification for them at the corresponding expense of others. Both of which alternatives necessitating pain, imply non-adaptation.

But why is not man adapted to the social state?

Simply because he yet partially retains the characteristics that adapted him for an antecedent state. The respects in which he is not fitted to society are the respects in which he is fitted for his original predatory life. His primitive circumstances required that he should sacrifice the welfare of other beings on his own; his present circumstances require that he should not do so; and in as far as his old attribute still clings to him, in so far is he unfit for the social state. All sins of men against each other, from the cannibalism of the Carrib to the crimes and venalities that we see around us; the felonies that fill our prisons, the trickeries of trade, the quarrelings of nation with nation, and of class with class, the corruptness of institutions, the jealousies of caste, and the scandal of drawing-rooms, have their causes comprehended under this generalization.

Concerning the present position of the human race, we must therefore say, that man needed one moral constitution to fit him for his original state; that he needs another to fit him for his present state; and that he has been, is, and will long continue to be, in process of adaptation. By the term *civilization* we signify the adaptation that has already taken place. The changes that constitute *progress* are the successive steps of the transition. And the belief in human perfectibility, merely amounts to the belief, that in virtue of this process, man will eventually become completely suited to his mode of life.

If there be any conclusiveness in the foregoing arguments, such a faith is well founded. As commonly supported by evidence drawn from history, it cannot be considered indisputable. The inference that as advancement has been hitherto the rule, it will be the rule henceforth, may be called a plausible speculation. But when it is shown that this advancement is due to the working of a universal law; and that in virtue of that law it must continue until the state we call perfection is reached, then the advent of such a state is removed out of the region of probability into that of certainty. If any one demurs to this, let him point out the error. Here are the several steps of the argument.

All imperfection is unfitness to the conditions of existence.

This unfitness must consist either in having a faculty or faculties in excess; or in having a faculty or faculties deficient; or in both.

A faculty in excess, is one which the conditions of existence do not afford full exercise to; and a faculty that is deficient, is one from which the conditions of existence demand more than it can perform.

But it is an essential principle of life that a faculty, to which circumstances do not allow full exercise diminishes; and that a faculty on which circumstances make excessive demands increases.

And so long as this excess and this deficiency continue, there must continue decrease on the one hand, and growth on the other.

Finally all excess and all deficiency must disappear; that is, all unfitness must disappear; that is, all imperfection must disappear.

Thus the ultimate development of the ideal man is logically certain—as certain as any conclusion in which we place the most implicit faith; for instance, that all men will die. For why do we infer that all men will die? Simply because, in an immense number of past experiences, death has uniformly occurred. Similarly then as the experiences of all people in all times—experiences that are embodied in maxims, proverbs, and moral precepts, and that are illustrated in biographies and histories, go to prove that organs, faculties, powers, capacities, or whatever else we call them, grow by use and diminish from disuse, it is inferred that they will continue to do so. And if this inference is unquestionable, then is the one above deduced from it—that humanity must in the end become completely adapted to its conditions—unquestionable also.

Progress, therefore, is not an accident, but a necessity. Instead of civilization being artificial, it is a part of nature; all of a piece with the development of the embryo or the unfolding of a flower. The modifications mankind have undergone, and are still undergoing, result from a law underlying the whole organic creation; and provided the human race continues, and the constitution of things remains the same, those modifications must end in completeness. As surely as the tree becomes bulky when it stands alone, and slender if one of a group; as surely as the same creature assumes the different forms of carthorse and race-horse, according as its habits demand strength or speed; as surely as a blacksmith's arm grows large, and the skin of a labourer's hand thick; as surely as the eye tends to become long-sighted in the sailor, and short-sighted in the student; as surely as the blind attain a more delicate sense of touch; as surely as a clerk acquires rapidity in writing and calculation; as surely as the musician learns to detect an error of a semitone amidst what seems to others a very babel of sounds; as surely as a passion grows by indulgence and diminishes when restrained; as surely as a disregarded conscience becomes inert, and one that is obeyed active; as surely as there is any efficacy in educational culture, or any meaning in such terms as habit, custom, practice;—so surely must the human faculties be moulded into complete fitness for the social state; so surely must the things we call evil and immorality disappear; so surely must man become perfect.

3

THE FIRST PRINCIPLE OF ETHICS

THERE WILL possibly be some for whom the *à priori* considerations set forth in the foregoing chapter, are too abstract for distinct comprehension. It is easy, however, to reason our way to that first principle of ethical science which we are about to follow out to its consequences, without any appeal to these. And it will be desirable now to do this. Starting afresh then, from the admitted truth, that human happiness is the Divine will, let us look at the means appointed for the obtainment of that happiness, and observe what conditions they presuppose.

Happiness is a certain state of consciousness. That state must be produced by the action upon consciousness of certain modifying influences—by certain affections of it. All affections of consciousness we term sensations. And amongst the rest, those affections of it which constitute happiness must be sensations.

But how do we receive sensations? Through what are called faculties. It is certain that a man cannot see without eyes. Equally certain is it that he can experience no impression of any kind, unless he is endowed with some power fitted to take in that impression; that is, a faculty. All the mental states which he calls feelings and ideas, are affections of his consciousness received through the faculties—sensations given to it by them.

There next comes the question—under what circumstances do the faculties yield those sensations of which happiness consists? The reply is—when they are exercised. It is from the activity of

From *Social Statics* (London: John Chapman, 1851), pp. 75–78.

one or more of them that all gratification arises. To the healthful performance of each function of mind or body attaches a pleasurable feeling. And this pleasurable feeling is obtainable only by the performance of the function; that is, by the exercise of the correlative faculty. Every faculty in turn affords its special emotion; and the sum of these constitutes happiness.

Or the matter may be briefly put thus. A desire is the need for some species of sensation. A sensation is producible only by the exercise of a faculty. Hence no desire can be satisfied except through the exercise of a faculty. But happiness consists in the due satisfaction of all the desires; that is, happiness consists in the due exercise of all the faculties.

Now if God wills man's happiness, and man's happiness can be obtained only by the exercise of his faculties, then God wills that man should exercise his faculties; that is, it is man's *duty* to exercise his faculties; his duty means fulfilment of the Divine will. That it *is* man's duty to exercise his faculties is further proved by the fact, that what we call *punishment* attaches to the neglect of that exercise.

. . . But as God wills man's happiness, that line of conduct which produces unhappiness is contrary to his will. Therefore the non-exercise of the faculties is contrary to his will. Either way then, we find that the exercise of the faculties is God's will and man's duty.

But the fulfilment of this duty necessarily presupposes freedom of action. Man cannot exercise his faculties without certain scope. He must have liberty to go and to come, to see, to feel, to speak, to work; to get food, raiment, shelter, and to provide for each and all of the needs of his nature. He must be free to do everything which is directly or indirectly requisite for the due satisfaction of every mental and bodily want. Without this he cannot fulfil his duty or God's will. But if he cannot fulfil God's will without it, then God commands him to take it. He has Divine authority, therefore, for claiming this freedom of action. God intended him to have it; that is, he has a *right* to it.

From this conclusion there seems no possibility of escape. Let us repeat the steps by which we arrive at it. God wills man's happiness. Man's happiness can only be produced by the exercise of his faculties. Then God wills that he should exercise his faculties. But to exercise his faculties he must have liberty to do all that his faculties naturally impel him to do. Then God intends he should have that liberty. Therefore he has a *right* to that liberty.

This, however, is not the right of one but of all. All are endowed with faculties. All are bound to fulfil the Divine will by exercising them. All therefore must be free to do those things in which the exercise of them consists. That is, all must have rights to liberty of action.

And hence there necessarily arises a limitation. For if men have like claims to that freedom which is needful for the exercise of their faculties, then must the freedom of each be bounded by the similar freedom of all. When, in the pursuit of their respective ends, two individuals clash, the movements of the one remain free only in so far as they do not interfere with the like movements of the other. This sphere of existence into which we are thrown not affording room for the unrestrained activity of all, and yet all possessing in virtue of their constitutions similar claims to such unrestrained activity, there is no course but to apportion out the unavoidable restraint equally. Wherefore we arrive at the general proposition, that every man may claim the fullest liberty to exercise his faculties compatible with the possession of like liberty by every other man.

4

SOCIAL STATICS AND SOCIAL DYNAMICS

SOCIAL philosophy may be aptly divided (as political economy has been) into statics and dynamics; the first treating of the equilibrium of a perfect society, the second of the forces by which society is advanced towards perfection. To determine what laws we must obey for the obtainment of complete happiness is the object of the one, whilst that of the other is to analyze the influences which are making us competent to obey these laws. Hitherto we have concerned ourselves chiefly with the statics, touching upon the dynamics only occasionally for purposes of elucidation. Now, however, the dynamics claim special attention. Some of the phenomena of progress already referred to need further explanation, and many others associated with them remain to be noticed. There are also sundry general considerations not admissible into foregoing chapters, which may here be fitly included.

And first let us mark, that the course of civilization could not possibly have been other than it has been. Whether a perfect social state might have been at once established; and why, if it might have been, it was not—why for unnumbered ages the world was filled with inferior creatures only—and why mankind were left to make it fit for human life by clearing it of these—are questions that need not be discussed here. But given an unsubdued earth; given the being—man, appointed to overspread and occupy it;

From *Social Statics* (London: John Chapman, 1851), p. 409–17, 431–42, 468–75.

given the laws of life what they are; and no other series of changes than that which has taken place, could have taken place.

For be it remembered, that the ultimate purpose of creation—the production of the greatest amount of happiness—can be fulfilled only under certain fixed conditions. Each member of the race fulfilling it, must not only be endowed with faculties enabling him to receive the highest enjoyment in the act of living, but must be so constituted that he may obtain full satisfaction for every desire, without diminishing the power of others to obtain like satisfaction: nay, to fulfil the purpose perfectly, must derive pleasure from seeing pleasure in others. Now, for beings thus constituted to multiply in a world already tenanted by inferior creatures—creatures that must be dispossessed to make room—is a manifest impossibility. By the definition such beings must lack all desire to exterminate the races they are to supplant. They must, indeed, have a repugnance to exterminating them, for the ability to derive pleasure from seeing pleasure, involves the liability to pain from seeing pain: the sympathy by which either of these results is effected, simply having for its function to reproduce observed emotions, irrespective of their kind. Evidently, therefore, having no wish to destroy—to destroy giving them, on the contrary, disagreeable sensations—these hypothetical beings, instead of subjugating and overspreading the earth, must themselves become the prey of pre-existing creatures, in whom destructive desires predominate. How then are the circumstances of the case to be met? Evidently the aboriginal man must have a constitution adapted to the work he has to perform, joined with a dormant capability of developing into the ultimate man when the conditions of existence permit. To the end that he may prepare the earth for its future inhabitants—his descendants, he must possess a character fitting him to clear it of races endangering his life, and races occupying the space required by mankind. Hence he must have a desire to kill, for it is the universal law of life that to every needful act must attach a gratification, the desire for which may serve as a stimulus. He must further be devoid of sympathy, or must have but the germ of it, for he would otherwise be incapacitated for his destructive office. In other words, he must be what we call a savage, and must be left to acquire fitness for social life as fast as the conquest of the earth renders social life possible.

Whoever thinks that a thoroughly-civilized community could be formed out of men qualified to wage war with the pre-existing occupants of the earth—that is, whoever thinks that men might behave sympathetically to their fellows, whilst behaving unsympathetically to inferior creatures, will discover his error on looking at the facts. He will find that human beings are cruel to one another, in proportion as their habits are predatory. The Indian, whose life is spent in the chase, delights in torturing his brother man as much as in killing game. His sons are schooled into fortitude by long days of torment, and his squaw made prematurely old by hard treatment. The treachery and vindictiveness which Bushmen or Australians show to one another and to Europeans, are accompaniments of that never-ceasing enmity existing between them and the denizens of the wilderness. Amongst partially-civilized nations the two characteristics have ever borne the same relationship. Thus the spectators in the Roman amphitheatres were as much delighted by the slaying of gladiators as by the death-struggles of wild beasts. The ages during which Europe was thinly peopled, and hunting a chief occupation, were also the ages of feudal violence, universal brigandage, dungeons, tortures. Here in England a whole province depopulated to make game preserves, and a law sentencing to death the serf who killed a stag, show how great activity of the predatory instinct and utter indifference to human happiness coexisted. In later days, when bull-baiting and cock-fighting were common pastimes, the penal code was far more severe than now; prisons were full of horrors; men put in the pillory were maltreated by the populace; and the inmates of lunatic asylums, chained naked to the wall, were exhibited for money, and tormented for the amusement of visitors. Conversely, amongst ourselves a desire to diminish human misery is accompanied by a desire to ameliorate the condition of inferior creatures. Whilst the kindlier feeling of men is seen in all varieties of philanthropic effort, in charitable societies, in association for improving the dwellings of the labouring classes, in anxiety for popular education, in attempts to abolish capital punishment, in zeal for temperance reformation, in ragged schools, in endeavours to protect climbing boys, in inquiries concerning "labour and the poor," in emigration funds, in the milder treatment of children, and so on, it also shows itself in societies for the prevention of cruelty to animals, in acts of parliament to put down the use of dogs for purpose of draught, in the condemnation of steeplechases and *battues*, in the late inquiry why the pursuers of a stag should not be punished as much as the carter who maltreats his horse, and lastly, in vegetarianism. Moreover, to make the evidence complete, we have the fact that men, partially adapted to the social state, retrograde on being placed in circumstances which call forth the old propensities. The barbarizing of colonists, who live under aboriginal conditions, is universally remarked. The back settlers of America, amongst whom unavenged murderers, rifle duels, and Lynch law prevail—or, better still, the trappers, who leading a savage life have descended to savage habits, to scalping, and occasionally even to cannibalism—sufficiently exemplify it.

But why, it may be asked, has this adaptation gone on so slowly? Judging from the rapidity with which habits are formed in the individual, and seeing how those habits, or rather the latent tendencies towards them, become hereditary, it would seem that the needful modification should have been completed long ago. How, then, are we to understand the delay?

The answer is that the new conditions to which adaptation has been taking place have themselves grown up but slowly. Only when a revolution in circumstances is at once both marked and permanent, does a decisive alteration of character follow. If the demand for increase of power in some particular faculty is great and unceasing, development will go on with proportionate speed. And conversely, there will be an appreciable dwindling in a faculty altogether deprived of exercise. But the conditions of human life have undergone no changes sudden enough to produce these immediate results. . . .

Hitherto, then, human character has changed but slowly, because it has been subject to two conflicting sets of conditions. On the one hand, the discipline of the social state has been developing it into the sympathetic form; whilst on the other hand, the necessity for self-defence partly of man against brute, partly of man against man, and partly of societies against each other, has been maintaining the old unsympathetic form. And only where the influence of the first set of conditions has exceeded that of the last, and then only in proportion to the excess, has modification taken place. Amongst tribes who have kept each other's anti-social characteristics in full activity by constant conflict, no advance has been possible. But where warfare against man and beast has ceased to be continuous, or where it has become the employment of but a portion of the people, the effects of living in the associated state have become greater than the effects of barbarizing antagonisms, and progress has resulted.

Regarded thus, civilization no longer appears to be a regular unfolding after a specific plan; but seems rather a development of man's latent capabilities under the action of favourable circumstances; which favourable circumstances, mark, were certain some time or other to occur. . . .

Whilst the continuance of the old predatory instinct after the fulfilment of its original purpose, has retarded civilization by giving rise to conditions at variance with those of social life, it has subserved civilization by clearing the earth of inferior races of men. The forces which are working out the great scheme of perfect happiness, taking no account of incidental suffering, exterminate such sections of mankind as stand in their way, with the same sternness that they exterminate beasts of prey and herds of useless ruminants. Be he human being, or be he brute, the hindrance must be got rid of. Just as the savage has taken the place of lower creatures, so must he, if he have remained too long a savage, give place to his superior. Evidently, therefore, from the very beginning, the conquest of one people over another has been, in the main, the conquest of the social man over the anti-social man; or, strictly speaking, of the more adapted over the less adapted.

In another mode, too, the continuance of the unsympathetic character has indirectly aided civilization whilst it has directly hindered it; namely, by giving rise to slavery. It has been observed

—and, as it seems, truly enough—that only by such stringent coercion as is exercised over men held in bondage, could the needful power of continuous application have been developed. Devoid of this, as from his habits of life the aboriginal man necessarily was (and as, indeed, existing specimens show), probably the severest discipline continued for many generations was required to make him submit contentedly to the necessities of his new state. And if so, the barbarous selfishness which maintained that discipline, must be considered as having worked a collateral benefit, though in itself so radically bad.

Let not the reader be alarmed. Let him not fear that these admissions will excuse new invasions and new oppressions. Nor let any one who fancies himself called upon to take Nature's part in this matter, by providing discipline for idle negroes or others, suppose that these dealings of the past will serve for precedents. Rightly understood, they will do no such thing. That phase of civilization during which forcible supplantings of the weak by the strong, and systems of savage coercion, are on the whole advantageous, is a phase which spontaneously and necessarily gives birth to these things. . . .

The process by which a change of political arrangements is affected, when the incongruity between them and the popular character becomes sufficient, must be itself in keeping with that character, and must be violent or peaceful accordingly. There are not a few who exclaim against all revolutions wrought out by force of arms, forgetting that the quality of a revolution, like that of an institution, is determined by the natures of those who make it. Moral suasion is very admirable; good for us; good, indeed, for all who can be induced to use it. But to suppose that, in the earlier stages of social growth, moral suasion can be employed, or, if employed, would answer, is to overlook the conditions. Stating the case mechanically, we may say that as, in proportion to their unfitness for associated life, the framework within which men are restrained must be strong, so must the efforts required to break up that framework, when it is no longer fit, be convulsive. The existence of a government which does not bend to the popular will—a despotic government—presupposes several circumstances which make any change but a violent one impossible. First, for coercive rule to have been practicable, implies in the people a predominance of that awe of power ever indicative of still lingering savageness. Moreover, with a large amount of power-worship present, disaffection can take place only when the cumulative evils of misgovernment have generated great exasperation. Add to which, that as abundance of the sentiment upholding external rule, involves lack of the sentiments producing internal rule, no such check to excesses as that afforded by a due regard for the lives and claims of others, can be operative. And where there are comparatively active destructive propensities, extreme anger, and deficient self-restraint, violence is inevitable. Peaceful revolutions occur under quite different circumstances. They become possible only when society, no longer consisting of members so antagonistic, begins to cohere from its own internal organization, and needs not be kept together by unyielding external restraints; and when, by consequence, the force required to effect change is less. They become possible only when men, having acquired greater adaptation to the social state, will neither inflict on each other, nor submit to, such extreme oppressions, and when, therefore, the causes of popular indignation are diminished. They become possible only when character has grown more sympathetic, and when, as a result of this, the tendency towards angry retaliation is partially neutralized. Indeed, the very idea that reforms may and ought to be effected peacefully implies a large endowment of the moral sense. Without this, such an idea cannot even be conceived, much less carried out; with this, it may be both.

Hence, we must look upon social convulsions as upon other natural phenomena, which work themselves out in a certain inevitable, unalterable way. We may lament the bloodshed—may wish it had been avoided; but it is folly to suppose that, the popular character remaining the same, things could have been managed differently. *If* such and such events had not occurred, say you, the result would have been otherwise; *if* this or that man had lived, he would have prevented the catastrophe. Do not be thus deceived. These changes are brought about by a power far above individual wills. Men who seem the prime movers, are merely the tools with which it works; and were they absent, it would quickly find others, Incongruity between character and institutions is the disturbing force, and a revolution is the act of restoring equilibrium. Accidental circumstances modify the process, but do not perceptibly alter the effect. They precipitate; they retard; they intensify or ameliorate; but, let a few years elapse, and the same end is arrived at, no matter what the special events passed through. . . .

From the point of view now arrived at, we may discern how what is termed in our artificial classifications of truth, *morality*, is essentially one with physical truth—is, in fact, a species, of transcendental physiology. That condition of things dictated by the law of equal freedom—that condition in which the individuality of each may be unfolded without limit, save the like individualities of others—that condition towards which, as we have just seen, mankind are progressing, is a condition towards which the whole creation tends. Already it has been incidentally pointed out that only by entire fulfilment of the moral law can life become complete; and now we shall find that all life whatever may be defined as a quality, of which aptitude to fulfil this law is the highest manifestation.

A theory of life developed by Coleridge has prepared the way for this generalization. "By life," says he, "I everywhere mean the true idea of life, or that most general form under which life manifests itself to us, which includes all other forms. This I have stated to be the *tendency to individuation;* and the degrees or intensities of life to consist in the progressive realizations of this tendency." To make this definition intelligible, a few of the facts sought to be expressed by it must be specified—facts exemplifying the contrast between low and high types of structure, and low and high degrees of vitality. . . . [There follows a list of biological instances of this rule.] And when the change at present going on is complete—when each possesses an active instinct of freedom, together with an active sympathy—then will all the still existing limitations to individuality, be they governmental restraints, or be they the aggressions of men on one another, cease. Then, none will be hindered from duly unfolding their natures; for whilst every one maintains his own claims, he will respect the like claims of others. Then, there will no longer be legislative restrictions and legislative burdens; for by the same process these will have become both needless and impossible. Then, for the first time in the history of the world, will there exist beings whose individualities can be expanded to the full in all directions. And thus, as before said, in the ultimate man perfect morality, perfect individuation, and perfect life will be simultaneously realized.

Yet must this highest individuation be joined with the greatest mutual dependence. Paradoxical though the assertion looks, the progress is at once towards complete separateness and complete union. But the separateness is of a kind consistent with the most complex combinations for fulfilling social wants; and the union is of a kind that does not hinder entire development of each personality. Civilization is evolving a state of things and a kind of character, in which two apparently conflicting requirements are reconciled. To achieve the creative purpose—the greatest sum of happiness, there must on the one hand exist an amount of population maintainable only by the best possible system of production; that is, by the most elaborate subdivision of labour; that is, by the extremest mutual dependence: whilst on the other hand, each individual must have the opportunity to do whatever his desires prompt. Clearly these two conditions can be harmonized only by that adaptation humanity is undergoing—that process during which all desires inconsistent with the most perfect social organization are dying out, and other desires corresponding to such an organization are being developed. How this will eventuate in producing at once perfect individuation and perfect mutual dependence, may not be at once obvious. But probably an illustration will sufficiently elucidate the matter. Here are certain domestic affections, which can be gratified only by the establishment of relationships with other beings. In the absence of those beings, and the consequent dormancy of the feelings with which they are regarded, life is incomplete—the individuality is shorn of its fair proportions. Now as the normal unfolding of the conjugal and parental elements of the individuality depends on having a family, so, when civilization becomes complete, will the normal unfolding of all other elements of the individuality depend upon the existence of the civilized state. Just that kind of individuality will be acquired which finds in the most highly-organized community the fittest sphere for its manifestation—which finds in each social arrangement a condition answering to some faculty in itself—which could not, in fact, expand at all, if otherwise circumstanced. The ultimate man will be one whose private requirements coincide with public ones. He will be that manner of man, who, in spontaneously fulfilling his own nature, incidentally performs the functions of a social unit; and yet is only enabled so to fulfil his own nature, by all others doing the like. . . .

The admission that social arrangements can be conformed to the moral law only in as far as the people are themselves moral, will probably be thought a sufficient plea for claiming liberty to judge how far the moral law may safely be acted upon. For if congruity between political organization and popular character is necessary; and if, by consequence, a political organization in advance of the age will need modification to make it fit the age; and if this process of modification must be accompanied by great inconvenience, and even suffering; then it would seem to follow that for the avoidance of these evils our endeavour should be to at first adapt such organization to the age. That is to say, men's ambition to realize an ideal excellence must be checked by prudential considerations.

"Progress, and at the same time resistance,"—that celebrated saying of M. Guizot, with which the foregoing position is in substance identical—no doubt expresses a truth; but not at all the order of truth usually supposed. To look at society from afar off, and to perceive that such and such are the principles of its development, is one thing: to adopt these as rules for our daily government, will turn out on examination to be quite a different thing. Just as we saw that it is very possible for the attainment of greatest happiness to be from one point of view the recognised end of morality, and yet to be of no value for immediate guidance, so, it is very possible for "progress, and at the same time resistance," to be a law of social life, without being a law by which individual citizens may regulate their actions. . . .

That the aspiration after things as they should be, needs restraining by an attachment to things as they are, is fully admitted. The two feelings answer to the two sides of our present mixed nature—the side on which we continue adapted to old conditions of existence, and the side on which we are becoming adapted to new ones. Conservatism defends those coercive arrangements which a still-lingering savageness makes requisite. Radicalism endeavours to realize a state more in harmony with the character of the ideal man. The strengths of these sentiments are proportionate to the necessity for the institutions they respond to. And the social organization proper for a given people at a given time, will be one bearing the impress of these sentiments in the ratio of their prevalence amongst that people at that time. Hence the necessity for a vigorous and constant manifestation of both of them. Whilst, on the one hand, love of what is abstractedly just, indignation against every species of aggression, and enthusiasm on behalf of reform, are to be rejoiced over; we must, on the other hand, tolerate, as indispensable, these displays of an antagonistic tendency; be they seen in the detailed opposition to every improvement, or in the puerile sentimentalisms of Young England, or even in some frantic effort to bring back the age of hero-worship. Of all these nature has need, so long as they represent sincere beliefs. From time to time the struggle eventuates in change; and by composition of forces there is produced a *resultant*, embodying the right amount of movement in the right direction. Thus understood, then, the theory of "progress, and at the same time resistance," is correct.

Mark now, however, that for this resistance to be beneficial, it must come from those who think the institutions they defend really the best, and the innovations proposed absolutely wrong. It must not come from those who secretly approve of change, but think a certain opposition to it expedient. For if the true end of this conflict of opinion is to keep social arrangements in harmony with the average character of the people; and if (rejecting that temporary kind of opinion generated by revolutionary passion) the *honest* opinion held by each man of any given state of things is not an intellectual accident, but indicates a preponderating fitness or unfitness of that state of things to his moral condition; then it follows that only by a universal manifestation of *honest* opinions can harmony between social arrangements and the average popular character be preserved. If, concealing their real sympathies, some of the movement party join the stationary party, merely with the view of preventing too rapid an advance, they must inevitably disturb the adaptation between the community and its institutions. So long as the natural conservatism ever present in society is left to restrain the progressive tendency, things will go right; but add to this natural conservatism an artificial conservatism—a conservatism not founded on love of the old, but on a theory that conservatism is needful—and the proper ratio between the two forces is destroyed; the *resultant* is no longer in the right direction; and the effect produced by it is more or less vitiated. Whilst, therefore, there is truth in the belief that "progress, and at the same time resistance," is the law of social change, there is a fatal error in the inference that resistance should be factitiously created. It is a mistake to suppose this the kind of resistance called for; and, as M. Guizot's own experience testifies, it is a further mistake to suppose that any one can say how far resistence should be carried.

But, indeed, without entering upon a criticism like this, the man of moral insight sees clearly enough that no such self-contradicting behaviour can answer. Successful methods are always genuine, sincere. The affairs of the universe are not carried on after a system of benign double-dealing. In nature's doings all things show their true qualities—exert whatsoever of influence is really in them. It is manifest that a globe built up partly of semblances instead of facts, would not be long on this side chaos. And it is certain that a community composed of men whose acts are not in harmony with their innermost beliefs, will be equally unstable. To know in our hearts that some proposed measure is essentially right, and yet to say by our deeds that it is not right, will never prove really beneficial. Society cannot prosper by lies. . . .

The candid reader may now see his way out of the dilemma in which he feels placed, between a conviction, on the one hand, that the perfect law is the only safe guide, and a consciousness, on the other, that the perfect law cannot be fulfilled by imperfect men. Let him but duly realize the fact that opinion is the agency through which character adapts external arrangements to itself—that *his* opinion rightly forms part of this agency—is a unit of force, constituting, with other such units, the general power which works out social changes—and he will then perceive that he may properly give full utterance to his *innermost conviction;* leaving it to produce what effect it may. It is not for nothing that he has in him these sympathies with some principles, and repugnance to others. He, with all his capacities, and desires, and beliefs, is not an accident, but a product of the time. Influences that have acted upon preceding generations; influences that have been brought to bear upon him; the education that disciplined his childhood; together with the circumstances in which he has since lived; have conspired to make him what he is. And the result thus wrought out in him has a purpose. He must remember that whilst he is a child of the past, he is a parent of the future. The moral sentiment developed in him, was intended to be instrumental in producing further progress; and to gag it, or to conceal the thoughts it generates, is to balk creative design. He, like every other man, may properly consider himself as an agent through whom nature works; and when nature gives birth in him to a certain belief, she thereby authorizes him to profess and to act out that belief.

II. From Progress to Evolution

5

POPULATION AND PROGRESS

[SPENCER has been arguing that throughout the animal kingdom fertility is inversely correlated with brain size, declining as the evolutionary scale is ascended, and that as the struggle for survival forces the latter to increase, the former will be lessened] That an enlargement of the nervous centres is going on in mankind, is an ascertained fact. Not alone from a general survey of human progress—not alone from the greater power of self-preservation shown by civilized races, are we left to infer such enlargement; it is proved by actual measurement. The mean capacities of the crania in the leading divisions of the species have been found to be—

In the Australian	. . . . .	75 cubic inches.
" African	. . . . . .	82 "
" Malayan	. . . . . .	86 "
" Englishmen	. . . . .	96 "

showing an increase in the course of the advance from the savage state of our present phase of civilization, amounting to nearly 30 per cent on the original size. That this increase will be continuous, might be reasonably assumed; and to infer a future decrease of fertility would be tolerably safe, were no further evidence forthcoming. But it may be shown why a greater development of the nervous system *must* take place, and why, consequently, there

From *Westminister Review*, 1852, pp. 32–35, "A Theory of Population deduced from the General Law of Animal Fertility."

must be a diminution of the present excess of fertility; and further, it may be shown that the sole agency needed to work out this change is—*the excess of fertility itself.*

For, as we all know, this excess of fertility entails a constant pressure of population upon the means of subsistence; and, as long as it exists, must continue to do this. Looking only at the present and the immediate future, it is unquestionably true, that, if unchecked, the rate of increase of people would exceed the rate of increase of food. It is clear that the wants of their redundant numbers constitute the only stimulus mankind have to a greater production of the necessaries of life; for, were not the demand beyond the supply, there would be no motive to increase the supply. Moreover, this excess of demand over supply, and this pressure of population, of which it is the index, cannot be eluded. Though by the emigration that takes place when the pressure arrives at a certain intensity, a partial and temporary relief may be obtained, yet, as by this process all habitable countries must gradually become peopled, it follows, that in the end the pressure, whatever it may then be, must be borne in full.

But this inevitable redundancy of numbers—this constant increase of people beyond the means of subsistence—involving as it does an increasing stimulus to better the modes of producing food and other necessaries—involves also an increasing demand for skill, intelligence, and self-control—involves, therefore, a constant exercise of these, that is—involves a gradual growth of them. Every improvement is at once the product of a higher form of humanity, and demands that higher form of humanity to carry it into practice. The application of science to the arts is simply the bringing to bear greater intelligence for satisfying our wants; and implies continued increase of that intelligence. To get more produce from the acre, the farmer must study chemistry—must adopt new mechanical appliances—and must, by the multiplication of tools and processes, cultivate both his own powers and the powers of his labourers. To meet the requirements of the market, the manufacturer is perpetually improving his old machines, and inventing new ones; and by the premium of high wages incites artizans to acquire greater skill. The daily-widening ramifications of commerce entail upon the merchant a need for more knowledge and more complex calculations; whilst the lessening profits of the ship-owner force him to employ greater science in building, to get captains of higher intelligence, and better crews. In all cases, increase of numbers is the efficient cause. Were it not for the competition this entails, more thought would not daily be brought to bear upon the business of life; greater activity of mind would not be called for; and development of mental power would not take place. Difficulty in getting a living is alike the incentive to a higher education of children, and to a more intense and long-continued application in adults. In the mother it induces foresight, economy, and skilful housekeeping; in the father, laborious days and constant self-denial. Nothing but necessity could make men submit to this discipline, and nothing but this discipline could produce a continued progression. The contrast between a Pacific Islander, all whose wants are supplied by Nature, and an Englishman, who, generation after generation, has had to bring to the satisfaction of his wants ever-increasing knowledge and skill, illustrates at once the need for, and the effects of, such discipline. And this being admitted, it cannot be denied that a further continuance of such discipline, possibly under a yet more intense form, must produce a further progress in the same direction—a further enlargement of the nervous centres, and a further decline of fertility.

And here it must be remarked, that the effect of pressure of population, in increasing the ability to maintain life, and decreasing the ability to multiply, is not a uniform effect, but an average one. In this case, as in many others, Nature secures each step in advance by a succession of trials, which are perpetually repeated, and cannot fail to be repeated, until success is achieved. All mankind in turn subject themselves more or less to the discipline described; they either may or may not advance under it; but, in the nature of things, only those who *do* advance under it eventually survive. For, necessarily, families and races whom this increasing difficulty of getting a living which excess of fertility entails, does not stimulate to improvements in production—that is, to greater mental activity—are on the high road to extinction; and must ultimately by supplanted by those whom the pressure does so stimulate. This truth we have recently seen exemplified in Ireland. And here, indeed, without further illustration, it will be seen that premature death, under all its forms, and from all its causes, cannot fail to work in the same direction. For as those prematurely carried off must, in the average of cases, be those in whom the power of self-preservation is the least, it unavoidably follows, that those left behind to continue the race must be those in whom the power of self-preservation is the greatest—must be the select of their generation. So that, whether the dangers to existence be of the kind produced by excess of fertiltiy, or of any other kind, it is clear, that by the ceaseless exercise of the faculties needed to contend with them, and by the death of all men who fail to contend with them successfully, there is ensured a constant progress towards a higher degree of skill, intelligence, and self-regulation—a better co-ordination of actions—a more complete life.

There now remains but to inquire towards what limit this progress tends. Evidently, so long as the fertility of the race is more than sufficient to balance the diminution by deaths, population must continue to increase: so long as population continues to increase, there must be pressure on the means of subsistence: and so long as there is pressure on the means of subsistence, further mental development must go on, and further diminution of fertility must result. Hence, the change can never cease until the rate of multiplication is just equal to the rate of mortality; that is—can never cease until, on the average, each pair brings to maturity but two children. Probably this involves that each pair will rarely produce more than two offspring; seeing that with the greatly-increased ability to preserve life, which the hypothesis presupposes, the amount of the infant and juvenile mortality must become very small. Be this as it may, however, it is manifest that, in the end, pressure of population and its accompanying evils will entirely disappear; and will leave a state of things which will require from each individual no more than a normal and pleasurable activity. That this last inference is a legitimate corollary will become obvious on a little consideration. For, a cessation in the decrease of fertility implies a cessation in the development of the nervous system; and this implies that the nervous system has become fully equal to all that is demanded of it—has not to do more than is natural to it. But that exercise of faculties which does not exceed what is natural constitutes gratification. Consequently, in the end, the obtainment of subsistence will require just that kind and that amount of action needful to perfect health and happiness.

Thus do we see how simple are the means by which the greatest and most complex results are worked out. From the point of view now reached, it becomes plain that the necessary antagonism of individuation and reproduction not only fulfils with precision the *a priori* law of maintenance of race, from the monad up to man, but ensures the final attainment of the highest form of this maintenance—a form in which the amount of life shall be the greatest possible, and the births and deaths the fewest possible. In the nature of things, the antagonism could not fail to work out the results we see it working out. The gradual diminution and ultimate disappearance of the original excess of fertility could take place only through the process of civilization; and, at the same, time, the excess of fertility has itself rendered the process of civilization inevitable. From the beginning, pressure of population has been the proximate cause of progress. It produced the original diffusion of the race. It compelled men to abandon predatory habits and take to agriculture. It led to the clearing of the earth's surface. It forced men into the social state; made social organization inevitable; and has developed the social sentiments. It has stimulated to progressive improvements in production, and to increased skill and intelligence. It is daily pressing us into closer contact and more mutually-dependent relationships. And after having caused, as it ultimately must, the due peopling of the globe, and the bringing of all its habitable parts into the highest state of culture—after having brought all processes for the satisfaction of human wants to the greatest perfection—after having, at the same time, developed the intellect into complete competency for its work, and the feelings into complete fitness for social life—after having done all this, we see that the pressure of population, as it gradually finishes its work, must gradually bring itself to an end.

6

PROGRESS: ITS LAW AND CAUSE

THE CURRENT conception of Progress is somewhat shifting and indefinite. Sometimes it comprehends that more than simple growth—as of a nation in the number of its members and the extent of territory over which it has spread. Sometimes it has reference to quantity of material products—as when the advance of agriculture and manufactures is the topic. Sometimes the superior quality of these products is contemplated: and sometimes the new or improved appliances by which they are produced. When, again, we speak of moral or intellectual progress, we refer to the state of the individual or people exhibiting it; while, when the progress of Knowledge, of Science, of Art, is commented upon, we have in view certain abstract results of human thought and action. Not only, however, is the current conception of Progress more or less vague, but it is in great measure erroneous. It takes in not so much the reality of Progress as its accompaniments—not so much the substance as the shadow. That progress in intelligence seen during the growth of the child into the man, or the savage into the philosopher, is commonly regarded as consisting in the greater number of facts known and laws understood: whereas the actual progress consists in those internal modifications of which this increased knowledge is the expression. Social progress is supposed to consist in the produce of a greater quantity and variety of the articles required for satisfying man's wants; in

---

From "Progress: its Law and Cause" (1857), reprinted in *Essays* (vol. 1, 1868), pp. 1–59.

the increasing security of person and property; in widening freedom of action: whereas, rightly understood, social progress consists in those changes of structure in the social organism which have entailed these consequences. The current conception is a teleological one. The phenomena are contemplated solely as bearing on human happiness. Only those changes are held to constitute progress which directly or indirectly tend to heighten human happiness. And they are thought to constitute progress simply *because* they tend to heighten human happiness. But rightly to understand progress, we must inquire what is the nature of these changes, considered apart from our interests. Ceasing, for example, to regard the successive geological modifications that have taken place in the Earth, as modifications that have gradually fitted it for the habitation of Man, and as *therefore* a geological progress, we must seek to determine the character common to these modifications—the law to which they all conform. And similarly in every other case. Leaving out of sight concomitants and beneficial consequences, let us ask what Progress is in itself.

In respect to that progress which individual organisms display in the course of their evolution, this question has been answered by the Germans. The investigations of Wolff, Goethe, and Von Baer, have established the truth that the series of changes gone through during the development of a seed into a tree, or an ovum into an animal, constitute an advance from homogeneity of structure to heterogeneity of structure. In its primary stage, every germ consists of a substance that is uniform throughout, both in texture and chemical composition. The first step is the appearance of a difference between two parts of this substance; or, as the phenomenon is called in physiological language, a differentiation. Each of these differentiated divisions presently begins itself to exhibit some contrast of parts; and by and by these secondary differentiations become as definite as the original one. This process is continuously repeated—is simultaneously going on in all parts of the growing embryo; and by endless such differentiations there is finally produced that complex combination of tissues and organs constituting the adult animal or plant. This is the history of all organisms whatever. It is settled beyond dispute that organic progress consists in a change from the homogeneous to the heterogeneous.

Now, we propose in the first place to show, that this law of organic progress is the law of all progress. Whether it be in the development of the Earth, in the development of Life upon its surface, in the development of Society, of Government, of Manufactures, of Commerce, of Language, Literature, Science, Art, this same evolution of the simple into the complex, through successive differentiations, holds throughout. From the earliest traceable cosmical changes down to the latest results of civilization, we shall find that the transformation of the homogeneous into the heterogeneous, is that in which Progress essentially consists. . . .

Whether an advance from the homogeneous to the heterogeneous is or is not displayed in the biological history of the globe, it is clearly enough displayed in the progress of the latest and most heterogeneous creature—Man. It is alike true that, during the period in which the Earth has been peopled, the human organism has grown more heterogeneous among the civilized divisions of the species; and that the species, as a whole, has been growing more heterogeneous in virtue of the multiplication of races and the differentiation of these races from each other.

In proof of the first of these positions, we may cite the fact that, in the relative development of the limbs, the civilized man departs more widely from the general type of the placental mammalia than do the lower human races. While often possessing well-developed body and arms, the Papuan has extremely small legs: thus reminding us of the quadrumana, in which there is no great contrast in size between the hind and fore limbs. But in the European, the greater length and massiveness of the legs has become very marked—the fore and hind limbs are relatively more heterogeneous. Again, the greater ratio which the cranial bones bear to the facial bones illustrates the same truth. Among the vertebrata in general, progress is marked by an increasing heterogeneity in the vertebral column, and more especially in the vertebræ constituting the skull: the higher forms being distinguished by the relatively larger size of the bones which cover the brain, and the relatively smaller size of those which form the jaw, &c. Now, this characteristic, which is stronger in Man than in any other creature, is stronger in the European than in the savage. Moreover, judging from the greater extent and variety of faculty he exhibits, we may infer that the civilized man has also a more complex or heterogeneous nervous system than the uncivilized man: and indeed the fact is in part visible in the increased ratio which his cerebrum bears to the subjacent ganglia.

If further elucidation be needed, we may find it in every nursery. The infant European has sundry marked points of resemblance to the lower human races; as in the flatness of the alæ of the nose, the depression of its bridge, the divergence and forward opening of the nostrils, the form of the lips, the absence of a frontal sinus, the width between the eyes, the smallness of the legs. Now, as the developmental process by which these traits are turned into those of the adult European, is a continuation of that change from the homogeneous to the heterogeneous displayed during the previous evolution of the embryo, which every physiologist will admit; it follows that the parallel development process by which the like traits of the barbarous races have been turned into those of the civilized races, has also been a continuation of the change from the homogeneous to the heterogeneous. The truth of the second position—that Mankind, as a whole, have become more heterogeneous—is so obvious as scarcely to need illustration. Every work on Ethnology, by its divisions and subdivisions of races, bears testimony to it. Even were we to admit the hypothesis that Mankind originated from several separate stocks, it would still remain true, that as, from each of these stocks, there have sprung many now widely different tribes, which are proved by philological evidence to have had a common origin, the race as a whole is far less homogeneous than it once was. Add to which, that we have, in the Anglo-Americans, an example of a new variety arising within these few generations; and that, if we may trust to the description of observers, we are likely soon to have another such example in Australia.

On passing from Humanity under its individual form, to Humanity as socially embodied, we find the general law still more variously exemplified. The change from the homogeneous to the heterogeneous is displayed equally in the progress of civilization as a whole, and in the progress of every tribe or nation; and is still going on with increasing rapidity. As we see in existing barbarous tribes, society in its first and lowest form is a homogeneous aggregation of individuals having like powers and like functions: the only marked difference of function being that which accompanies difference of sex. Every man is warrior, hunter, fisherman, tool-maker, builder; every woman performs the same drudgeries; every family is self-sufficing, and save for purposes of aggression and defence, might as well live apart from the rest. Very early, however, in the process of social evolution, we find an incipient differentiation between the governing and the governed. Some kind of chieftainship seems coeval with the first advance from the state of separate wandering families to that of a nomadic tribe. The authority of the strongest makes itself felt among a body of savages as in a herd of animals, or a posse of schoolboys. At first however, it is indefinite, uncertain; is shared by others of scarcely inferior power; and is unaccompanied by any difference in occupation or style of living: the first ruler kills his own game, makes his own weapons, builds his own hut, and economically considered, does not differ from others of his tribe. Gradually, as the tribe progresses, the contrast between the governing and the governed grows more decided. Supreme power becomes hereditary in one family; the head of that family, ceasing to provide for his own wants, is served by others; and he begins to assume the sole office of ruling.

At the same time there has been arising a co-ordinate species of government—that of Religion. As all ancient records and traditions prove, the earliest rulers are regarded as divine personages. The maxims and commands they uttered during their lives are held sacred after their deaths, and are enforced by their divinely-descended successors; who in their turns are promoted to the pantheon of the race, there to be worshipped and propitiated along with their predecessors: the most ancient of whom is the supreme god, and the rest subordinate gods. For a long time these connate forms of government—civil and religious—continue closely associated. For many generations the king continues to be the chief priest, and the priesthood to be members of the royal race. For many ages religious law continues to contain more or less of civil regulations, and civil law to possess more or less of religious sanction; and even among the most advanced nations these two controlling agencies are by no means completely differentiated from each other.

Having a common root with these, and gradually diverging from them, we find yet another controlling agency—that of Manners or ceremonial usages. All titles of honour are originally the names of the god-king; afterwards of God and the king; still later of persons of high rank; and finally come, some of them, to be used between man and man. All forms of complimentary address were at first the expressions of submission from prisoners to their conqueror or from subjects to their ruler, either human or divine—expressions that were afterwards used to propitiate subordinate authorities, and slowly descended into ordinary intercourse. All models of salutation were once obeisances made before the monarch and used in worship of him after his death. Presently others of the god-descended race were similarly saluted; and by degrees some of the salutations have become the due of all. Thus, no sooner does the originally homogeneous social mass differentiate into the governed and the governing parts, than this last exhibits an incipient differentiation into religious and secular—Church and State; while at the same time there begins to be differentiated from both, that less definite species of government which rules our daily intercourse—a species of government which, as we may see in heralds' colleges, in books of the peerage, in masters of ceremonies, is not without a certain embodiment of its own. Each of these is itself subject to successive differentiations. In the course of ages, there arises, as among ourselves, a highly complex political organization of monarch, ministers, lords and commons, with their subordinate administrative departments, courts of justice, revenue offices, &c., supplemented in the provinces by municipal governments, county governments, parish or union governments—all of them more or less elaborated. By its side there grows up a highly complex religious organization, with its various grades of officials, from archbishops down to sextons, its colleges, convocations, ecclesiastical courts, &c.; to all which must be added the ever multiplying independent sects, each with its general and local authorities. And at the same time there is developed a highly complex aggregation of customs, manners, and temporary fashions, enforced by society at large, and serving to control those minor transactions between man and man which are not regulated by civil and religious law. Moreover it is to be observed that this ever increasing heterogeneity in the government appliances of each nation, has been accompanied by an increasing heterogeneity in the governmental appliances of different nations; all of which are more or less unlike in their political systems and legislation, in their creeds and religious institutions, in their customs and ceremonial usages.

Simultaneously there has been going on a second differentiation of a more familiar kind; that, namely, by which the mass of the community has been segregated into distinct classes and orders of workers. While the governing part has undergone the complex development above detailed, the governed part has undergone an equally complex development, which has resulted in that minute division of labour characterizing advanced nations. It is needless to trace out this progress from its first stages, up through the caste divisions of the East and the incorporated guilds of Europe, to the elaborate producing and distributing organization existing among ourselves. Political economists have long since described the evolution which, beginning with a tribe whose members severally perform the same actions each for himself, ends with a civilized community whose members severally perform different actions for each other; and they have further pointed out the changes through which the solitary producer of any one commodity is transformed into a combination of producers who, united under a master, take separate parts in the manufacture of such commodity. But there are yet other and higher phases of this advance from the homogeneous to the heterogeneous in the industrial organization of society.

Long after considerable progress has been made in the division of labour among different classes of workers, there is still little or no division of labour among the widely separated parts of the community; the nation continues comparatively homogeneous in the respect that in each district the same occupations are pursued. But when roads and other means of transit become numerous and good, the different districts begin to assume different functions, and to become mutually dependent. The calico manufacture locates itself in this county, the woollen-cloth manufacture in that; silks are produced here, lace there; stockings in one place, shoes in another; pottery, hardware, cutlery, come to have their special towns; and ultimately every locality becomes more or less distinguished from the rest by the leading occupation carried on in it. Nay, more, this subdivision of functions shows itself not only among the different parts of the same nation, but among different nations. That exchange of commodities which free-trade promises so greatly to increase, will ultimately have the effect of specializing, in a greater or less degree, the industry of each people. So that beginning with a barbarous tribe, almost if not quite homogeneous in the functions of its members, the progress has been, and still is, towards an economic aggregation of the whole human race; growing ever more heterogeneous in respect of the separate functions assumed by separate nations, the separate functions assumed by the local sections of each nation, the separate functions assumed by the many kinds of makers and traders in each town, and the separate functions assumed by the workers united in producing each commodity.

Not only is the law thus clearly exemplified in the evolution of the social organism, but it is exemplified with equal clearness in the evolution of all products of human thought and action, whether concrete or abstract, real or ideal. Let us take Language as our first illustration. . . . [Spencer considers the evolution of language, painting, sculpture, poetry, music and musical instruments from their origin in religion.]

But doubtless the reader is already weary of illustrations; and our promise has been amply fulfilled. We believe we have shown beyond question, that that which the German physiologists have found to be the law of organic development, is the law of all development. The advance from the simple to the complex, through a process of successive differentiations, is seen alike in the earliest changes of the Universe to which we can reason our way back; and in the earliest changes which we can inductively establish; it is seen in the geologic and climatic evolution of the Earth, and of every single organism on its surface; it is seen in the evolution of Humanity, whether contemplated in the civilized individual, or in the aggregation of races; it is seen in the evolution of Society in respect alike of its political, its religious, and its economical organization; and it is seen in the evolution of all those endless concrete and abstract products of human activity which constitute the environment of our daily life. From the remotest past which Science can fathom, up to the novelties of yesterday, that in which Progress essentially consists, is the transformation of the homogeneous into the heterogeneous.

And now, from this uniformity of procedure, may we not infer some fundamental necessity whence it results? May we not rationally seek for some all-pervading principle which determines this all-pervading process of things? Does not the universality of the *law* imply a universal *cause?*

That we can fathom such cause, noumenally considered, is not to be supposed. To do this would be to solve that ultimate mystery which must ever transcend human intelligence. But it still may be possible for us to reduce the law of all Progress, above established, from the condition of an empirical generalization, to the condition of a rational generalization. Just as it was possible to interpret Kepler's laws as necessary consequences of the law of gravitation; so it may be possible to interpret this law of Progress, in its multiform manifestations, as the necessary consequence of some similarly universal principle. As gravitation was assignable as the *cause* of each of the groups of phenomena which Kepler formulated; so may some equally simple attribute of things be assignable as the cause of each of the groups of phenomena formulated in the foregoing pages. We may be able to affiliate all these varied and complex evolutions of the homogeneous into the heterogeneous, upon certain simple facts of immediate experience, which, in virtue of endless repetition, we regard as necessary.

The probability of a common cause, and the possibility of

formulating it, being granted, it will be well, before going further, to consider what must be the general characteristics of such cause, and in what direction we ought to look for it. We can with certainty predict that it has a high degree of generality; seeing that it is common to such infinitely varied phenomena: just in proportion to the universality of its application must be the abstractness of its character. We need not expect to see in it an obvious solution of this or that form of Progress; because it equally refers to forms of Progress bearing little apparent resemblance to them: its association with multi-form orders of facts, involves its dissociation from any particular order of facts. Being that which determines Progress of every kind—astronomic, geologic, organic, ethnologic, social, economic, artistic, &c.—it must be concerned with some fundamental attribute possessed in common by these; and must be expressible in terms of this fundamental attribute. The only obvious respect in which all kinds of Progress are alike, is, that they are modes of *change;* and hence, in some characteristic of changes in general, the desired solution will probably be found. We may suspect *a priori* that in some law of change lies the explanation of this universal transformation of the homogeneous into the heterogeneous.

Thus much premised, we pass at once to the statement of the law, which is this:—*Every active force produces more than one change—every cause produces more than one effect.*

Before this law can be duly comprehended, a few examples must be looked at. . . . [Some examples from Chemistry follow.]

. . . This multiplication of results, which is displayed in every event of to-day, has been going on from the beginning; and is true of the grandest phenomena of the universe as of the most insignificant. From the law that every active force produces more than one change, it is an inevitable corollary that through all time there has been an ever-growing complication of things. Starting with the ultimate fact that every cause produces more than one effect, we may readily see that throughout creation there must have gone on, and must still go on, a never-ceasing transformation of the homogeneous into the heterogeneous. But let us trace out this truth in detail. . . . [Spencer applies it to cosmology and biology with tendencies to an increasing variety of species and to the internal differentiation of each one.]

Observe, now, however, a further consequence. There must arise not simply a tendency towards the differentiation of each race of organisms into several races; but also a tendency to the occasional production of a somewhat higher organism. Taken in the mass these divergent varieties which have been caused by fresh physical conditions and habits of life, will exhibit changes quite indefinite in kind and degree; and changes that do not necessarily constitute an advance. Probably in most cases the modified type will be neither more nor less heterogeneous than the original one. In some cases the habits of life adopted being simpler than before, a less heterogeneous structure will result: there will be a retrogradation. But it *must* now and then occur, that some division of a species, falling into circumstances which give it rather more complex experiences, and demand actions somewhat more involved, will have certain of its organs further differentiated in proportionately small degrees,—will become slightly more heterogeneous.

Thus, in the natural course of things, there will from time to time arise an increased heterogeneity both of the Earth's flora and fauna, and of individual races included in them. Omitting detailed explanations, and allowing for the qualifications which cannot here be specified, we think it is clear that geological mutations have all along tended to complicate the forms of life, whether regarded separately or collectively. The same causes which have led to the evolution of the Earth's crust from the simple into the complex, have simultaneously led to a parallel evolution of the Life upon its surface. In this case, as in previous ones, we see that the transformation of the homogeneous into the heterogeneous is consequent upon the universal principle, that every active force produces more than one change. . . .

If the advance of Man towards greater heterogeneity is traceable to the production of many effects by one cause, still more clearly may the advance of Society towards greater heterogeneity be so explained. Consider the growth of an industrial organization. When, as must occasionally happen, some individual of a tribe displays unusual aptitude for making an article of general use—a weapon, for instance—which was before made by each man for himself, there arises a tendency towards the differentiation of that individual into a maker of such weapons. His companions—warriors and hunters all of them,—severally feel the importance of having the best weapons that can be made; and are therefore certain to offer strong inducements to this skilled individual to make weapons for them. He, on the other hand, having not only an unusual faculty, but an unusual liking, for making such weapons (the talent and the desire for any occupation being commonly associated), is predisposed to fulfil these commissions on the offer of an adequate reward: especially as his love of distinction is also gratified. This first specialization of function, once commenced, tends ever to become more decided. On the side of the weapon-maker continued practice gives increased skill—increased superiority to his products: on the side of his clients, cessation of practice entails decreased skill. Thus the influences that determine this division of labour grow stronger in both ways; and the incipient heterogeneity is, on the average of cases, likely to become permanent for that generation, if no longer.

Observe now, however, that this process not only differentiates the social mass into two parts, the one monopolizing, or almost monopolizing, the performance of a certain function, and the other having lost the habit, and in some measure the power, of performing that function; but it tends to imitate other differentiations. The advance we have described implies the introduction of barter,—the maker of weapons has, on each occasion, to be paid in such other articles as he agrees to take in exchange. But he will not habitually take in exchange one kind of article, but many kinds. He does not want mats only, or skins, or fishing gear, but he wants all these; and on each occasion will bargain for the particular things he most needs. What follows? If among the members of the tribe there exist any slight differences of skill in the manufacture of these various things, as there are almost sure to do, the weapon-maker will take from each one the thing which that one excels in making: he will exchange for mats with him whose mats are superior, and will bargain for the fishing gear of whoever has the best. But he who has bartered away his mats or his fishing gear, must make other mats or fishing gear for himself; and in so doing must, in some degree, further develop his aptitude. Thus it results that the small specialties of faculty possessed by various members of the tribe, will tend to grow more decided. If such transactions are from time repeated, these specializations may become appreciable. And whether or not there ensue distinct differentiations of other individuals into makers of particular articles, it is clear that incipient differentiations take place throughout the tribe: the one original cause produces not only the first dual effect, but a number of secondary dual effects, like in kind, but minor in degree. This process, of which traces may be seen among groups of schoolboys, cannot well produce any lasting effects in an unsettled tribe; but where there grows up a fixed and multiplying community, these differentiations become permanent, and increase with each generation. A larger population, involving a greater demand for every commodity, intensifies the functional activity of each specialized person or class; and this renders the specialization more definite where it already exists, and establishes it where it is nascent. By increasing the pressure on the means of subsistence, a larger population again augments these results; seeing that each person is forced more and more to confine himself to that which he can do best, and by which he can gain most. This industrial progress, by aiding future production, opens the way for a further growth of population, which reacts as before: in all which the multiplication of effects is manifest. . . .

Our limits will not allow us to follow out this process in its higher complications: else might we show how the localization of special industries in special parts of a kingdom, as well as the minute subdivision of labour in the making of each commodity, are similarly determined. Or, turning to a somewhat different order of illustrations, we might dwell on the multitudinous changes —material, intellectual, moral,—caused by printing; or the further extensive series of changes wrought by gunpowder. But leaving the intermediate phases of social development, let us take a few illustrations from its most recent and its passing phases. To trace the effects of steam-power, in its manifold applications to mining, navigation, and manufactures of all kinds, would carry us into unmanageable detail. Let us confine ourselves to the latest embodiment of steam-power—the locomotive engine.

This, as the proximate cause of our railway system, has changed the face of the country, the course of trade, and the habits of the people. Consider, first, the complicated sets of changes that precede the making of every railway—the provisional arrangements, the meetings, the registration, the trial section, the parliamentary survey, the lithographed plans, the books of reference, the local deposits and notices, the application to Parliament, the passing Standing-Orders Committee, the first, second, and third readings: each of which brief heads indicates a multiplicity of transactions, and the development of sundry occupations—as those of engineers, surveyors, lithographers, parliamentary agents, share-brokers; and the creation of sundry others—as those of traffic-takers, reference-takers. Consider, next, the yet more marked changes implied in railway construction—the cutting, embankings, tunnellings, diversions of roads; the building of bridges and stations; the laying down of ballast, sleepers, and rails; the making of engines, tenders, carriages and waggons: which processes, acting upon numerous trades, increase the importation of timber, the quarrying of stone, the manufacture of iron, the mining of coal, the burning of bricks: institute a variety of special manufactures weekly advertised in the *Railway Times;* and, finally, open the way to sundry new occupations, as those of drivers, stokers, cleaners, plate-layers, &c., &c. And then consider the changes, more numerous and involved still, which railways in action produce on the community at large. The organization of every business is more or less modified: ease of communication makes it better to do directly what was before done by proxy; agencies are established where previously they would not have paid; goods are obtained from remote wholesale houses instead of near retail ones; and commodities are used which distance once rendered inaccessible. Again, the rapidity and small cost of carriage tend to specialize more than ever the industries of different districts—to confine each manufacture to the parts in which, from local advantages, it can be best carried on. Further, the diminished cost of carriage, facilitating distribution, equalizes prices, and also, on the average, lowers prices: thus bringing divers articles within the means of those before unable to buy them, and so increasing their comforts and improving their habits. At the same time the practice of travelling is immensely extended. Classes who never before thought of it, take annual trips to the sea; visit their distant relations; make tours; and so we are benefited in body, feelings, and intellect. Moreover, the more prompt transmission of letters and of news produces further changes—makes the pulse of the nation faster. Yet more, there arises a wide dissemination of cheap literature through railway book-stalls, and of advertisements in railway carriages: both of them aiding ulterior progress.

And all the innumerable changes here briefly indicated are consequent on the invention of the locomotive engine. The social organism has been rendered more heterogeneous in virtue of the many new occupations introduced, and the many old ones further specialized; prices in every place have been altered; each trader has, more or less, modified his way of doing business; and almost every person has been affected in his actions, thoughts, emotions. . . .

. . . It will be seen that as in each event of to-day, so from the beginning, the decomposition of every expended force into several forces has been perpetually producing a higher complication; that the increase of heterogeneity so brought about is still going on, and must continue to go on; and that thus Progress is not an accident, not a thing within human control, but a beneficent necessity.

7

THE SOCIAL ORGANISM

SIR JAMES MACINTOSH got great credit for the saying, that "constitutions are not made, but grow." In our day, the most significant thing about this saying is, that it was ever thought so significant. As from the surprise displayed by a man at some familiar fact, you may judge of his general culture; so from the admiration which an age accords to a new thought, its average degree of enlightenment may be inferred. That this apophthegm of Macintosh should have been quoted and re-quoted as it has, shows how profound has been the ignorance of social science. A small ray of truth has seemed brilliant, as a distant rushlight looks like a star in the surrounding darkness.

Such a conception could not, indeed, fail to be startling when let fall in the midst of a system of thought to which it was utterly alien. Universally in Macintosh's day, things were explained on the hypothesis of manufacture, rather than that of growth: as indeed they are, by the majority, in our own day. It was held that the planets were severally projected round the sun from the Creator's hand; with exactly the velocity required to balance the sun's attraction. The formation of the Earth, the separation of sea from land, the production of animals, were mechanical works from which God rested as a labourer rests. Man was supposed to be moulded after a manner somewhat akin to that in which a modeller makes a clay-figure. And of course, in harmony with such ideas, societies were

From "The Social Organism" (1860), reprinted in *Essays*, vol. 1 (1868), pp. 388–430.

tacitly assumed to be arranged thus or thus by direct interposition of Providence; or by the regulations of law-makers; or by both.

Yet that societies are not artificially put together, is a truth so manifest, that it seems wonderful men should have ever overlooked it. Perhaps nothing more clearly shows the small value of historical studies, as they have been commonly pursued. You need but to look at the changes going on around, or observe social organization in its leading peculiarities, to see that these are neither supernatural, nor are determined by the wills of individual men, as by implication historians commonly teach; but are consequent on general natural causes. The one case of the division of labour suffices to show this. It has not been by command of any ruler that some men have become manufacturers, while others have remained cultivators of the soil. In Lancashire, millions have devoted themselves to the making of cotton-fabrics; in Yorkshire, another million lives by producing woollens; and the pottery of Staffordshire, the cutlery of Sheffield, the hardware of Birmingham, severally occupy their hundreds of thousands. These are large facts in the structure of English society; but we can ascribe them neither to miracle, nor to legislation. It is not by "the hero as king," any more than by "collective wisdom," that men have been segregated into producers, wholesale distributors, and retail distributors.

The whole of our industrial organization, from its main outlines down to its minutest details, has become what it is, not simply without legislative guidance, but, to a considerable extent, in spite of legislative hindrances. It has arisen under the pressure of human wants and activities. While each citizen has been pursuing his individual welfare, and none taking thought about division of labour, or, indeed, conscious of the need for it, division of labour has yet been ever becoming more complete. It has been doing this slowly and silently: scarcely any having observed it until quite modern times. By steps so small, that year after year the industrial arrangements have seemed to men just what they were before—by changes as insensible as those through which a seed passes into a tree; society has become the complex body of mutually-dependent workers which we now see. And this economic organization, mark, is the all-essential organization. Through the combination thus spontaneously evolved, every citizen is supplied with daily necessaries; while he yields some product or aid to others. That we are severally alive to-day, we owe to the regular working of this combination during the past week; and could it be suddenly abolished, a great proportion of us would be dead before another week ended. If these most conspicuous and vital arrangements of our social structure, have arisen without the devising of any one, but through the individual efforts of citizens to satisfy their own wants; we may be tolerably certain that the less important arrangements have similarly arisen.

"But surely," it will be said, "the social changes directly produced by law, cannot be classed as spontaneous growths. When parliaments or kings order this or that thing to be done, and appoint officials to do it, the process is clearly artificial; and society to this extent becomes a manufacture rather than a growth." No, not even these changes are exceptions, if they be real and permanent changes. The true sources of such changes lie deeper than the acts of legislators. To take first the simplest instance. We all know that the enactments of representative governments ultimately depend on the national will: they may for a time be out of harmony with it, but eventually they must conform to it. And to say that the national will finally determines them, is to say that they result from the average of individual desires; or, in other words—from the average of individual natures. A law so initiated, therefore, really grows out of the popular character.

In the case of a Government representing a dominant class, the same thing holds, though not so manifestly. For the very existence of a class monopolizing all power, is due to certain sentiments in the commonalty. But for the feeling of loyalty on the part of retainers, a feudal system could not exist. We see in the protest of the Highlanders against the abolition of heritable jurisdictions, that they preferred that kind of local rule. And if to the popular nature, must thus be ascribed the growth of an irresponsible ruling class; then to the popular nature must be ascribed the social arrangements which that class creates in the pursuit of its own ends. Even where the Government is despotic, the doctrine still holds. The character of the people is, as before, the original source of this political form; and, as we have abundant proof, other forms suddenly created will not act, but rapidly retrograde to the old form. Moreover, such regulations as a despot makes, if really operative, are so because of their fitness to the social state. His acts being very much swayed by general opinion—by precedent, by the feeling of his nobles, his priesthood, his army—are in part immediate results of the national character; and when they are out of harmony with the national character, they are soon practically abrogated.

The failure of Cromwell permanently to establish a new social condition, and the rapid revival of suppressed institutions and practices after his death, show how powerless is a monarch to change the type of the society he governs. He may disturb, he may retard, or he may aid the natural process of organization; but the general course of this process is beyond his control. Nay, more than this is true. Those who regard the histories of societies as the histories of their great men, and think that these great men shape the fates of their societies, overlook the truth that such great men are the products of their societies. Without certain antecedents—without a certain average national character, they could neither have been generated nor could have had the culture which formed them. If their society is to some extent re-moulded by them, they were, both before and after birth, moulded by their society—were the results of all those influences which fostered the ancestral character they inherited, and gave their own early bias, their creed, morals, knowledge, aspirations. So that such social changes as are immediately traceable to individuals of unusual power, are still remotely traceable to the social causes which produced these individuals, and hence, from the highest point of view, such social changes also, are parts of the general developmental process.

Thus that which is so obviously true of the industrial structure of society, is true of its whole structure. The fact that "constitutions are not made, but grow," is simply a fragment of the much larger fact, that under all its aspects and through all its ramifications, society is a growth and not a manufacture.

A perception that there exists some analogy between the body politic and a living individual body, was early reached; and from time to time re-appeared in literature. But this perception was necessarily vague and more or less fanciful. In the absence of physiological science, and especially of those comprehensive generalizations which it has but recently reached, it was impossible to discern the real parallelisms. . . . [Spencer goes on to criticize Plato and Hobbes.]

Let us set out by succinctly stating the points of similarity and the points of difference. Societies agree with individual organisms in four conspicuous peculiarities:—

1. That commencing as small aggregations, they insensibly augment in mass: some of them eventually reaching ten thousand times what they originally were.

2. That while at first so simple in structure as to be considered structureless, they assume, in the course of their growth, a continually-increasing complexity of structure

3. That though in their early, undeveloped states, there exists in them scarcely any mutual dependence of parts, their parts gradually acquire a mutual dependence; which becomes at last so great, that the activity and life of each part is made possible only by the activity and life of the rest.

4. That the life and development of a society is independent of, and far more prolonged than, the life and development of any of its component units; who are severally born, grow, work reproduce, and die, while the body politic composed of them survives generation after generation, increasing in mass, completeness of structure, and functional activity.

These four parallelisms will appear the more significant the more we contemplate them. While the points specified, are points in which societies agree with individual organisms, they are points in which individual organisms agree with each other, and disagree with all things else. In the course of its existence, every plant and animal increases in mass, in a way not paralleled by inorganic objects: even such inorganic objects as crystals, which arise by growth, show us no such definite relation between growth and existence as organisms do. The orderly progress from simplicity to complexity, displayed by bodies politic in common with all living bodies, is a characteristic which distinguishes living bodies from the inanimate bodies amid which they move. That functional dependence of parts, which is scarcely more manifest in animals or plants than nations, has no counterpart elsewhere. And in no aggregate except an organic, or a social one, is there a perpetual removal and replacement of parts, joined with a continued integrity of the whole.

Moreover, societies and organisms are not only alike in these peculiarities, in which they are unlike all other things; but the highest societies, like the highest organisms, exhibit them in the greatest degree. We see that the lowest animals do not increase to anything like the sizes of the higher ones; and, similarly, we see that aboriginal societies, are comparatively limited in their growths. In complexity, our large civilized nations as much exceed primitive savage tribes, as a vertebrate animal does a zoophyte. Simple communities, like simple creatures, have so little mutual dependence of parts, that subdivision or mutilation causes but little inconvenience; but from complex communities, as from complex creatures, you cannot remove any considerable organ without producing great disturbance or death of the rest. And in societies of low type, as in inferior animals, the life of the aggregate, often cut short by division or dissolution, exceeds in length the lives of the component units, very far less than in civilized communities and superior animals; which outlive many generations of their component units.

On the other hand, the leading differences between societies and individual organisms are these:—

1. That societies have no specific external forms. This, however, is a point of contrast which loses much of its importance, when we remember that throughout the vegetal kingdom, as well as in some lower divisions of the animal kingdom, the forms are often very indefinite—definiteness being rather the exception than the rule: and that they are manifestly in part determined by surrounding physical circumstances, as the forms of societies are. If, too, it should eventually be shown, as we believe it will, that the

form of every species of organism has resulted from the average play of the external forces to which it has been subject during its evolution as a species; then, that the external forms of societies should depend, as they do, on surrounding conditions, will be a further point of community.

2. That though the living tissue whereof an individual organism consists, forms a continuous mass, the living elements of a society do not form a continuous mass; but are more or less widely dispersed over some portion of the Earth's surface. This, which at first sight appears to be a fundamental distinction, is one which yet to a great extent disappears when we contemplate all the facts. For, in the lower divisions of the animal and vegetal kingdoms, there are types of organization much more nearly allied, in this respect, to the organization of a society, than might be supposed—types in which the living units essentially composing the mass, are dispersed through an inert substance, that can scarcely be called living in the full sense of the word. . . .

3. That while the ultimate living elements of an individual organism, are mostly fixed in their relative positions, those of the social organism are capable of moving from place to place, seems a marked disagreement. But here, too, the disagreement is much less than would be supposed. For while citizens are locomotive in their private capacities, they are fixed in their public capacities. As farmers, manufacturers, or traders, men carry on their business at the same spots, often throughout their whole lives; and if they go away occasionally, they leave behind others to discharge their functions in their absence. Each great centre of production, each manufacturing town or district, continues always in the same place; and many of the firms in such town or district, are for generations carried on either by the descendants or successors of those who founded them. Just as in a living body, the cells that make up some important organ, severally perform their functions for a time and then disappear, leaving others to supply their places; so, in each part of a society, the organ remains, though the persons who compose it change. Thus, in social life, as in the life of an animal, the units as well as the larger agencies formed of them, are in the main

stationary as respects the places where they discharge their duties and obtain their sustenance. And hence the power of individual locomotion does not practically affect the analogy.

4. The last and perhaps the most important distinction, is, that while in the body of an animal, only a special tissue is endowed with feeling; in a society, all the members are endowed with feeling. Even this distinction, however, is by no means a complete one. For in some of the lowest animals, characterized by the absence of a nervous system, such sensitiveness as exists is possessed by all parts. It is only in the more organized forms that feeling is monopolized by one class of the vital elements. Moreover, we must remember that societies, too, are not without a certain differentiation of this kind. Though the units of a community are all sensitive, yet they are so in unequal degrees. The classes engaged in agriculture and laborious occupations in general, are much less susceptible, intellectually and emotionally, than the rest; and especially less so than the classes of highest mental culture. Still, we have here a tolerably decided contrast between bodies politic and individual bodies. And it is one which we should keep constantly in view. For it reminds us that while in individual bodies, the welfare of all other parts is rightly subservient to the welfare of the nervous system, whose pleasurable or painful activities make up the good or evil of life; in bodies politic, the same thing does not hold, or holds to but a very slight extent. It is well that the lives of all parts of an animal should be merged in the life of the whole; because the whole has a corporate consciousness capable of happiness or misery. But it is not so with a society; since its living units do not and cannot lose individual consciousness; and since the community as a whole has no corporate consciousness. And this is an everlasting reason why the welfare of citizens cannot rightly be sacrificed to some supposed benefit of the State; but why, on the other hand, the State is to be maintained solely for the benefit of citizens. The corporate life must here be subservient to the lives of the parts; instead of the lives of the parts being subservient to the corporate life.

Such, then, are the points of analogy and the points of difference. May we not say that the points of difference serve but to bring into clearer light the points of analogy. . . . The *principles* of organization are the same; and the differences are simply differences of application.

Here ending this general survey of the facts which justify the comparison of a society to a living body; let us look at them in detail. We shall find that the parallelism becomes the more marked the more closely it is traced. . . . [The structure of various Protozoa is described.]

. . . But these little societies of monads, or cells, or whatever else we may call them, are societies only in the lowest sense: there is no subordination of parts among them—no organization. Each of the component units lives by and for itself; neither giving nor receiving aid. There is no mutual dependence, save that consequent on mere mechanical union.

Now do we not here discern analogies to the first stages of human societies? Among the lowest races, as the Bushmen, we find but incipient aggregation: sometimes single families: sometimes two or three families wandering about together. The number of associated units is small and variable; and their union inconstant. No division of labour except between the sexes; and the only kind of mutual aid is that of joint attack or defence. We see nothing beyond an undifferentiated group of individuals, forming the germ of a society; just as in the homogeneous groups of cells above described we see only the initial stage of animal and vegetable organization.

The comparison may now be carried a step higher. . . . [More complex Polyps are described.]

Turning to societies, we find these stages parallel in the majority of aboriginal tribes. When, instead of such small variable groups as are formed by Bushmen, we come to the larger and more permanent groups formed by savages not quite so low, we begin to find traces of social structure. Though industrial organization scarcely shows itself, except in the different occupations of the sexes: yet there is always more or less of governmental organization. While all the men are warriors and hunters, only a part of them are included in the council of chiefs; and in this council of chiefs some one has commonly supreme authority. There is thus a certain distinction of classes and powers; and through this slight specialization of functions, is effected a rude co-operation among the increasing mass of individuals, whenever the society has to act in its corporate capacity. . . . [Composite forms of the Hydra are described.]

Now in these various forms and degrees of aggregation, may we not see paralleled the union of groups of connate tribes into nations? Though in regions where circumstances permit, the separate tribes descended from some original tribe, migrate in all directions, and become far removed and quite separate; yet, in other cases, where the territory presents barriers to distant migration, this does not happen: the small kindred communities are held in closer contact, and eventually become more or less united into a nation. The contrast between the tribes of American Indians and the Scottish clans, illustrates this. And a glance at our own early history, or the early histories of continental nations, shows this fusion of small simple communities taking place in various ways and to various extents. . . . [Instances of further complexifications in marine animals.]

Well, in the evolution of a society, we see a primary differentiation of analogous kind; which similarly underlies the whole future structure. As already pointed out, the only manifest contrast of parts in primitive societies, is that between the governing and the governed. In the least organized tribes, the council of chiefs may be a body of men distinguished simply by greater courage or experience. In more organized tribes, the chief-class is definitely separated from the lower class, and often regarded as different in nature—sometimes as god-descended. And later, we find these two becoming respectively freemen and slaves, or nobles and serfs. A glance at their respective functions, makes it obvious that the great divisions thus early formed, stand to each other in a relation similar to that in which the primary divisions of the embryo stand to each other. For, from its first appearance, the class of chiefs is that by which the external acts of the society are controlled: alike in war, in negotiation, and in migration. Afterwards, while the upper class grows distinct from the lower, and at the same time becomes more exclusively regulative and defensive in its functions, alike in the persons of kings and subordinate rulers, priests, and military leaders; the inferior class becomes more and more exclusively occupied in providing the necessaries of life for the community at large. From the soil, with which it comes in most direct contact, the mass of the people takes up and prepares for use, the food and such rude articles of manufacture as are known; while the overlying mass of superior men, maintained by the working population, deals with circumstances external to the community—circumstances with which, by position, it is more immediately concerned. Ceasing by-and-by to have any knowledge of, or power over, the concerns of the society as a whole, the serf-class becomes devoted to the processes of alimentation; while the noble class, ceasing to take any part in the processes of alimentation, becomes devoted to the co-ordinated movements of the entire body public.

Equally remarkable is a further analogy of like kind. After the mucous and serous layers of the embryo have separated, there presently arises between the two, a third, known to physiologists as the vascular layer—a layer out of which are developed the chief blood-vessels. . . . Well, may we not trace a parallel step in social progress?

Between the governing and the governed, there at first exists no intermediate class; and even in some societies that have reached considerable sizes, there are scarcely any but the nobles and their kindred on the one hand, and the serfs on the other: the social structure being such, that the transfer of commodities takes place directly from slaves to their masters. But in societies of a higher type, there grows up between these two primitive classes, another—the trading or middle class. Equally, at first as now, we may see that, speaking generally, this middle class is the analogue of the middle layer in the embryo. For all traders are essentially distributors. . . .

Another fact which should not be passed over, is that in the evolution of a large society out of an aggregation of small ones, there is a gradual obliteration of the original lines of separation—a change to which, also, we may see analogies in living bodies. . . . [Biological examples from the Annulosa and Crustacea.] In feudal times, the minor communities governed by feudal lords, were severally organized in the same rude way; and were held together only by the fealty of their respective rulers to some suzerain. But along with the growth of a central power, the demarcations of these local communities disappeared; and their separate organizations merged into the general organization. The like is seen on a larger scale in the fusion of England, Wales, Scotland, and Ireland; and, on the Continent, in the coalescence of provinces into kingdoms. Even in the disappearance of law-made divisions, the process is analogous. Among the Anglo-Saxons, England was divided into tithings, hundreds, and counties: there were county courts, courts of hundred, and courts of tithing. The courts of tithing disappeared first; then the courts of hundred, which have, however, left traces; while the county-jurisdiction still exists.

But chiefly it is to be noted, that there eventually grows up an organization which has no reference to these original divisions, but traverses them in various directions, as is the case in creatures belonging to the sub-kingdom just named; and, further, that in both cases it is the sustaining organization which thus traverses old boundaries, while in both cases it is the governmental, or co-ordinating organization in which the original boundaries continue traceable. Thus, in the highest *Annulosa*, the exo-skeleton and the muscular system, never lose all traces of their primitive segmentation; but throughout a great part of the body, the contained viscera do not in the least conform to the external divisions. Similarly, with a nation, we see that while, for governmental purposes, such divisions as counties and parishes still exist, the structure developed for carrying out the nutrition of society, wholly ignores these boundaries: our great cotton-manufacture spreads out of Lancashire into North Derbyshire; Leicestershire and Nottinghamshire have long divided the stocking-trade between them; one great centre for the production of iron and iron-goods, includes parts of Warwickshire, Staffordshire, Worcestershire; and those various specializations of agriculture which have made different parts of England noted for different products, show no more respect to county-boundaries than do our growing towns to the boundaries of parishes.

If, after contemplating these analogies of structure, we inquire whether there are any such analogies between the processes of organic change, the answer is—yes. The causes which lead to increase of bulk in any part of the body politic, are of like nature with those which lead to increase of bulk in any part of an individual body. In both cases the antecedent is greater functional activity, consequent on greater demand. Each limb, viscus, gland, or other member of an animal, is developed by exercise—by actively discharging the duties which the body at large requires of it; and similarly, any class of labourers or artisans, any manufacturing centre, or any official agency, begins to enlarge when the community devolves on it an increase of work. In each case, too, growth has its conditions and its limits. That any organ in a living being may grow by exercise, there needs a due supply of blood: all action implies waste; blood brings the materials for repair; and before there can be growth, the quantity of blood supplied must be more than that requisite for repair.

So is it in a society. If to some district which elaborates for the community particular commodities—say the woollens of Yorkshire—there comes an augmented demand; and if, in fulfilment of this demand, a certain expenditure and wear of the manufacturing organization are incurred; and if, in payment for the extra supply of woollens sent away, there comes back only such quantity of commodities as replaces the expenditure, and makes good the waste of life and machinery; there can clearly be no growth. That there may be growth, the commodities obtained in return must be more than sufficient for these ends; and just in proportion as the surplus is great will the growth be rapid. Whence it is manifest that what in commercial affairs we call *profit*, answers to the excess of nutrition over waste in a living body. . . .

The last few paragraphs introduce the next division of our subject. Almost unawares we have come upon the analogy which exists between the blood of a living body, and the circulating mass of commodities in the body politic. We have now to trace out this analogy from its simplest to its most complex manifestations. . . .

Thus far, we have considered the analogy between the blood in a living body and the consumable and circulating commodities in the body politic. Let us now compare the appliances by which they are respectively distributed. We shall find in the development of these appliances, parallelisms not less remarkable than those above set forth. Already we have shown that, as classes, wholesale and retail distributors discharge in a society, the office which the vascular system discharges in an individual creature; that they come into existence later than the other two great classes, as the vascular layer appears later than the mucous and serous layers; and that they occupy a like intermediate position. Here, however, it remains to be pointed out that a complete conception of the circulating system in a society, includes not only the active human agents who propel the currents of commodities, and regulate their distribution; but includes, also, the channels of communication. It is the formation and arrangement of these, to which we now direct attention.

Going back once more to those lower animals in which there is found nothing but a partial diffusion, not of blood, but only of crude nutritive fluids, it is to be remarked that the channels through which the diffusion takes place, are mere excavations through the half-organized substance of the body: they have no lining membranes, but are mere *lacunæ* traversing a rude tissue. Now countries in which civilization is but commencing, display a like condition: there are no roads properly so called; but the wilderness of vegetal life covering the earth's surface, is pierced by tracks, through which the distribution of crude commodities takes place. And while in both cases, the acts of distribution occur only at long intervals (the currents, after a pause, now setting towards a general centre, and now away from it), the transfer is in both cases slow and difficult. But among other accompaniments of progress, common to animals and societies, comes the formation of more definite and complete channels of communication. Blood-vessels acquire distinct walls; roads are fenced and gravelled. This advance is first seen in those roads or vessels that are nearest to the chief centres of distribution; while the peripheral roads and peripheral vessels, long continue in their primitive states. At a yet later stage of development, where comparative finish of structure is found throughout the system as well as near the chief centres, there remains in both cases the difference, that the main channels are comparatively broad and straight, while the subordinate ones are narrow and tortuous in proportion to their remoteness. . . .

These parallelisms in the evolutions and structures of the circulating systems, introduce us to others in the kinds and rates of the movements going on through them. In the lowest societies, as in the lowest creatures, the distribution of crude nutriment is by slow gurgitations and regurgitations. In creatures that have rude vascular systems, as in societies that are beginning to have roads and some transfer of commodities along them, there is no regular circulation in definite courses; but instead, periodical changes of the currents—now towards this point, and now towards that. Through each part of an inferior mollusk's body, the blood flows for a while in one direction, then stops, and flows in the opposite direction; just as through a rudely-organized society, the distribution of merchandise is slowly carried on by great fairs, occurring in different localities, to and from which the currents periodically set. Only animals of tolerably complete organizations, like advanced communities, are permeated by constant currents that are definitely directed. In living bodies, the local and variable currents disappear when there grow up great centres of circulation, generating more powerful currents, by a rhythm which ends in a quick, regular pulsation. And when in social bodies, there arise great centres of commercial activity, producing and exchanging large quantities of commodities, the rapid and continuous streams drawn in and emitted by these centres, subdue all minor and local circulations: the slow rhythm of fairs merges into the faster one of weekly markets, and in the chief centres of distribution, weekly markets merge into daily markets; while in place of the languid transfer from place to place, taking place at first weekly, then twice or thrice a week, we by-and-by get daily transfer, and finally transfer many times a day—the original sluggish, irregular rhythm, becomes a rapid, equable pulse. . . .

We come at length to the nervous system. . . . We have now to compare the appliances by which a society, as a whole, is regulated, with those by which the movements of an individual creature are regulated. We shall find here, parallelisms equally striking with those already detailed. . . .

Again, in the unmodified ectoderm, as we see it in the *Hydra*, the units are all endowed both with impressibility and contractility; but as we ascend to higher types of organization, the ectoderm differentiates into classes of units which divide those two functions between them: some, becoming exclusively impressible, cease to be contractile; while some, becoming exclusively contractile, cease to be impressible. Similarly with societies. In an aboriginal tribe, the directive and executive functions are diffused in a mingled form throughout the whole governing class. Each minor chief commands those under him, and if need be, himself coerces them into obedience. The council of chiefs itself carries out on the battle-field its own decisions. The head chief not only makes laws, but administers justice with his own hands. In larger and more settled communities, however, the directive and executive agencies begin to grow distinct from each other. As fast as his duties accumulate, the head chief or king confines himself more and more to directing public affairs, and leaves the execution of his will to others: he deputes others to enforce submission, to inflict punsihments, or to carry out minor acts of offence and defence; and only on occasions when, perhaps, the safety of the society and his own supremacy are at stake, does he begin to act as well as direct. As this differentiation establishes itself, the characteristics of the ruler begin to change. No longer, as in an aboriginal tribe, the strongest and most daring man, the tendency is for him to become the man of greatest cunning, foresight, and skill in the management of others; for in societies that have advanced beyond the first stage, it is chiefly such qualities that insure success in gaining supreme power, and holding it, against internal and external enemies. Thus that member of the governing class who comes to be the chief directing agent, and so plays the same part that a rudimentary nervous centre does in an unfolding organism, is usually one endowed with some superiorities of nervous organization. . . . [Spencer now considers more complex systems of control.]

The cerebrum co-ordinates the countless heterogeneous considerations which affect the present and future welfare of the individual as a whole; and the legislature co-ordinates the countless heterogeneous considerations which affect the immediate and remote welfare of the whole community. We may describe the office of the brain as that of *averaging* the interests of life, physical, intellectual, moral, social; and a good brain is one in which the desires answering to these respective interests are so balanced, that the conduct they jointly dictate, sacrifices none of them. Similarly, we may describe the office of a Parliament as that of *averaging* the interests of the various classes in a community; and a good Parliament is one in which the parties answering to these respective interests are so balanced, that their united legislation concedes to each class as much as consists with the claims of the rest. Besides being comparable in their duties, these great directive centres, social and individual, are comparable in the processes by which their duties are discharged.

It is now an acknowledged truth in psychology, that the cerebrum is not occupied with direct impressions from without, but with the ideas of such impressions: instead of the actual sensations produced in the body, and directly appreciated by the sensory ganglia or primitvie nervous centres, the cerebrum receives only the representations of these sensations; and its consciousness is called *representative* consciousness, to distinguish it from the original or *presentative* consciousness. Is it not significant that we have hit on the same word to distinguish the function of our House of Commons? We call it a *representative* body, because the interests with which it deals—the pains and pleasures about which it consults—are not directly presented to it, but represented to it by its various members; and a debate is a conflict of representations of the evils or benefits likely to follow from a proposed course—a description which applies with equal truth to a debate in the individual consciousness. In both cases, too, these great governing masses take no part in the executive functions. As, after a conflict in the cerebrum, those desires which finally predominate, act on the subjacent ganglia, and through their instrumentality determine the bodily actions; so the parties which, after a parliamentary struggle, gain the victory, do not themselves carry out their wishes, but get them carried out by the executive divisions of the Government. The fulfilment of all legislative decisions still devolves on the original directive centres—the impulse passing from the Parliament to the Ministers, and from the Ministers to the King, in whose name everything is done; just as those smaller, first-developed ganglia, which in the lowest vertebrata are the chief controlling agents, are still, in the brains of the higher vertebrata, the agents through which the dictates of the cerebrum are worked out.

Moreover, in both cases these original centres become increasingly automatic. In the developed vertebrate animal, they have little function beyond that of conveying impressions to, and executing the determinations of, the larger centres. In our highly organized government, the monarch has long been lapsing into a passive agent of Parliament; and now, ministers are rapidly falling into the same position.

8

EVOLUTION DEFINED

It is true that Evolution, under its primary aspect, is a change from a less coherent state to a more coherent state, consequent on the dissipation of motion and integration of matter; but this is far from being the whole truth. Along with a passage from the incoherent, there goes on a passage from the uniform to the multiform. Such, at least, is the fact wherever Evolution is compound; which it is in the immense majority of cases. While there is a progressing concentration of the aggregate, caused either by the closer approach of the matter within its limits, or by the drawing in of further matter, or by both; and while the more or less distinct parts into which the aggregate divides and subdivides are also severally concentrating; these parts are simultaneously becoming unlike—unlike in size, or in form, or in texture, or in composition, or in several or all of these. The same process is exhibited by the whole and by its members. The entire mass is integrating and at the same time differentiating from other masses; while each member of it is also integrating and at the same time differentiating from other members.

Our conception, then, must unite these characters. As we now understand it, Evolution is definable as a change from an incoherent homogeneity to a coherent heterogeneity, accompanying the dissipation of motion and integration of matter. . . .

From *First Principles,* 6th ed. (London: Williams and Norgate [1862], 1904), pp. 291, 438.

The law of Evolution has been thus far contemplated as holding true of each order of existences, considered as a separate order. But the induction as so presented falls short of that completeness which it gains when we contemplate these several orders of existences as forming together one natural whole. While we think of Evolution as divided into astronomic, geologic, biologic, psychologic, sociologic, &c., it may seem to some extent a coincidence that the same law of metamorphosis holds throughout all its divisions. But when we recognize these divisions as mere conventional groupings, made to facilitate the arrangement and acquisition of knowledge—when we remember that the different existences with which they severally deal are component parts of one Cosmos; we see at once that there are not several kinds of Evolution having certain traits in common, but one Evolution going on everywhere after the same manner.

III. A Methodology for Social Science

9

THE NEED FOR SOCIOLOGY

Over his pipe in the village ale-house, the labourer says very positively what Parliament should do about the "foot and mouth disease." At the farmer's market-table, his master makes the glasses jingle as, with his fist, he emphasizes the assertion that he did not get half enough compensation for his slaughtered beasts during the cattle-plague. These are not hesitating opinions. On a matter affecting the agricultural interest, statements are still as dogmatic as they were during the Anti-Corn-Law agitation, when, in every rural circle, you heard that the nation would be ruined if the lightly-taxed foreigner was allowed to compete in our markets with the heavily-taxed Englishman: a proposition held to be so self-evident that dissent from it implied either stupidity or knavery.

Now, as then, may be daily heard among other classes, opinions just as decided and just as unwarranted. By men called educated, the old plea for extravagant expenditure, that "it is good for trade," is still continually urged with full belief in its sufficiency. Scarcely any decrease is observable in the fallacy that whatever gives employment is beneficial: no regard being had to the value for ulterior purposes of that which the labour produces; no question being asked what would have resulted had the capital which paid for the labour taken some other channel and paid for some other labour. Neither criticism nor explanation appreciably modifies these beliefs. When there is again an opening for them they are expressed

---

From *The Study of Sociology* (London: Williams and Norgate, 1873), pp. 1–3, 11–22.

with undiminished confidence. Along with delusions of this kind go whole families of others. People who think that the relations between expenditure and production are so simple, naturally assume simplicity in other relations among social phenomena. Is there distress somewhere? They suppose nothing more is required than to subscribe money for relieving it. On the one hand, they never trace the reactive effects which charitable donations work on bank accounts, on the surplus-capital bankers have to lend, on the productive activity which the capital now abstracted would have set up, on the number of labourers who would have received wages and who now go without wages—they do not perceive that certain necessaries of life have been withheld from one man who would have exchanged useful work for them, and given to another who perhaps persistently evades working. Nor, on the other hand, do they look beyond the immediate mitigation of misery. They deliberately shut their eyes to the fact that as fast as they increase the provision for those who live without labour, so fast do they increase the number of those who live without labour; and that with an ever-increasing distribution of alms, there comes an ever-increasing outcry for more alms. Similarly throughout all their political thinking. Proximate causes and proximate results are alone contemplated. There is scarcely any consciousness that the original causes are often numerous and widely different from the apparent cause; and that beyond each immediate result there will be multitudinous remote results, most of them quite incalculable.

Minds in which the conceptions of social actions are thus rudimentary, are also minds ready to harbour wild hopes of benefits to be achieved by administrative agencies. In each such mind there seems to be the unexpressed postulate that every evil in a society admits of cure; and that the cure lies within the reach of law. . . . Just as the perpetual-motion schemer hopes, by a cunning arrangement of parts, to get from one end of his machine more energy than he puts in at the other; so the ordinary political schemer is convinced that out of a legislative apparatus, properly devised and worked with due dexterity, may be had beneficial State-action without any detrimental reaction. He expects to get out of a stupid people the effects of intelligence, and to evolve from inferior citizens superior conduct.

But while the prevalence of crude political opinions among those whose conceptions about simple matters are so crude, might be anticipated, it is surprising that the class disciplined by scientific culture should bring to the interpretation of social phenomena, methods but little in advance of those used by others. Now that the transformation and equivalence of forces is seen by men of science to hold not only throughout all inorganic actions, but throughout all organic actions; now that even mental changes are recognized as the correlatives of cerebral changes, which also conform to this principle; and now, that there must be admitted the corollary, that all actions going on in a society are measured by certain antecedent energies, which disappear in effecting them, while they themselves become actual or potential energies from which subsequent actions arise; it is strange that there should not have arisen the consciousness that these highest phenomena are to be studied as lower phenomena have been studied—not, of course, after the same physical methods, but in conformity with the same principles. And yet scientific men rarely display such a consciousness. . . .

This immense incongruity between the attitude in which the most disciplined minds approach other orders of natural phenomena presented by societies, will be best illustrated by a series of antitheses thus:—

The material media through which we see things, always more or less falsify the facts: making, for example, the apparent direction of a star slightly different from its real direction, and sometimes, as when a fish is seen in the water, the apparent place is so far from the real place, that great misconception results unless large allowance is made for refraction; but sociological observations are not thus falsified: through the daily press light comes without any bending of its rays, and in studying past ages it is easy to make allowance for the refraction due to the historic medium. The motions of gases, though they conform to mechanical laws which are well understood, are nevertheless so involved, that the art of controlling currents of air in a house is not yet mastered; but the waves and currents of feeling running through a society, and the consequent directions and amounts of social activities, may be readily known beforehand. Though molecules of inorganic substances are very simple, yet prolonged study is required to understand their modes of behavior to one another, and even the most instructed frequently meet with interactions of them producing consequences they never anticipated; but where the interacting bodies are not molecules but living beings of highly-complex natures, it is easy to foresee all results which will arise. Physical phenomena are so connected that between seeming probability and actual truth, there is apt to be a wide difference, even where but two bodies are acting: instance the natural supposition that during our northern summer the Earth is nearer to the Sun than during the winter, which is just the reverse of the fact; but among sociological phenomena, where the bodies are so multitudinous, and the forces by which they act on one another so many, and so multiform, and so variable, the probability and the actuality will of course correspond. Matter often behaves paradoxically, as when two cold liquids added together become boiling hot, or as when the mixing of two clear liquids produces an opaque mud, or as when water immersed in sulphurous acid freezes on a hot iron plate; but what we distinguish as Mind, especially when massed together in the way which causes social action, evolves no paradoxical results—always such results come from it as seem likely to come.

The acceptance of contradictions like these, tacitly implied in the beliefs of the scientifically cultivated, is the more remarkable when we consider how abundant are the proofs that human nature is difficult to manipulate; that methods apparently the most rational disappoint expectation; and that the best results frequently arise from courses which common sense thinks unpractical. . . . How obvious it appears that when minds go deranged, there is no remedy but replacing the weak internal control by a strong external control. Yet the "non-restraint system" has had far more success than the system of strait-waistcoats. Dr. Batty Tuke, a physician of much experience in treating the insane, has lately testified that the desire to escape is great when locks and keys are used, but almost disappears when they are disused: the policy of unlocked doors has had 95 per cent. of success and 5 per cent. of failure. And in further evidence of the mischief often done by measures supposed to be curative, here is Dr. Maudsley, also an authority on such questions, speaking of "asylum-made lunatics." Again, is it not clear that the repression of crime will be effectual in proportion as the punishment is severe? Yet the great amelioration in our penal code, initiated by Romilly, has not been followed by increased criminality but by decreased criminality; and the testimonies of those who have had most experience—Maconochie in Norfolk Island, Dickson in Western Australia, Obermier in Germany, Montesinos in Spain—unite to show that in proportion as the criminal is left to suffer no other penalty than that of maintaining himself under such restraints only as are needful for social safety, the reformation is great: exceeding, indeed, all anticipation. . . .

. . . We habitually assume that only by legal restraints are men to be kept from aggressing on their neighbours; and yet there are facts which should lead us to qualify our assumption. So-called debts of honour, for the non-payment of which there is no legal penalty, are held more sacred than debts that can be legally enforced; and on the Stock-Exchange, where only pencil memoranda in the respective note-books of two brokers guarantee the sale and purchase of many thousands, contracts are safer than those which, in the outside world, are formally registered in signed and sealed parchments.

Multitudes of cases might be accumulated showing how, in other directions, men's thoughts and feelings produce kinds of conduct which, *a priori*, would be judged very improbable. And if, going beyond our own society and our own time, we observe what has happened among other races, and among the earlier generations of our own race, we meet, at every step, workings-out of human nature utterly unlike those which we assume when making political forecasts. Who, generalizing the experiences of his daily life, would suppose that men, to please their gods, would swing for hours from hooks drawn through the muscles of their backs, or let their nails grow through the palms of their clenched hands, or roll over and over hundreds of miles to visit a shrine? Who would have thought it possible that a public sentiment and a private feeling might be as in China, where a criminal can buy a substitute to be executed in his stead: the substitute's family having the money? Or, to take hsitorical cases more nearly concerning ourselves—Who foresaw that the beliefs in purgatory and priestly intercession would cause one-half of England to lapse into the hands of the Church? or who foresaw that a defect in the law of mortmain would lead to bequests of large estates consecrated as graveyards? Who could have imagined that robber-kings and bandit-barons, with vassals to match, would, generation after generation, have traversed all Europe through hardships and dangers to risk their lives in getting possession of the reputed burial place of one whose injunction was to turn the left cheek when the right was smitten? Or who, again, would have anticipated that when, in Jerusalem, this same teacher disclaimed political aims, and repudiated political instrumentalities, the professed successors of his disciples would by and by become rulers dominating over all the kings of Europe? Such a result could be as little foreseen as it could be foreseen that an instrument of torture used by the Pagans would give the ground-plans to Christian temples throughout Europe; and as little as it could be foreseen that the process of this torture, recounted in Christian narratives, might come to be mistaken for a Christian institution, as it was by the Malay chief who, being expostulated with for crucifying some rebels, replied that he was following "the English practice," which he read in "their sacred books."

Look where we will at the genesis of social phenomena, we shall similarly find that while the particular ends contemplated and arranged for have commonly not been more than temporarily attained if attained at all, the changes actually brought about have arisen from causes of which the very existence was unknown.

To such considerations as these, set down to show the inconsistency of those who think that prevision of social phenomena is possible without much study, though much study is needed for prevision of other phenomena, it will doubtless be replied that time does not allow of systematic inquiry. From the scientific, as from the unscientific, there will come the plea that, in his capacity of citizen, each man has to act—must vote, and must decide before he votes—must conclude to the best of his ability on such information as he has.

In this plea there is some truth, mingled with a good deal more that looks like truth. It is a product of that "must-do-something" impulse which is the origin of much mischief, individual and social. An amiable anxiety to undo or neutralize an evil, often prompts to rash courses, as you may see in the hurry with which one who has fallen is snatched up by those at hand; just as though there were danger in letting him lie, which there is not, and no danger in incautiously raising him, which there is. Always you find among people in proportion as they are ignorant, a belief in specifics, and a great confidence in pressing the adoption of them. . . .

. . . But as fast as crude conceptions of diseases and remedial measures grow up into Pathology and Therapeutics, we find increasing caution, along with increasing proof that evil is often done instead of good. This contrast is traceable not only as we pass from popular ignorance to professional knowledge, but as we pass from the smaller professional knowledge of early times to the greater professional knowledge of our own. The question with the modern physician is not as with the ancient—shall the treatment be blood-letting? shall cathartics, or shall diaphoretics be given? or shall mercurials be administered? But there rises the previous question —shall there be any treatment beyond a wholesome regimen? And even among existing physicians it happens that in proportion as the judgment is most cultivated, there is the least yielding to the "must-do-something" impulse.

Is it not possible, then—is it not even probable, that this supposed necessity for immediate action, which is put in as an excuse for drawing quick conclusions from few data, is the concomitant of deficient knowledge? Is it not probable that as in Biology so in Sociology, the accumulation of more facts, the more critical comparison of them, and the drawing of conclusions on scientific methods, will be accompanied by increasing doubt about the benefits to be secured, and increasing fear of the mischiefs which may be worked? Is it not probable that what in the individual organism is improperly, though conveniently, called the *vis medicatrix naturæ*, may be found to have its analogue in the social organism? and will there not very likely come along with the recognition of this, the consciousness that in both cases the one thing needful is to maintain the conditions under which the natural actions have fair play? Such a consciousness, to be anticipated from increased knowledge, will diminish the force of this plea for prompt decision after little inquiry; since it will check this tendency to think of a remedial measure as one that may do good and cannot do harm. Nay more, the study of Sociology, scientifically carried on by tracing back proximate causes to remote ones, and tracing down primary effects to secondary and tertiary effects which multiply as they diffuse, will dissipate the current illusion that social evils admit of radical cures. Given an average defect of nature among the units of a society, and no skilful manipulation of them will prevent that defect from producing its equivalent of bad results. It is possible to change the form of these bad results; it is possible to change the places at which they are manifested; but it is not possible to get rid of them. The belief that faulty character can so organize itself socially, as to get out of itself a conduct which is not proportionately faulty, is an utterly-baseless belief. You may alter the incidence of the mischief, but the amount of it must inevitably be borne somewhere. . . .

10

SOCIOLOGY AGAINST HISTORY

My position, stated briefly, is that until you have got a true theory of humanity, you cannot interpret history; and when you have got a true theory of humanity *you do not want history*. You can draw no inference from the facts and alleged facts of history without your conceptions of human nature entering into that inference: and unless your conceptions of human nature are true your inference will be vicious. But if your conceptions of human nature be true you need none of the inferences drawn from history for your guidance. If you ask how is one to get a true theory of humanity, I reply—study it in the facts you see around you and in the general laws of life. For myself, looking as I do at humanity as the highest result yet of the evolution of life on the earth, I prefer to take in the whole series of phenomena from the beginning as far as they are ascertainable. I, too, am a lover of history; but it is the history of the Cosmos as a whole. I believe that you might as reasonably expect to understand the nature of an adult man by watching him for an hour (being in ignorance of all his antecedents), as to suppose that you can fathom humanity by studying the last few thousand years of its evolution.

[Spencer has been criticizing the vulgar attribution of phenomena to divine agency.] An allied class, equally unprepared to

From *Life and Letters of Herbert Spencer*, by D. Duncan (London: Williams and Norgate, 1908), p. 62; *The Study of Sociology* (London: Williams and Norgate, 1873), pp. 31–35; *Education* (London: Williams and Norgate, 1861), pp. 39–43; *The Study of Sociology*, pp. 37–47.

interpret sociological phenomena scientifically, is the class which sees in the course of civilization little else than a record of remarkable persons and their doings. One who is conspicuous as the exponent of this view writes:—"As I take it, universal history, the history of what man has accomplished in this world, is at bottom the history of the great men who have worked here." And this, not perhaps distinctly formulated, but everywhere implied, is the belief in which nearly all are brought up. Let us glance at the genesis of it.

Round their camp-fire assembled savages tell the events of the day's chase; and he among them who has done some feat of skill or agility is duly lauded. On a return from the war-path, the sagacity of the chief and the strength or courage of this or that warrior, are the all-absorbing themes. When the day, or the immediate past, affords no remarkable deed, the topic is the achievement of some noted leader lately dead, or some traditional founder of the tribe: accompanied, it may be, with a dance dramatically representing those victories which the chant recites. Such narratives, concerning, as they do, the prosperity and indeed the very existence of the tribe, are of the intensest interest; and in them we have the common root of music, of the drama, of poetry, of biography, of history, and of literature in general. Savage life furnishes little else worthy of note; and the chronicles of tribes contain scarcely anything more to be remembered. Early historic races show us the same thing. [Instances from Egypt, Assyria and Greece.] The lessons given to every civilized child tacitly imply, like the traditions of the uncivilized and semi-civilized, that throughout the past of the human race, the doings of conspicuous persons have been the only things worthy of remembrance. . . . "Arms and the man" form the end of the story as they form its beginning. After the mythology, which of course is all-essential, come the achievements of rulers and soldiers from Agamemnon down to Cæsar: what knowledge is gained of social organization, manners, ideas, morals, being little more than the biographical statements involve. And the value of the knowledge is so ranked that while it would be a disgrace to be wrong about the amours of Zeus, and while inability to name the commander at Marathon would be discreditable, it is excusable to know nothing of the social condition that preceded Lycurgus or of the origin and functions of the Areopagus.

Thus the great-man-theory of History finds everywhere a ready-prepared conception—is, indeed, but the definite expression of that which is latent in the thoughts of the savage, tacitly asserted in all early traditions, and taught to every child by multitudinous illustrations. The glad acceptance it meets with has sundry more special causes. There is, first, this universal love of personalities, which, active in the aboriginal man, dominates still—a love seen in the urchin who asks you to tell him a story, meaning, thereby, somebody's adventures; a love gratified in adults by police-reports, court-news, divorce-cases, accounts of accidents, and lists of births, marriages, and deaths; a love displayed even by conversations in the streets, where fragments of dialogue, heard in passing, show that mostly between men, and always between women, the personal pronouns recur every instant. If you want roughly to estimate any one's mental calibre, you cannot do it better than by observing the ratio of generalities to personalities in his talk—how far simple truths about individuals are replaced by truths abstracted from numerous experiences of men and things. And when you have thus measured many, you find but a scattered few likely to take anything more than a biographical view of human affairs. In the second place, this great-man-theory commends itself as promising instruction along with amusement. Being already fond of hearing about people's sayings and doings, it is pleasant news that, to understand the course of civilization, you have only to read diligently the lives of distinguished men. . . . And then, in the third place, the interpretation of things thus given is so beautifully simple—seems so easy to comprehend. Providing you are content with conceptions that are out of focus, as most people's conceptions are, the solutions it yields appear quite satisfactory. . . .

But now, if, dissatisfied with vagueness, we demand that our ideas shall be brought into focus and exactly defined, we discover the hypothesis to be utterly incoherent. If, not stopping at the explanation of social progress as due to the great man, we go back a step and ask whence comes the great man, we find that the theory breaks down completely. The question has two conceivable answers: his origin is supernatural, or it is natural. Is his origin supernatural? Then he is a deputy-god, and we have Theocracy once removed—or, rather, not removed at all; for we must then agree with Mr. Schomberg, quoted above, that "the determination of Cæsar to invade Britain" was divinely inspired, and that from him, down to "George III, the GREAT and the GOOD," the successive rulers were appointed to carry out successive designs. Is this an unacceptable solution? Then the origin of the great man is natural; and immediately this is recognized he must be classed with all other phenomena in the society that gave him birth, as a product of its antecedents. Along with the whole generation of which he forms a minute part—along with its institutions, language, knowledge, manners, and its multitudinous arts and appliances, he is a resultant of an enormous aggregate of forces that have been co-operating for ages. . . . If it be a fact that the great man may modify his nation in its structure and actions, it is also a fact that there must have been those antecedent modifications constituting national progress before he could be evolved. Before he can re-make his society, his society must make him. So that all those changes of which he is the proximate initiator have their chief causes in the generations he descended from. If there is to be anything like a real explanation of these changes, it must be sought in that aggregate of conditions out of which both he and they have arisen. . . .

. . . Our school-courses contain certain studies which, nominally at least, bear upon political and social duties. Of these the only one that occupies a prominent place is History.

But, as already hinted, the information commonly given under this head, is almost valueless for purposes of guidance. Scarcely any of the facts set down in our school-histories, and very few of those contained in the more elaborate works written for adults, illustrate the right principles of political action. The biographies of monarchs (and our children learn little else) throw scarcely any light upon the science of society. Familiarity with court intrigues, plots, usurpations, or the like, and with all the personalities accompanying them, aids very little in elucidating the causes of national progress. We read of some squabble for power, that it led to a pitched battle; that such and such were the names of the generals and their leading subordinates; that they had each so many thousand infantry and cavalry, and so many cannon; that they arranged their forces in this and that order; that they manœuvred, attacked, and fell back in certain ways; that at this part of the day such disasters were sustained, and at that such advantages gained; that in one particular movement some leading officer fell, while in another a certain regiment was decimated; that after all the changing fortunes of the fight, the victory was gained by this or that army; and that so many were killed and wounded on each side, and so many captured by the conquerors. And now, out of the accumulated details making up the narrative, say which it is that helps you in deciding on your conduct as a citizen. Supposing even that you diligently read, not only *The Fifteen Decisive Battles of the World*, but accounts of all other battles that history mentions; how much more judicious would your vote be at the next election? "But these are facts—interesting facts," you say. Without doubt they are facts (such, at least, as are not wholly or partially fictions); and to many they may be interesting facts. But this by no means implies that they are valuable. . . . They are facts from which no conclusions can be drawn—*unorganizable* facts; and therefore facts of no service in establishing principles of conduct, which is the chief use of facts. Read them, if you like, for amusement; but do not flatter yourself they are instructive.

That which constitutes History, properly so called, is in great part omitted from works on the subject. Only of late years have historians commenced giving us, in any considerable quantity, the truly valuable information. As in past ages the king was everything and the people nothing; so, in past histories the doings of the king fill the entire picture, to which the national life forms but an obscure background. While only now, when the welfare of nations rather than the rulers is becoming the dominant idea, are historians beginning to occupy themselves with the phenomena of social progress. The thing it really concerns us to know is the natural history of society. We want all facts which help us to understand how a nation has grown and organized itself. Among these, let us of course have an account of its government; with as little as may be of gossip about the men who officered it, and as much as possible about the structure, principles, methods, prejudices, corruptions, etc., which it exhibited; and let this account include not only the nature and actions of the central government, but also those of local governments, down to their minutest ramifications. Let us of course also have a parallel description of the ecclesiastical government—its organization, its conduct, its power, its relations to the State; and accompanying this, the ceremonial, creed, and religious ideas—not only those nominally believed, but those really believed and acted upon. Let us at the same time be informed of the control exercised by class over class, as displayed in social observances—in titles, salutations, and forms of address. Let us know, too, what were all the other customs which regulated the popular life out of doors and indoors: including those concerning the relations of the sexes, and the relations of parents to children. The superstitions, also, from the more important myths down to the charms in common use, should be indicated. Next should come a delineation of the industrial system: showing to what extent the division of labour was carried; how trades were regulated, whether by caste, guilds, or otherwise; what was the connection between employers and employed; what were the agencies for distributing commodities; what were the means of communication; what was the circulating medium. Accompanying all which should be given an account of the industrial arts technically considered: stating the processes in use, and the quality of the products. Further, the intellectual condition of the nation in its various grades should be depicted; not only with respect to the kind and amount of education, but with respect to the progress made in science, and the prevailing manner of thinking. The degree of æsthetic culture, as displayed in architecture, sculpture, painting, dress, music, poetry, and fiction, should be described. Nor should there be omitted a sketch of the daily lives of the people—their food, their homes, and their amusements. And lastly, to connect the whole, should be exhibited the morals, theoretical and practical, of all classes as indicated in their laws, habits, proverbs, deeds. These facts, given with as much brevity as consists with clearness and accuracy, should be so grouped and arranged that they may be comprehended in their *ensemble*, and contemplated as mutually-dependent parts of one great whole. The aim should be so to present them that men may readily trace the *consensus* subsisting among them; with the view of learning what social phenomena coexist with what others. And then the corresponding delineations of succeeding ages should be so managed as to show how each belief, institution, custom, and arrangement was modified; and how the *consensus* of preceding structures and functions was developed into the *consensus* of succeeding ones. Such alone is the kind of information respecting past times, which can be of service to the citizen for the regulation of his conduct. The only history that is of practical value, is what may be called Descriptive Sociology. And the highest office which the historian can discharge, is that of so narrating the lives of nations, as to furnish materials for a Comparative Sociology; and for the subsequent determination of the ultimate laws to which social phenomena conform.

But now mark, that even supposing an adequate stock of this truly valuable historical knowledge has been acquired, it is of comparatively little use without the key. And the key is to be found only in Science. In the absence of the generalizations of biology and psychology, rational interpretation of social phenomena is impossible. . . .

In addition to that passive denial of a Social Science implied by these two allied doctrines, one or other of which is held by nine men out of ten, there comes from some an active denial of it—either entire or partial. Reasons are given for the belief that no such thing is possible. The invalidity of these reasons can be shown only after the essential nature of Social Science, overlooked by those who give them, has been pointed out; and to point this out here would be to forestal the argument. Some minor criticisms may, however, fitly precede the major criticism. Let us consider first the positions taken up by Mr. Froude:—

When natural causes are liable to be set aside and neutralized by what is called volition, the word Science is out of place. If it is free to a man to choose what he will do or not do, there is no adequate science of him. If there is a science of him, there is no free choice, and the praise or blame with which we regard one another are impertinent and out of place.

It is in this marvellous power in men to do wrong . . . that the impossibility stands of forming scientific calculations of what men will do before the fact, or scientific explanations of what they have done after the fact.

Mr. Buckle would deliver himself from the eccentricities of this and that individual by a doctrine of averages. . . . Unfortunately the average of one generation need not be the average of the next: . . . no two generations are alike.

There [in history] the phenomena never repeat themselves. There we are dependent wholly on the record of things said to have happened once, but which never happen or can happen a second time. There no experiment is possible; we can watch for no recurring fact to test the worth of our conjectures.[1]

Here Mr. Froude changes the venue, and joins issue on the old battle-ground of free will *versus* necessity: declaring a Social Science to be incompatible with free will. The first extract implies, not simply that indivdual volition is incalculable—that "there is no adequate science of" man (no Science of Psychology); but it also asserts, by implication, that there are no causal relations among his states of mind: the volition by which "natural causes are liable to be set aside," being put in antithesis to natural, must be supernatural. Hence we are, in fact, carried back to that primitive form of interpretation contemplated at the outset. A further comment is, that because volitions of some kinds cannot be foreseen, Mr. Froude argues as though no volitions can be foreseen: ignoring the fact that the simple volitions determining the ordinary conduct, are so regular that prevision having a high degree of probability is easy. If, in crossing a street, a man sees a carriage coming upon him, you may safely assert that, in nine hundred and ninety-nine cases out of a thousand, he will try to get out of the way. If, being pressed to catch a train, he knows that by one route it is a mile to the station and by another two miles, you may conclude with considerable confidence that he will take the one-mile route; and

1 J. A. Froude (1818–94), a personal friend of Kingsley's, turned to history after he had lost his faith and resigned holy orders. His *History of England* (1856), moralistic, Carlylean, very popular in its day, is more to be admired for its style than its scholarship.—Ed.

should he be aware that losing the train will lose him a fortune, it is pretty certain that, if he has but ten minutes to do the mile in, he will either run or call a cab. If he can buy next door a commodity of daily consumption better and cheaper than at the other end of the town, we may affirm that, if he does not buy next door, some special relation between him and the remoter shop-keeper furnishes a strong reason for taking a worse commodity at greater cost of money and trouble. And though, if he has an estate to dispose of, it is within the limits of possibility that he will sell it to A for £1,000, though B has offered £2,000 for it; yet the unusual motives leading to such an act need scarcely be taken into account as qualifying the generalization that a man will sell to the highest bidder. Now, since the predominant activities of citizens are determined by motives of this degree of regularity, there must be resulting social phenomena that have corresponding degrees of regularity—greater degrees, indeed, since in them the effects of exceptional motives become lost in the effects of the aggregate of ordinary motives. Another comment may be added. Mr. Froude exaggerates the antithesis he draws by using a conception of science which is too narrow: he speaks as though there were no science but exact science. Scientific previsions, both qualitative and quantitative, have various degrees of definiteness; and because among certain classes of phenomena the previsions are approximate only, it is not, therefore, to be said that there is no science of those phenomena: if there is *some* prevision, there is *some* science. Take, for example, Meteorology. The Derby has been run in a snow-storm, and you may occasionally want a fire in July; but such anomalies do not prevent us from being perfectly certain that the coming summer will be warmer than the past winter. Our south-westerly gales in the autumn may come early or may come late, may be violent or moderate, at one time or at intervals; but that there will be an excess of wind from the south-west at that part of the year we may be sure. The like holds with the relations of rain and dry weather to the quantity of water in the air and the weight of the atmospheric column: though exactly-true predictions cannot be made, approximately-true ones can. So that, even were there not among social phenomena more definite relations than these (and the all-important ones are far more definite), there would still be a Social Science. Once more, Mr. Froude contends that the facts presented in history do not furnish subject-matter for science, because they "never repeat themselves,"—because "we can watch for no recurring fact to test the worth of our conjectures." I will not meet this assertion by the counter-assertion often made, that historic phenomena *do* repeat themselves; but, admitting that Mr. Froude here touches on one of the great difficulties of the Social Science (that social phenomena are in so considerable a degree different in each case from what they were in preceding cases), I still find a sufficient reply. For in no concrete science is there absolute repetition; and in some concrete sciences the repetition is no more specific than in Sociology. Even in the most exact of them, Astronomy, the combinations are never the same twice over: the repetitions are but approximate. And on turning to Geology, we find that, though the processes of denudation, deposition, upheaval, subsidence, have been ever going on in conformity with laws more or less clearly generalized, the effects have been always new in their proportions and arrangements; though not so completely new as to forbid comparisons, consequent deductions, and approximate previsions based on them.

Were there no such replies as these to Mr. Froude's reasons, there would still be the reply furnished by his own interpretations of history; which make it clear that his denial must be understood as but a qualified one. Against his professed theory may be set his actual practice, which, as it seems to me, tacitly asserts that explanations of some social phenomena in terms of cause and effect are possible, if not explanations of all social phenomena. Thus, respecting the Vagrancy Act of 1547, which made a slave of a confirmed vagrant, Mr. Froude says:—"In the condition of things which was now commencing . . . neither this nor any other penal act against idleness could be practically enforced." That is to say, the operation of an agency brought into play was neutralized by the operation of natural causes coexisting. . . . And elsewhere he says that "the miseries and horrors which are now destroying the Chinese Empire are the direct and organic results of the moral profligacy of its inhabitants." Each of these statements tacitly asserts that certain social relations, and actions of certain kinds, are inevitably beneficial, and others inevitably detrimental—an historic induction furnishing a basis for positive deduction. So that we must not interpret Mr. Froude too literally when he alleges the "impossibility of forming scientific calculations of what men will do before the fact, or scientific explanations of what they have done after the fact."

Another writer who denies the possibility of a Social Science, or who, at any rate, admits it only as a science which has its relations of phenomena so traversed by providential influences that it does not come within the proper definition of a science, is Canon Kingsley.[2] In his address on *The Limits of Exact Science as applied to History*, he says:—

> You say that as the laws of matter are inevitable, so probably are the laws of human life? Be it so: but in what sense are the laws of matter inevitable? Potentially or actually? Even in the seemingly most uniform and universal law, where do we find the inevitable or the irresistable? Is there not in nature a perpetual competition of law against law, force against force, producing the most endless and unexpected variety of results? Cannot each law be interfered with at any moment by some other law, so that the first law, though it may struggle for the mastery, shall be for an indefinite time utterly defeated? The law of gravity is immutable enough: but do all stones veritably fall to the ground? Certainly not, if I choose to catch one, and keep it in my hand. It remains there by laws; and the law of gravity is there, too, making it feel heavy in my hand: but it has not fallen to the ground, and will not, till I let it. So much for the inevitable action of the laws of gravity, as of others. Potentially, it is immutable; but actually, it can be conquered by other laws.

This passage, severely criticized, if I remember rightly, when the address was originally published, it would be scarcely fair to quote

2 Rev. Charles Kingsley (1819–75) achieved fame as a Christian Socialist and a novelist; his *Alton Locke* (1850) deals with the "two nations" question. From 1860 to 1869 he was Regius Professor of History at Cambridge, despite complete lack of competence and distinction as a historian; and his inaugural lecture is the target of Spencer's criticisms here. In both political and intellectual matters his views were entirely opposed to Spencer's.—Ed.

were it not that Canon Kingsley has repeated it at a later date in his work, *The Roman and the Teuton.* The very unusual renderings of scientific ideas which it contains, need here be only enumerated. Mr. Kingsley differs profoundly from philosophers and men of science, in regarding a law as itself a power or force, and so in thinking of one law as "conquered by other laws"; whereas the accepted conception of law is that of an established *order*, to which the manifestations of a power or force conform. He enunciates, too, a quite-exceptional view of gravitation. As conceived by astronomers and physicists, gravitation is a universal and ever-acting *force*, which portions of matter exercise on one another when at sensible distances; and the *law* of this force is that it varies directly as the mass and inversely as the square of the distance. Mr. Kingsley's view, is that the law of gravitation is "defeated" if a stone is prevented from falling to the ground—that the law "struggles" (not the force), and that because it no longer produces motion, the "inevitable action of the laws of gravity" (not of gravity) is suspended: the truth being that neither the force nor its law is in the slightest degree modified. Further, the theory of natural processes which Mr. Kingsley has arrived at, seems to be that when two or more forces (or laws, if he prefers it) come into play, there is a partial or complete suspension of one by another. Whereas the doctrine held by men of science is, that the forces are all in full operation, and the effect is their *resultant*; so that, for example, when a shot is fired horizontally from a cannon, the force impressed on it produces in a given time just the same amount of horizontal motion as though gravity were absent, while gravity produces in that same time a fall just equal to that which it would have produced had the shot been dropped from the mouth of the cannon. Of course, holding these peculiar views of causation as displayed among simple physical phenomena, Canon Kingsley is consistent in denying historical sequence; and in saying that "as long as man has the mysterious power of breaking the laws of his own being, such a sequence not only cannot be discovered, but it cannot exist." At the same time it is manifest that until he comes to some agreement with men of science respecting conceptions of forces, of their laws, and of the modes in which phenomena produced by compositions of forces are interpretable in terms of compound laws, no discussion of the question at issue can be carried on with profit. . . .

Reduced to a more concrete form, the case may be put thus:—Mr. Froude and Canon Kingsley both believe to a considerable extent in the efficiency of legislation—probably to a greater extent than it is believed in by some of those who assert the existence of a Social Science. To believe in the efficiency of legislation is to believe that certain prospective penalties or rewards will act as deterrents or incentives—will modify individual conduct, and therefore modify social action. Though it may be possible to say that a given law will produce a foreseen effect on a particular person, yet no doubt is felt that it will produce a foreseen effect on the mass of persons. Though Mr. Froude, when arguing against Mr. Buckle, says that he "would deliver himself from the eccentricities of this and that individual by a doctrine of averages," but that "unfortunately, the average of one generation need not be the average of the next"; yet Mr. Froude himself so far believes in the doctrine of averages as to hold that legislative interdicts, with threats of death or imprisonment behind them, will restrain the great majority of men in ways which can be predicted. While he contends that the results of individual will are incalculable, yet, by approving certain laws and condemning others, he tacitly affirms that the results of the aggregate of wills are calculable. And if this be asserted of the aggregate of wills as affected by legislation, it must be asserted of the aggregate of wills as affected by social influences at large. If it be held that the desire to avoid punishment will so act on the average of men as to produce an average foreseen result; then it must also be held that on the average of men, the desire to get the greatest return for labour, the desire to rise into a higher rank of life, the desire to gain applause, and so forth, will each of them produce a certain average result. And to hold this is to hold that there can be prevision of social phenomena, and therefore Social Science.

In brief, then, the alternative positions are these. On the one hand, if there is no natural causation throughout the actions of incorporated humanity, government and legislation are absurd. Acts of Parliament may, as well as not, be made to depend on the drawing of lots or the tossing of a coin; or, rather, there may as well be none at all: social sequences having no ascertainable order, no effect can be counted upon—everything is chaotic. On the other hand, if there is natural causation, then the combination of forces by which every combination of effects is produced, produces that combination of effects in conformity with the laws of the forces. And if so, it behoves us to use all diligence in ascertaining what the forces are, what are their laws, and what are the ways in which they co-operate.

11

METHODOLOGICAL INDIVIDUALISM

Given the natures of the units, and the nature of the aggregate they form is pre-determined. I say the *nature*, meaning, of course, the essential traits, and not including the incidental. By the characters of the units are necessitated certain limits within which the characters of the aggregate must fall. The circumstances attending aggregation greatly modify the results; but the truth here to be recognized is, that these circumstances, in some cases perhaps preventing aggregation altogether, in other cases impending it, in other cases facilitating it more or less, can never give to the aggregate, characters that do not consist with the characters of the units. No favouring conditions will give the labourer power to pile cannon-shot into a vertical wall; no favouring conditions will make it possible for common salt, which crystallizes on the regular system, to crystallize, like sulphate of soda, on the oblique prismatic system; no favouring conditions will enable the fragment of a polype to take on the structure of a mollusk.

Among such social aggregates as inferior creatures fall into, more or less definitely, the same truth holds. Whether they live in a mere assemblage, or whether they live in something like an organized union with division of labour among its members, as happens in many cases, is unquestionably determined by the properties of the units. Given the structures and consequent instincts of the individuals as we find them, and the community they form will

---

From *The Study of Sociology* (London: Williams and Norgate, 1873), pp. 50–59.

inevitably present certain traits; and no community having such traits can be formed out of individuals having other structures and instincts.

Those who have been brought up in the belief that there is one law for the rest of the Universe and another law for mankind, will doubtless be astonished by the proposal to include aggregates of men in this generalization. And yet that the properties of the units determine the properties of the whole they make up, evidently holds of societies as of other things. A general survey of tribes and nations, past and present, shows clearly enough that it is so; and a brief consideration of the conditions shows, with no less clearness, that it must be so.

Ignoring for the moment the special traits of races and individuals, observe the traits common to members of the species at large; and consider how these must affect their relations when associated.

They have all needs for food, and have corresponding desires. To all of them exertion is physiological expense; must bring a certain return in nutriment, if it is not to be detrimental; and is accompanied by repugnance when pushed to excess, or even before reaching it. They are all of them liable to bodily injury, with accompanying pain, from various extreme physical actions, and they are liable to emotional pains, of positive and negative kinds, from one another's actions.

Conspicuous, however, as is this possession of certain fundamental qualities by all individuals, there is no adequate recognition of the truth that from these individual qualities must result certain qualities in an assemblage of individuals; that in proportion as the individuals forming one assemblage are like in their qualities to the individuals forming another assemblage, the two assemblages will have likenesses; and that the assemblages will differ in their characters in proportion as the component individuals of the one differ from those of the other. Yet when this, which is almost a truism, has been admitted, it cannot be denied that in every community there is a group of phenomena growing naturally out of the phenomena presented by its members—a set of properties in the aggregate determined by the sets of properties in the units; and that the relations of the two sets form the subject-matter of a science. It needs but to ask what would happen if men avoided one another, as various inferior creatures do, to see that the very possibility of a society depends on a certain emotional property in the individual. It needs but to ask what would happen if each man liked best the men who gave him most pain, to perceive that social relations, supposing them to be possible, would be utterly unlike the social relations resulting from the greater liking which men individually have for others who give them pleasure. It needs but to ask what would happen if, instead of ordinarily preferring the easiest ways of achieving their ends, men preferred to achieve their ends in the most troublesome ways, to infer that then, a society, if one could exist, would be a widely-different society from any we know. And if, as these extreme cases show us, cardinal traits in societies are determined by cardinal traits in men, it cannot be questioned that less-marked traits in societies are determined by less-marked traits in men; and that there must everywhere be a *consensus* between the special structures and actions of the one and the special structures and actions of the other.

Setting out, then, with this general principle, that the properties of the units determine the properties of the aggregate, we conclude that there must be a Social Science expressing the relations between the two, with as much definiteness as the natures of the phenomena permit. Beginning with types of men who form but small and incoherent social aggregates, such a science has to show in what ways the individual qualities, intellectual and emotional, negative further aggregation. It has to explain how slight modifications of individual nature, arising under modified conditions of life, make somewhat larger aggregates possible. It has to trace out, in aggregates of some size, the genesis of the social relations, regulative and operative, into which the members fall. It has to exhibit the stronger and more prolonged social influences which, by further modifying the characters of the units, facilitate further aggregation with consequent further complexity of social structure. Among societies of all orders and sizes, from the smallest and rudest up to the largest and most civilized, it has to ascertain what traits there are in common, determined by the common traits of human beings; what less-general traits, distinguishing certain groups of societies, result from traits distinguishing certain races of men; and what peculiarities in each society are traceable to the peculiarities of its members. In every case it has for its subject-matter the growth, development, structure, and functions of the social aggregate, as brought about by the mutual actions of individuals whose natures are partly like those of all men, partly like those of kindred races, partly distinctive.

These phenomena of social evolution have, of course, to be explained with due reference to the conditions each society is exposed to—the conditions furnished by its locality and by its relations to neighbouring societies. . . . What Biography is to Anthropology, History is to Sociology—History, I mean, as commonly conceived. The kind of relation which the sayings and doings that make up the ordinary account of a man's life, bear to an account of his bodily and mental evolution, structural and functional, is like the kind of relation borne by that narrative of a nation's actions and fortunes its historian gives us, to a description of its institutions, regulative and operative, and the ways in which their structures and functions have gradually established themselves. And if it is an error to say that there is no Science of Man, because the events of a man's life cannot be foreseen, it is equally an error to say that there is no Science of Society, because there can be no prevision of the occurrences which make up ordinary history.

Of course, I do not say that the parallel between an individual organism and a social organism is so close, that the distinction to be clearly drawn in the one case may be drawn with like clearness in the other. The structures and functions of the social organism are obviously far less specific, far more modifiable, far more dependent on conditions that are variable and never twice alike. All I mean is that, as in the one case so in the other, there lie underneath the phenomena of conduct, not forming subject-matter for science, certain vital phenomena, which do form subject-matter for science. Just as in the man there are structures and functions which make possible the doings his biographer tells of, so in the nation there are structures and functions which make possible the doings its historian tells of; and in both cases it is with these structures and functions, in their origin, development, and decline, that science is concerned.

To make better the parallel, and further to explain the nature of the Social Science, we must say that the morphology and physiology of Society, instead of corresponding to the morphology and physiology of Man, correspond rather to morphology and physiology in general. Social organisms, like individual organisms, are to be arranged into classes and sub-classes—not, indeed, into classes and sub-classes having anything like the same definiteness or the same constancy, but nevertheless having likenesses and differences which justify the putting of them into major groups most-markedly contrasted, and, within these, arranging them in minor groups less-markedly contrasted. And just as Biology discovers certain general traits of development, structure, and function, holding throughout all organisms, others holding throughout certain great groups, others throughout certain sub-groups these contain; so Sociology has to recognize truths of social development, structure, and function, that are some of them universal, some of them general, some of them special.

12

DIFFICULTIES OF THE SOCIAL SCIENCE

From the intrinsic natures of its facts, from our own natures as observers of its facts, and from the peculiar relation in which we stand towards the facts to be observed, there arise impediments in the way of Sociology greater than those in the way of any other science.

The phenomena to be generalized are not of a directly-perceptible kind—cannot be noted by telescope and clock, like those of Astronomy; cannot be measured by dynamometer and thermometer, like those of Physics; cannot be elucidated by scales and test-papers, like those of Chemistry; are not to be got at by scalpel and microscope, like the less obvious biological phenomena; nor are to be recognized by introspection, like the phenomena Psychology deals with. They have severally to be established by putting together many details, no one of which is simple, and which are dispersed, both in Space and Time, in ways that make them difficult of access. Hence the reason why even cardinal truths in Sociology, such as the division of labour, remain long unrecognized. That in advanced societies men follow different occupations, was indeed a generalization easy to make; but that this form of social arrangement had neither been specially created, nor enacted by a king, but had grown up without forethought of any one, was a conclusion which could be reached only after many transactions of many kinds between men had been noted, remembered, and

---

From *The Study of Sociology* (London: Williams and Norgate, 1873), pp. 72–74, 101–5, 114–16, 118–22, 126–31.

accounted for, and only after comparisons had been made between these transactions and those taking place between men in simpler societies and in earlier times. And when it is remembered that the data for the inference that labour becomes specialized, are far more accessible than the data for most other sociological inferences, it will be seen how greatly the advance of Sociology is hindered by the nature of its subject-matter.

The characters of men as observers, add to this first difficulty a second that is perhaps equally great. Necessarily men take with them into sociological inquiries, the modes of observation and reasoning which they have been accustomed to in other inquiries—those of them, at least, who make any inquiries worthy to be so called. Passing over the great majority of the educated, and limiting ourselves to the very few who consciously collect data, compare them, and deliberately draw conclusions; we may see that even these have to struggle with the difficulty that the habits of thought generated by converse with relatively-simple phenomena, partially unfit them for converse with these highly-complex phenomena. Faculty of every kind tends always to adjust itself to its work. Special adjustment to one kind of work involves more or less non-adjustment to other kinds. And hence, intellects disciplined in dealing with less-involved classes of facts, cannot successfully deal with this most-involved class of facts without partially unlearning the methods they have learnt. From the emotional nature, too, there arise great obstacles. Scarcely any one can contemplate social arrangements and actions with the unconcern felt when contemplating arrangements and actions of other kinds. For correct observation and correct drawing of inferences, there needs the calmness that is ready to recognize or to infer one truth as readily as another. But it is next to impossible thus to deal with the truths of Sociology. In the search for them, each is moved by feelings, more or less strong, which make him eager to find this evidence, oblivious of that which is at variance with it, reluctant to draw any conclusion but that already drawn. And though perhaps one in ten among those who think, is conscious that his judgment is being warped by prejudice, yet even in him the warp is not adequately allowed for. Doubtless in nearly every field of inquiry emotion is a perturbing intruder: mostly there is some preconception, and some *amour propre* that resists disproof of it. But a peculiarity of Sociology is, that the emotions with which its facts and conclusions are regarded, have unusual strength. The personal interests are directly affected; or there is gratification or offence to sentiments that have grown out of them; or else other sentiments which have relation to the existing form of society, are excited, agreeably or disagreeably.

And here we are introduced to the third kind of difficulty—that caused by the position occupied, in respect to the phenomena to be generalized. In no other case has the inquirer to investigate the properties of an aggregate in which he is himself included. His relation towards the facts he here studies, we may figure to ourselves by comparing it to the relation between a single cell forming part of a living body, and the facts which that living body presents as a whole. Speaking generally, the citizen's life is made possible only by due performance of his function in the place he fills; and he cannot wholly free himself from the beliefs and sentiments generated by the vital connexions hence arising between himself and his society. Here, then, is a difficulty to which no other science presents anything analogous. To cut himself off in thought from all his relationships of race, and country, and citizenship—to get rid of all those interests, prejudices, likings, superstitions, generated in him by the life of his own society and his own time—to look on all the changes societies have undergone and are undergoing, without reference to nationality, or creed, or personal welfare; is what the average man cannot do at all, and what the exceptional man can do very imperfectly. . . .

A further great difficulty to which we are thus introduced is, that the comparisons by which alone we can finally establish relations of cause and effect among social phenomena, can rarely be made between cases in all respects fit for comparison. Every society differs specifically, if not generically, from every other. Hence it is a peculiarity of the Social Science that parallels drawn between different societies, do not afford grounds for decided conclusions—will not, for instance, show us with certainty, what is an essential phenomenon in a given society and what is a non-essential one. Biology deals with numerous individuals of a species, and with many species of a genus, and by comparing them can see what traits are specifically constant and what generically constant; and the like holds more or less with the other concrete sciences. But comparisions between societies, among which we may almost say that each individual is a species by itself, yield much less definite results: the necessary characters are not thus readily distinguishable from the accidental characters. . . .

In a society living, growing, changing, every new factor becomes a permanent force; modifying more or less the direction of movement determined by the aggregate of forces. Never simple and direct, but, by the co-operation of so many causes, made irregular, involved, and always rhythmical, the course of social change cannot be judged of in its general direction by inspecting any small portion of it. Each action will inevitably be followed, after a while, by some direct or indirect reaction, and this again by a re-action; and until the successive effects have shown themselves, no one can say how the total motion will be modified. You must compare positions at great distances from one another in time, before you can perceive rightly whither things are tending. Even so simple a thing as a curve of single curvature cannot have its nature determined unless there is a considerable length of it. See here these four points close together. The curve passing through them may be a circle, an ellipse, a parabola, an hyperbola; or it may be a catenarian, a cycloid, a spiral. Let the points be further apart, and it becomes possible to form some opinion of the nature of the curve—it is obviously not a circle. Let them be more remote still, and it may be seen that it is neither an elipse nor a parabola. And when the distances are relatively great, the mathematician can say with certainty what curve alone will pass through them all. Surely, then, in such complex and slowly-evolving movements as those of a nation's life, all the smaller and greater rhythms of which fall within certain general directions, it is impossible that such general directions can be traced by looking at stages that are close together—it is impossible that the effect wrought on any general direction by some additional force, can be truly computed from observations extending over but a few years, or but a few generations.

For, in the case of these most-involved of all movements, there is the difficulty, paralleled in no other movements (being only approached in those of individual evolution), that each new factor, besides modifying in an immediate way the course of a movement, modifies it also in a remote way, by changing the amounts and directions of all other factors. A fresh influence brought into play on a society, not only affects its members directly in their acts, but also indirectly in their characters. Continuing to work on their characters generation after generation, and altering by inheritance the feelings which they bring into social life at large, this influence alters the intensities and bearings of all other influences throughout the society. By slowly initiating modifications of nature, it brings into play forces of many kinds, incalculable in their strengths and tendencies, that act without regard to the original influence, and may cause quite opposite effects. . . .

I recall this and kindred cases to the reader's mind, for the purpose of exemplifying a necessity and a difficulty. The necessity is that in dealing with other beings and interpreting their actions, we must represent their thoughts and feelings in terms of our own. The difficulty is that in so representing them we can never be more than partially right, and are frequently very wrong. The conception which any one frames of another's mind, is inevitably more or less after the pattern of his own mind—is automorphic; and in proportion as the mind of which he has to frame a conception differs from his own, his automorphic interpretation is likely to be wide of the truth.

That measuring other person's actions by the standards our own thoughts and feelings furnish, often causes misconstruction, is a remark familiar even to the vulgar. But while among members of the same society, having natures nearly akin, it is seen that automorphic explanations are often erroneous, it is not seen with due clearness how much more erroneous such explanations commonly are, when the actions are those of men of another race, to whom the kinship in nature is comparatively remote. We do, indeed, perceive this, if the interpretations are not our own; and if both the interpreters and the interpreted are mentally alien to us. When, as in early English literature, we find Greek history conceived in terms of feudal institutions, and the heroes of antiquity spoken of as princes, knights, and squires, it becomes clear that the ideas concerning ancient civilization must have been utterly wrong. When we find Virgil named in religious stories of the middle ages as one among the prophets who visited the cradle of Christ—when an illustrated psalter gives scenes from the life of Christ in which there repeatedly figures a castle with a portcullis—when even the crucifixion is described by Langland in the language of chivalry, so that the man who pierced Christ's side with a spear is considered as a knight who disgraced his knighthood—when we read of the Crusaders calling themselves "vassals of Christ"; we need no further proof that by carrying their own sentiments and ideas to the interpretation of social arrangements and transactions among the Jews, our ancestors were led into absurd misconceptions. But we do not recognize the fact that in virtue of the same tendency, we are ever framing conceptions which, if not so grotesquely untrue, are yet very wide of the truth. How difficult it is to imagine mental states remote from our own so correctly that we can understand how they issue in individual actions, and consequently in social actions, an instance will make manifest.

The feeling of vague wonder with which he received his first lessons in the Greek mythology, will most likely be dimly remembered by every reader. . . . He interpreted them automorphically —carrying with him not simply his own faculties developed to a stage of complexity considerably beyond that reached by the faculties of the savage, but also the modes of thinking in which he was brought up, and the stock of information he had acquired. Probably it has never since occurred to him to do otherwise. Even if he now attempts to see things from the savage's point of view, he most likely fails entirely; and if he succeeds at all, it is but partially. Yet only by seeing things as the savage sees them can his ideas be understood, his behaviour accounted for, and the resulting social phenomena explained. These apparently-strange superstitions are quite natural—quite rational, in a certain sense, in their respective times and places. The laws of intellectual action are the same for civilized and uncivilized. The difference between civilized and uncivilized is in complexity of faculty and in amount of knowledge accumulated and generalized. Given, reflective powers developed only to that lower degree in which they are possessed by the aboriginal man—given, his small stock of ideas, collected in a narrow area of space, and not added to by records extending through time—given, his impulsive nature incapable of patient inquiry; and these seemingly-monstrous stories of his become in reality the most feasible explanations he can find of surrounding things. Yet even after concluding that this must be so, it is not easy to think from the savage's stand-point, clearly enough to follow the effects of his ideas on his acts, through all the relations of life, social and other. . . .

. . . I have here to dwell on the misleading effects of certain mental states which similarly appear unlikely to co-exist, and which yet do habitually co-exist. I refer to the belief which, even while I write, I find repeated in the leading journal, that "the deeper a student of history goes, the more does he find man the same in all time"; and to the opposite belief embodied in current politics, that human nature may be readily altered. These two beliefs, which ought to cancel one another but do not, originate two classes of errors in sociological speculation; and nothing like correct conclusions in Sociology can be drawn until they have been rejected and replaced by a belief which reconciles them—the belief that human nature is indefinitely modifiable, but that no modification of it can be brought about rapidly. We will glance at the errors to which each of these beliefs leads.

While it was held that the stars are fixed and that the hills are everlasting, there was a certain congruity in the notion that man continues unchanged from age to age; but now when we know that all stars are in motion, and that there are no such things as everlasting hills—now when we find all things throughout the Universe to be in a ceaseless flux, it is time for this crude conception of human nature to disappear out of our social conceptions; or rather—it is time for its disappearance to be followed by that of the many narrow notions respecting the past and the future of society, which have grown out of it, and which linger notwithstanding the loss of their root. For, avowedly by some and tacitly by others, it continues to be thought that the human heart is as "desperately wicked" as it ever was, and that the state of society hereafter will be very much like the state of society now. If, when the evidence has been piled mass upon mass, there comes a reluctant admission that aboriginal man, of troglodyte or kindred habits, differed somewhat from man as he was during feudal times, and that the customs and sentiments and beliefs he had in feudal times, imply a character appreciably unlike that which he has now—if, joined with this, there is a recognition of the truth that along with these changes in man there have gone still more conspicuous changes in society; there is, nevertheless, an ignoring of the implication that hereafter man and society will continue to change, until they have diverged as widely from their existing types as their existing types have diverged from those of the earliest recorded ages. It is true that among the more cultured the probability, or even the certainty, that such transformations will go on, may be granted; but the granting is but nominal—the admission does not become a factor in the conclusions drawn. The first discussion on a political or social topic, reveals the tacit assumption that, in times to come, society will have a structure substantially like its existing structure. If, for instance, the question of domestic service is raised, it mostly happens that its bearings are considered wholly in reference to those social arrangements which exist around us: only a few proceed on the supposition that these arrangements are probably but transitory. It is so throughout. Be the subject industrial organization, or class-relations, or rule by fashion, the thought which practically moulds the conclusions, if not the thought theoretically professed, is, that whatever changes they may undergo, our institutions will not cease to be recognizably the same. Even those who have, as they think, deliberately freed themselves from this perverting tendency—even M. Comte and his disciples, believing in an entire transformation of society, nevertheless betray an incomplete emancipation; for the ideal society expected by them, is one under regulation by a hierarchy essentially akin to hierarchies such as mankind have known. So that everywhere sociological thinking is more or less impeded by the difficulty of bearing in mind that the social states towards which our race is being carried, are probably as little conceivable by us as our present social state was conceivable by a Norse pirate and his followers.

Note, now, the opposite difficulty, which appears to be surmountable by scarcely any of our parties, political or philanthropic,—the difficulty of understanding that human nature, though indefinitely modifiable, can be modified but very slowly; and that all laws and institutions and appliances which count on getting from it, within a short time, much better results than present ones, will inevitably fail. If we glance over the programmes of societies, and sects, and schools of all kinds, from Rousseau's disciples in the French Convention up to the members of the United Kingdom Alliance, from the adherents of the Ultramontane propaganda up to the enthusiastic advocates of an education exclusively secular, we find in them one common trait. They are all pervaded by the conviction, now definitely expressed and now taken as a self-evident truth, that there needs but this kind of instruction or that kind of discipline, this mode of repression or that system of culture, to bring society into a very much better state. Here we read that "it is necessary completely to re-fashion the people whom one wishes to make free": the implication being that a re-fashioning is practicable. There it is taken as undeniable that when you have taught children what they ought to do to be good citizens, they will become good citizens. Elsewhere it is held to be a truth beyond question, that if by law temptations to drink are removed from men, they will not only cease to drink, but thereafter cease to commit crimes. And yet the delusiveness of all such hopes is obvious enough to any one not blinded by a hypothesis, or carried away by an enthusiasm. The fact, often pointed out to temperance-fanatics, that some of the soberest nations in Europe yield a proportion of crime higher than our own, might suffice to show them that England would not be suddenly moralized if they carried their proposed restrictions into effect. The superstition that good behaviour is to be forthwith produced by lessons learnt out of school-books, which was long ago statistically disproved, would, but for preconceptions, be utterly dissipated by observing to what a slight extent knowledge affects conduct—by observing that the dishonesty implied in the adulterations of tradesmen and manufacturers, in fraudulent bankruptcies, in bubble-companies, in "cooking" of railway accounts and financial prospectuses, differs only in form, and not in amount, from the dishonesty of the uneducated—by observing how amazingly little the teachings given to medical students affect their lives, and how even the most experienced medical men have their prudence scarcely at all increased by their information. Similarly, the Utopian ideas which come out afresh along with every new political scheme, from the "paper-constitutions" of the Abbé Sieyès down to the lately-published programme of M. Louis Blanc, and from agitations for vote-by-ballot up to those which have a Republic for their aim, might, but for this tacit belief we are contemplating, be extinguished by the facts perpetually and startlingly thrust on our attention. Again and again for three generations has France been showing to the world how impossible it is essentially to change the type of a social structure by any re-arrangement wrought out through a revolution. However great the transformation may for a time seem, the original thing re-appears in disguise. Out of the nominally-free government set up a new despotism arises, differing from the old by having a new shibboleth and new men to utter it; but identical with the old in the determination to put down opposition and in the means used to this end. Liberty, when obtained, is forthwith surrendered to an avowed autocrat; or, as we have seen within this year, is allowed to lapse into the hands of one who claims the reality of autocracy without its title. Nay, the change is, in fact, even less; for the regulative organization which ramifies throughout French society, continues unaltered by these changes at the governmental centre. The bureaucratic system persists equally under Imperialist, Constitutional, and Republican arrangements. As the Duc d'Audiffret-Pasquier pointed out, "Empires fall, Ministries pass away, but Bureaux remain." The aggregate of forces and tendencies embodied, not only in the structural arrangements holding the nation together, but in the ideas and sentiments of its units, is so powerful, that the excision of a part, even though it be the government, is quickly followed by the substitution of a like part. It needs but to recall the truth exemplified some chapters back, that the properties of the aggregate are determined by the properties of its units, to see at once that so long as the characters of citizens remain substantially unchanged, there can be no substantial change in the political organization which has slowly been evolved by them.

This double difficulty of thought, with the double set of delusions fallen into by those who do not surmount it, is, indeed, naturally associated with the once-universal, and still-general, belief that societies arise by manufacture, instead of arising, as they do, by evolution. Recognize the truth that incorporated masses of men grow, and acquire their structural characters through modification upon modification, and there are excluded these antithetical errors that humanity remains the same and that humanity is readily alterable; and along with exclusion of these errors comes admission of the inference, that the changes which have brought social arrangements to a form so different from past forms, will in future carry them on to forms as different from those now existing. Once become habituated to the thought of a continuous unfolding of the whole and of each part, and these misleading ideas disappear. . . .

The conceptions with which sociological science is concerned, are complex beyond all others. In the absence of faculty having a corresponding complexity, they cannot be grasped. Here, however, as in other cases, the absence of an adequately-complex faculty is not accompanied by any consciousness of incapacity. Rather do we find that deficiency in the required kind of mental grasp, is accompanied by extreme confidence of judgment on sociological questions, and a ridicule of those who, after long discipline, begin to perceive what there is to be understood, and how difficult is the right understanding of it. A simple illustration of this will prepare the way for more-involved illustrations.

A few months ago the *Times* gave us an account of the last achievement in automatic printing—the "Walter-Press," by which its own immense edition is thrown off in a few hours every morning. Suppose a reader of the description, adequately familiar with mechanical details, follows what he reads step by step with full comprehension: perhaps making his ideas more definite by going to see the apparatus at work and questioning the attendants. Now he goes away thinking he understands all about it. Possibly, under its aspect as a feat in mechanical engineering, he does so. Possibly also, under its biographical aspect, as implying in Mr. Walter and those who co-operated with him certain traits, moral and intellectual, he does so. But under its sociological aspect he probably has no notion of its meaning; and does not even suspect that it has a sociological aspect. Yet if he begins to look into the genesis of the thing, he will find that he is but on the threshold of the full explanation. On asking not what is its proximate but what is its remote origin, he finds, in the first place, that this automatic printing-machine is lineally descended from other automatic printing-machines, which have undergone successive developments —each pre-supposing others that went before: without cylinder printing-machines long previously used and improved, there would have been no "Walter-Press." He inquires a step further, and discovers that this last improvement became possible only by the help of *papier-mâché* stereotyping, which, first employed for making flat plates, afforded the possibility of making cyclindrical plates. And tracing this back, he finds that plaster-of-paris stereotyping came before it, and that there was another process before that. Again, he learns that this highest form of automatic printing, like the many less-developed forms preceding it, depended for its practicability on the introduction of rollers for distributing ink, instead of the hand-implements used by "printer's-devils" fifty years ago; which rollers, again, could never have been made fit for their present purposes, without the discovery of that curious elastic compound out of which they are cast. And then, on tracing the more remote antecedents, he finds an ancestry of hand printing-presses, which, through generations, had been successively improved. Now, perhaps, he thinks he understands the apparatus, considered as a sociological fact. Far from it. Its multitudinous parts, which will work together only when highly finished and exactly adjusted, came from machine-shops; where there are varieties of complicated, highly-finished engines for turning cylinders, cutting out wheels, planing bars, and so forth; and on the pre-existence of these the existence of this printing-machine depended. If he inquires into the history of these complex automatic tools, he finds they have severally been, in the slow course of mechanical progress, brought to their present perfection by the help of preceding complex automatic tools of various kinds, that co-operated to make their component parts—each larger, or more accurate, lathe or planing-machine having been made possible by pre-existing lathes and planing-machines, inferior in size or exactness. And so if he traces back the whole contents of the machine-shop, with its many different instruments, he comes in course of time to the blacksmith's hammer and anvil; and even, eventually, to still ruder appliances. The explanation is now completed, he thinks. Not at all. No such process as that which the "Walter-Press" shows us, was possible until there had been invented, and slowly perfected, a paper-machine capable of making miles of paper without break. Thus there is the genesis of the paper-machine involved, and that of the multitudinous appliances and devices which preceded it, and are at present implied by it. Have we now got to the end of the matter? No; we have just glanced at one group of the antecedents. All this development of mechanical appliances—this growth of the iron-manufacture, this extensive use of machinery made from iron, this production of so many machines for making machines—has had for one of its causes the abundance of the raw materials, coal and iron; has had for another of its causes the insular position which has favoured peace and the increase of industrial activity. There have been moral causes at work too. Without that readiness to sacrifice present ease to future benefit, which is implied by enterprise, there would never have arisen the machine in question, —nay, there would never have arisen the multitudinous improved instruments and processes that have made it possible. And beyond the moral traits which enterprise pre-supposes, there are those pre-supposed by efficient co-operation. Without mechanical engineers who fulfilled their contracts tolerably well, by executing work accurately, neither this machine itself nor the machines that made it, could have been produced; and without artizans having considerable conscientiousness, no master could insure accurate work. Try to get such products out of an inferior race, and you will find defective character an insuperable obstacle. So, too, will you find defective intelligence an insuperable obstacle. The skilled artizan is not an accidental product, either morally or intellectually. The intelligence needed for making a new thing is not everywhere to be found; nor is there everywhere to be found the accuracy of perception and nicety of execution without which no complex machine can be so made that it will act. Exactness of finish in machines has developed *pari passu* with exactness of perception in artizans. Inspect some mechanical appliance made a century ago, and you may see that, even had all other requisite conditions been fulfilled, want of the requisite skill in workmen would have been a fatal obstacle to the production of an engine requiring so many delicate adjustments. So that there are implied in this mechanical achievement, not only our slowly-generated industrial state, with its innumerable products and processes, but also the slowly-moulded moral and intellectual natures of masters and workmen. Has nothing now been forgotten? Yes, we have left out a whole division of all-important social phenomena—those which we group as the progress of knowledge. Along with the many other developments that have been necessary antecedents to this machine, there has been the development of Science. The growing and improving arts of all kinds, have been helped up, step after step, by those generalized experiences, becoming ever wider, more complete, more exact, which make up what we call Mathematics, Physics, Chemistry, &c. Without a considerably-developed Geometry, there could never have been the machines for making machines; still less this machine that has proceeded from them. Without a developed Physics, there would have been no steam-engine to move these various automatic appliances, primary and secondary; nor would the many implied metallurgic processes have been brought to the needful perfection. And in the absence of a developed Chemistry, many other requirements, direct and indirect, could not have been adequately fulfilled. So that, in fact, this organization of knowledge which began with civilization, had to reach something like its present stage before such a machine could come into existence; supposing all other pre-requisites to be satisfied. Surely we have now got to the end of the history. Not quite: there yet remains an essential factor. No one goes on year after year spending thousands of pounds and much time, and persevering through disappointment and anxiety, without a strong motive: the "Walter-Press" was not a mere *tour de force*. Why, then, was it produced? To meet an immense demand with great promptness—to print, with one machine, 16,000 copies per hour. Whence arises this demand? From an extensive reading public, brought in the course of generations to have a keen morning-appetite for news of all kinds—merchants who need to know the latest prices at home and the latest telegrams from abroad; politicians who must learn the result of last night's division, be informed of the new diplomatic move, and read the speeches at a meeting; sporting men who look for the odds and the result of yesterday's race; ladies who want to see the births, marriages, and deaths. And on asking the origin of these many desires to be satisfied, they prove to be concomitants of our social state in general—its trading, political, philanthropic, and other activities; for in societies where these are not dominant, the demand for news of various kinds rises to no such intensity. See, then, how enormously involved is the genesis of this machine, as a sociological phenomenon. A whole encyclopædia of mechanical inventions—some dating from the earliest times—go to the explanation of it. Thousands of years of discipline, by which the impulsive improvident nature of the savage has been evolved into a comparatively self-controlling nature, capable of sacrificing present ease to future good, are presupposed. There is pre-supposed the equally-long discipline by which the inventive faculty, almost wholly absent in the savage, has been evolved; and by which accuracy, not even conceived by the savage, has been cultivated. And there is further pre-supposed the slow political and social progress, at once cause and consequence of these other changes, that has brought us to a state in which such a machine finds a function to fulfil.

The complexity of a sociological fact, and the difficulty of adequately grasping it, will now perhaps be more apparent. For as in this case there has been a genesis, so has there been in every other case, be it of institution, arrangement, custom, belief, &c.; but while in this case the genesis is comparatively easy to trace, because of the comparatively-concrete character of process and product, it is in other cases difficult to trace, because the factors are mostly not of sensible kinds. And yet only when the genesis has been traced—only when the antecedents of all orders have been observed in their co-operation, generation after generation, through past social states—is there reached that interpretation of a fact which makes it a part of sociological science, properly understood.

IV. Evolution in General

13

THE FACTORS OF SOCIAL EVOLUTION

THE BEHAVIOUR of a single inanimate object depends on the co-operation between its own forces and the forces to which it is exposed: instance a piece of metal, the molecules of which keep the solid state or assume the liquid state, according partly to their natures and partly to the heat-waves falling on them. Similarly with any group of inanimate objects. Be it a cart-load of bricks shot down, a barrowful of gravel turned over, or a boy's bag of marbles emptied, the behaviour of the assembled masses—here standing in a heap with steep sides, here forming one with sides much less inclined, and here spreading out and rolling in all directions—is in each case determined partly by the properties of the individual members of the group, and partly by the forces of gravitation, impact, and friction, they are jointly and individually subjected to.

It is equally so when the discrete aggregate consists of organic bodies, such as the members of a species. For a species increases or decreases in numbers, widens or contracts its habitat, migrates or remains stationary, continues an old mode of life or falls into a new one, under the combined influences of its intrinsic nature and the environing actions, inorganic and organic.

It is thus, too, with aggregates of men. Be it rudimentary or be it advanced, every society displays phenomena that are ascribable to the characters of its units and to the conditions under which they exist. Here, then, are the factors as primarily divided.

From *The Principles of Sociology* (London: Williams and Norgate, 1876), vol. 1, part 1, pp. 9–15; part 2, pp. 455–62; part 8 (1896), p. 325.

These factors are re-divisible. Within each there are groups of factors that stand in marked contrasts.

Beginning with the extrinsic factors, we see that from the outset several kinds of them are variously operative. They need but barely enumerating. We have climate, hot, cold, or temperate, moist or dry, constant or variable. We have surface, much or little of which is available, and the available part of which is fertile in greater or less degree; and we have configuration of surface, as uniform or multiform. Next we have the vegetal productions, here abundant in quantities and kinds, and there deficient in one or both. And besides the Flora of the region we have its Fauna, which is highly influential in many ways; not only by the numbers of its species and individuals, but by the proportion between those that are useful and those that are injurious. On these sets of conditions, inorganic and organic, characterizing the environment, primarily depends the possibility of social evolution.

When we turn to the intrinsic factors we have to note, first, that, considered as a social unit, the individual man has physical characters which are potent in determining the growth and structure of the society. He is in every case more or less distinguished by emotional characters which aid, or hinder, or modify, the activities of the society, and the developments accompanying them. Always, too, his degree of intelligence and the tendencies of thought peculiar to him, become co-operating causes of social quiescence or social change.

Such being the original sets of factors, we have now to note the secondary or derived sets of factors, which social evolution itself brings into play.

First may be set down the progressive modifications of the environment, inorganic and organic, which the actions of societies effect.

Among these are the alterations of climate caused by clearing and by drainage. Such alterations may be favourable to social growth, as where a rainy region is made less rainy by cutting down forests, or a swampy surface rendered more salubrious and fertile by carrying off water; or they may be unfavourable, as where, by destroying the forests, a region already dry is made arid: witness the seat of the old Semitic civilizations, and, in a less degree, Spain.

Next come the changes wrought in the kind and quantity of plant-life over the surface occupied. These changes are three-fold. There is the increasing substitution of plants conducive to social growth, for plants not conducive to it; there is the gradual production of better varieties of these useful plants, causing, in time, extreme divergences from their originals; and there is, eventually, the introduction of new useful plants.

Simultaneously go on the kindred changes which social progress works in the Fauna of the region. We have the diminution or destruction of some or many injurious species. We have a fostering of useful species, which has the double effect of increasing their numbers and making their qualities more advantageous to society. Further, we have the naturalization of desirable species, brought from abroad.

It needs but to think of the immense contrast between a wolf-haunted forest or a boggy moor peopled with wild birds, and the fields covered with crops and flocks which eventually occupy the same area, to be reminded that the environment, inorganic and organic, of a society, undergoes a continuous transformation of a remarkable kind during the progress of the society; and that this transformation becomes an all-important secondary factor in social evolution.

Another secondary factor which must not be overlooked, is the increasing size of the social aggregate, accompanied, generally, by increasing density.

Apart from social changes otherwise produced, there are social changes produced by simple growth. Mass is both a condition to, and a result of, organization in a society. It is clear that heterogeneity of structure is made possible only by multiplicity of units. Division of labour cannot be carried far where there are but few to divide the labour among them. There can be no differentiation into classes in the absence of numbers. Complex co-operations, governmental and industrial, are impossible without a population large enough to supply many kinds and gradations of agents. And sundry developed forms of activity, both predatory and peaceful, are made practicable only by the power which large masses of men furnish.

Hence, then, a derivative factor which, like the rest, is at once a consequence and a cause of social progress, is social growth, considered simply as accumulation of numbers. Other factors co-operate to produce this, and this joins other factors in working further changes.

The next secondary or derivative factor to be noted, is the reciprocal influence of the society and its units—the influence of the whole on the parts, and of the parts on the whole.

As soon as a social combination acquires some permanence, there begin actions and reactions between the society as a whole and each member of it, such that either affects the nature of the other. The control exercised by the aggregate over its units, is one tending ever to mould their activities and sentiments and ideas into congruity with social requirements; and these activities, sentiments, and ideas, in so far as they are changed by changing circumstances, tend to re-mould the society into congruity with themselves.

In addition, therefore, to the original nature of the individuals and the original nature of the society they form, we have to take into account the induced natures of the two. Superposed modifications are continually undergone by the units; and the altered units are ever superposing modifications of social structure on the previous modifications. Eventually this co-operation becomes a potent cause of transformation in both.

Yet a further derivative factor of extreme importance remains. I mean the influence of the super-organic environment—the action and reaction between a society and neighbouring societies.

While there exist nothing but small, wandering assemblages of men, devoid of organization, the conflicts of these assemblages with one another cannot work changes of structure. But when once there have arisen the definite chieftainships which these conflicts themselves tend to initiate, and especially when the conflicts have ended in permanent subjugations, there arise the rudiments of political organization; and, as at first, so afterwards, the wars of societies with one another have all-important effects in developing the social structure, or rather, one moiety of it. For I may here, in passing, briefly indicate the fact to be hereafter exhibited in full, that while the industrial organization of a society is mainly determined by its inorganic and organic environments, its governmental organization is mainly determined by its super-organic environment—by the actions of those adjacent societies with which it carries on the struggle for existence.

There remains in the group of derived factors one more, the potency of which can scarcely be over-estimated. I mean that accumulation of super-organic products which we commonly distinguish as artificial, but which, philosophically considered, are no less natural than all others resulting from evolution. There are several orders of these.

First come the material appliances, which, beginning with roughly-chipped flints, end in the complex automatic tools of an engine-factory driven by steam; which from boomerangs rise to thirty-five ton guns; which from huts of branches and grass grow to cities with their palaces and cathedrals. Then we have language, able at first only to eke out gestures in communicating simple ideas, but eventually becoming capable of expressing highly-complex conceptions with precision. While from that stage in which it conveys thoughts only by sounds to one or a few other persons, we pass through picture-writing up to steam-printing: multiplying indefinitely the numbers communicated with, and making accessible in voluminous literatures the ideas and feelings of innumerable men in various places and times. Concomitantly there goes on the development of knowledge, ending in science. Counting on the fingers grows into far-reaching mathematics; observation of the moon's changes leads at length to a theory of the solar system; and at successive stages there arise sciences of which not even the germs can at first be detected. Meanwhile the once few and simple customs, becoming more numerous, definite, and fixed, end in systems of laws. From a few rude superstitions there grow up elaborate mythologies, theologies, cosmogonies. Opinion getting embodied in creeds, gets embodied, too, in accepted codes of propriety, good conduct, ceremony, and in established social sentiments. And then there gradually evolve also the products we call æsthetic; which of themselves form a highly-complex group. From necklaces of fish-bones we advance to dresses elaborate, gorgeous, and infinitely varied; out of discordant war-chants come symphonies and operas; cairns develop into magnificent temples; in place of caves with rude markings there arise at length galleries of paintings; and the recital of a chief's deeds with mimetic accompaniment gives origin to epics, dramas, lyrics, and the vast mass of poetry, fiction, biography, and history.

All these various orders of super-organic products, each evolving within itself new genera and species while daily growing into a larger whole, and each acting upon the other orders while reacted upon by them, form together an immensely-voluminous, immensely-complicated, and immensely-powerful set of influences. During social evolution these influences are ever modifying individuals and modifying society, while being modified by both. They gradually form what we may consider either as a non-vital part of the society itself, or else as an additional environment, which eventually becomes even more important than the original environments—so much more important that there arises the possibility of carrying on a high type of social life under inorganic and organic conditions which originally would have prevented it. . . .

[The following passage recapitulates Part I of the *Principles* and introduces the remainder.] After recognizing the truth that the phenomena of social evolution are determined partly by the external actions to which the social aggregate is exposed, and partly by the natures of its units; and after observing that these two sets of factors are themselves progressively changed as the society evolves; we glanced at these two sets of factors in their original forms.

A sketch was given of the conditions, inorganic and organic, on various parts of the earth's surface; showing the effects of cold and heat, of humidity and dryness, of surface, contour, soil, minerals, of floras and faunas. After seeing how social evolution in its earlier stages depends entirely on a favourable combination of circumstances; and after seeing that though, along with advancing development, there goes increasing independence of circumstances, these ever remain important factors; it was pointed out that while dealing with principles of evolution which are common to all societies, we might neglect those special external factors which determine some of their special characters.

Our attention was then directed to the internal factors as primitive societies display them. An account was given of "The Primitive Man—Physical": showing that by stature, structure, strength, as well as by callousness and lack of energy, he was ill fitted for overcoming the difficulties in the way of advance. Examination of "The Primitive Man—Emotional," led us to see that his improvidence and his explosiveness, restrained but little by sociality and by the altruistic sentiments, rendered him unfit for co-operation. And then, in the chapter on "The Primitive Man—Intellectual," we saw that while adapted by its active and acute perceptions to primitive needs, his type of mind is deficient in the faculties required for progress in knowledge.

After recognizing these as the general traits of the primitive social unit, we found that there remained to be noted certain more special traits, implied by his ideas and their accompanying sentiments. This led us to trace the genesis of those beliefs concerning his own nature and the nature of surrounding things, which were summed up in the last chapter. And now observe the general conclusion reached. It is that while the conduct of the primitive man is in part determined by the feelings with which he regards men around him, it is in part determined by the feelings with which he regards men who have passed away. From these two sets of feelings, result two all-important sets of social factors. While *the fear of the living* becomes the root of the political control, *the fear of the dead* becomes the root of the religious control. On remembering how large a share the resulting ancestor-worship had in regulating life among the people who, in the Nile-valley, first reached a high civilization—on remembering that the ancient Peruvians were subject to a rigid social system rooted in an ancestor-worship so elaborate that the living might truly be called slaves of the dead—on remembering that in China, too, there has been, and still continues, a kindred worship generating kindred restraints; we shall perceive, in the fear of the dead, a social factor which is, at first, not less important, if indeed it is not more important, than the fear of the living.

And thus is made manifest the need for the foregoing account of the origin and development of this trait in the social units, by which co-ordination of their actions is rendered possible.

Setting out with social units as thus conditioned, as thus constituted physically, emotionally, and intellectually, and as thus possessed of certain early-acquired ideas and correlative feelings, the Science of Sociology has to give an account of all the phenomena that result from their combined actions.

The simplest of such combined actions are those by which the successive generations of units are produced, reared, and brought into fitness for co-operation. The development of the family thus stands first in order. The respective ways in which the fostering of offspring is influenced by promiscuity, by polyandry, by polygyny, and by monogamy, have to be traced; as have also the results of exogamous marriage and endogamous marriage. These, considered first as affecting the maintenance of the race in number and quality, have also to be considered as affecting the domestic lives of adults. Moreover, beyond observing how the several forms of the sexual relations modify family-life, they have to be treated in connexion with public life; on which they act and which reacts on them. And then, after the sexual relations, have to be similarly dealt with the parental and filial relations.

Sociology has next to describe and explain the rise and development of that political organization which in several ways regulates affairs—which combines the actions of individuals for purposes of tribal or national offence and defence; which restrains them in certain of their dealings with one another; and which also restrains them in certain of their dealings with themselves. It has to trace the relations of this co-ordinating and controlling apparatus to the area occupied, to the amount and distribution of population, to the means of communication. It has to show the differences of form which this agency presents in the different social types, nomadic and settled, military and industrial. It has to describe the changing relations between this regulative structure which is unproductive, and those structures which carry on production and make national life possible. It has also to set forth the connexions between, and reciprocal influences of, the institutions carrying on civil government, and the other governmental institutions simultaneously developing—the ecclesiastical and the ceremonial. And then it has to take account of those modifications which persistent political restraints are ever working in the characters of the social units, as well as the modifications worked by the reactions of the changed characters of the units on the political organization.

There has to be similarly described the evolution of the ecclesiastical structures and functions. Commencing with these as united to, and often scarcely distinguishable from, the political structures and functions, their divergent developments must be traced. How the share of ecclesiastical agencies in political actions becomes gradually less; how, reciprocally, political agencies play a decreasing part in ecclesiastical actions; are phenomena to be set forth. How the internal organization of the priesthood, differentiating and integrating as the society grows, stands related in type to the co-existing organizations, political and other; and how changes of structure in it are connected with changes of structure in them; are also subjects to be dealt with. Further, there has to be shown the progressive divergence between the set of rules gradually framed into civil law, and the set of rules which the ecclesiastical organization enforces; and in this second set of rules there has to be traced the divergence between those which become a code of religious ceremonial and those which become a code of ethical precepts. Once more, the science has to note how the ecclesiastical agency in its structure, functions, laws, creed, and morals, stands related to the mental nature of the citizens; and how the actions and reactions of the two mutually modify them.

The simultaneously-evolving system of restraints whereby the minor actions of citizens are regulated in daily life, has next to be dealt with. Ancillary to the political and ecclesiastical controls, and at first inseparable from them, is the control embodied in ceremonial observances; which, beginning with rules of class-subordination, grow into rules of intercourse between man and man. The mutilations which mark conquest and become badges of servitude; the obeisances which are originally signs of submission made by the conquered; the titles which are words directly or metaphorically attributing mastery over those who utter them; the salutations which are also the flattering professions of subjection and implied inferiority—these, and some others, have to be traced in their genesis and development as a supplementary regulative agency. The growth of the structure which maintains observances; the accumulation, complication, and increasing definition of observances; and the resulting code of bye-laws of conduct which comes to be added to the civil and religious codes; have to be severally delineated. These regulative arrangements, too, must be considered in their relations to co-existing regulative arrangements; with which they all along maintain a certain congruity in respect of coerciveness. And the reciprocal influences exercised by these restraints on men's natures, and by men's natures on them, need setting forth.

Co-ordinating structures and functions having been dealt with, there have to be dealt with the structures and functions co-ordinated. The regulative and the operative are the two most generally contrasted divisions of every society; and the inquiries of highest importance in social science concern the relations between them. The stages through which the industrial part passes, from its original union with the governmental part to its ultimate separateness, have to be studied. An allied subject of study is the growth of those regulative structures which the industrial part develops within itself. For purposes of production the actions of its units have to be directed; and the various forms of the directive apparatus have to be dealt with—the kinds of government under which separate groups of workers act; the kinds of government under which workers in the same business and of the same class are combined (eventually differentiating into guilds and into unions); and the kind of government which keeps in balance the activities of the various industrial structures. The relations between the forms of these industrial governments and the forms of the co-existing political and ecclesiastical governments, have to be considered at each successive stage; as have also the relations between each of these successive forms and the natures of the citizens: there being here, too, a reciprocity of influences. After the regulative part of the industrial organization comes the operative part; also presenting its successive stages of differentiation and integration. The separation of the distributive system from the productive system having been first traced, there has to be traced the growing division of labour within each—the rise of grades and kinds of distributors as well as grades and kinds of producers. And then there have to be added the effects which the developing and differentiating industries produce on one another—the advances of the industrial arts themselves, caused by the help received from one another's improvements.

After these structures and functions which make up the organization and life of each society, have to be treated certain associated developments which aid, and are aided by, social evolution—the developments of language, knowledge, morals, æsthetics. Linguistic progress has to be considered first as displayed in language itself, while passing from a relatively incoherent, indefinite, homogeneous state, to states that are successively more coherent, definite, and heterogeneous. We have to note how increasing social complexity conduces to increasing complexity of language; and how, as a society becomes settled, it becomes possible for its language to acquire permanence. The connexion between the developments of words and sentences and the correlative developments of thought which they aid, and which are aided by them, has to be observed: the reciprocity being traced in the increasing multiplicity, variety, exactness, which each helps the other to gain.

Progress in intelligence, thus associated with progress in language, has also to be treated as an accompaniment of social progress; which, while furthering it, is furthered by it. From experiences which accumulate and are recorded, come comparisons leading to generalizations of simple kinds. Gradually the ideas of uniformity, order, cause, becoming nascent, gain clearness with each fresh truth established. And while there have to be noted the connexion between each phase of science and the concomitant phase of social life, there have also to be noted the stages through which, within the body of science itself, there is an advance from a few, simple, incoherent truths, to a number of specialized sciences forming a body of truths that are multitudinous, varied, exact, coherent.

The emotional modifications which, as indicated above, accompany social modifications, both as causes and as consequences, also demand separate attention. Besides observing the inter-actions of the social state and the moral state, we have to observe the associated modifications of those moral codes in which moral feelings get their intellectual expression. The kind of behaviour which each kind of *régime* necessitates, finds for itself a justification which acquires an ethical character; and hence ethics must be dealt with in their social dependences.

Then come the groups of phenomena we call æsthetic; which, as exhibited in art-products and in the correlative sentiments, have to be studied in their respective evolutions internally considered, and in the relations of those evolutions to accompanying social phenomena. Diverging as they do from a common root, architecture, sculpture, painting, together with dancing, music, and poetry, have to be severally treated as connected with the political and ecclesiastical stages, with the co-existing phases of moral sentiment, and with the degrees of intellectual advance.

Finally we have to consider the inter-dependence of structures, and functions, and products, taken in their totality. Not only do all the above-enumerated organizations, domestic, political, ecclesiastical, ceremonial, industrial, influence one another through their respective activities; and not only are they all daily influenced by the states of language, knowledge, morals, arts; but the last are severally influenced by them, and are severally influenced by one another. Among these many groups of phenomena there is a *consensus*; and the highest achievement in Sociology is so to grasp the vast heterogeneous aggregate, as to see how each group is at each stage determined partly by its own antecedents and partly by the past and present actions of the rest upon it. . . .

Like other kinds of progress, social progress is not linear but divergent and re-divergent. Each differentiated product gives origin to a new set of differentiated products. While spreading over the Earth mankind have found environments of various characters, and in each case the social life fallen into, partly determined by the social life previously led, has been partly determined by the influences of the new environment; so that the multiplying groups have tended ever to acquire differences, now major and now minor: there have arisen genera and species of societies.

14

THE ORGANIC ANALOGY RECONSIDERED

What is a Society?

THIS QUESTION has to be asked and answered at the outset. Until we have decided whether or not to regard a society as an entity; and until we have decided whether, if regarded as an entity, a society is to be classed as absolutely unlike all other entities or as like some others; our conception of the subject-matter before us remains vague.

It may be said that a society is but a collective name for a number of individuals. Carrying the controversy between nominalism and realism into another sphere, a nominalist might affirm that just as there exist only the members of a species, while the species considered apart from them has no existence; so the units of a society alone exist, while the existence of the society is but verbal. Instancing a lecturer's audience as an aggregate which by disappearing at the close of the lecture, proves itself to be not a thing but only a certain arrangement of persons, he might argue that the like holds of the citizens forming a nation.

But without disputing the other steps of his argument, the last step may be denied. The arrangement, temporary in the one case, is lasting in the other; and it is the permanence of the relations among component parts which constitutes the individuality of a

---

From *The Principles of Sociology* (London: Williams and Norgate, 1876), vol. 1, part 2, pp. 465–69, 613–16.

whole as distinguished from the individualities of its parts. A coherent mass broken into fragments ceases to be a thing; while, conversely, the stones, bricks, and wood, previously separate, become the thing called a house if connected in fixed ways.

Thus we consistently regard a society as an entity, because, though formed of discrete units, a certain concreteness in the aggregate of them is implied by the maintenance, for generations and centuries, of a general likeness of arrangement throughout the area occupied. And it is this trait which yields our idea of a society. For, withholding the name from an ever-changing cluster such as primitive men form, we apply it only where some constancy in the distribution of parts has resulted from settled life.

But now, regarding a society as a thing, what kind of thing must we call it? It seems totally unlike every object with which our senses acquaint us. Any likeness it may possibly have to other objects, cannot be manifest to perception, but can be discerned only by reason. If the constant relations among its parts make it an entity; the question arises whether these constant relations among its parts are akin to the constant relations among the parts of other entities. Between a society and anything else, the only conceivable resemblance must be one due *to parallelism of principle in the arrangement of components.*

There are two great classes of aggregates with which the social aggregate may be compared—the inorganic and the organic. Are the attributes of a society, considered apart from its living units, in any way like those of a not-living body? or are they in any way like those of a living body? or are they entirely unlike those of both?

The first of these questions needs only to be asked to be answered in the negative. A whole of which the parts are alive, cannot, in its general characters, be like lifeless wholes. The second question, not to be thus promptly answered, is to be answered in the affirmative. The reasons for asserting that the permanent relations among the parts of a society, are analogous to the permanent relations among the parts of a living body, we have now to consider.

A Society Is an Organism

When we say that growth is common to social aggregates and organic aggregates, we do not thus entirely exclude community with inorganic aggregates: some of these, as crystals, grow in a visible manner; and all of them, on the hypothesis of evolution, are concluded to have arisen by integration at some time or other. Nevertheless, compared with things we call inanimate, living bodies and societies so conspicuously exhibit augmentation of mass, that we may fairly regard this as characteristic of them both. Many organisms grow throughout their lives; and the rest grow throughout considerable parts of their lives. Social growth usually continues either up to times when the societies divide, or up to times when they are overwhelmed.

Here, then, is the first trait by which societies ally themselves with the organic world and substantially distinguish themselves from the inorganic world.

It is also a character of social bodies, as of living bodies, that while they increase in size they increase in structure. A low animal, or the embryo of a high one, has few distinguishable parts; but along with its acquirement of greater mass, its parts multiply and simultaneously differentiate. It is thus with a society. At first the unlikenesses among its groups of units are inconspicuous in number and degree; but as it becomes more populous, divisions and sub-divisions become more numerous and more decided. Further, in the social organism as in the individual organism, differentiations cease only with that completion of the type which marks maturity and precedes decay.

Though in inorganic aggregates also, as in the entire solar system and in each of its members, structural differentiations accompany the integrations; yet these are so relatively slow, and so relatively simple, that they may be disregarded. The multiplication of contrasted parts in bodies politic and in living bodies, is so great that it substantially constitutes another common character which marks them off from inorganic bodies.

This community will be more fully appreciated on observing that progressive differentiation of structures is accompanied by progressive differentiation of functions.

The multiplying divisions, primary, secondary, and tertiary, which arise in a developing animal, do not assume their major and minor unlikenesses to no purpose. Along with diversities in their shapes and compositions there go diversities in the actions they perform: they grow into unlike organs having unlike duties. Assuming the entire function of absorbing nutriment at the same time that it takes on its structural characters, the alimentary system becomes gradually marked off into contrasted portions; each of which has a special function forming part of the general function. A limb, instrumental to locomotion or prehension, acquires divisions and sub-divisions which perform their leading and their subsidiary shares in this office. So is it with the parts into which a society divides. A dominant class arising does not simply become unlike the rest, but assumes control over the rest; and when this class separates into the more and the less dominant, these, again, begin to discharge distinct parts of the entire control. With the classes whose actions are controlled it is the same. The various groups into which they fall have various occupations: each of such groups also, within itself, acquiring minor contrasts of parts along with minor contrasts of duties.

And here we see more clearly how the two classes of things we are comparing distinguish themselves from things of other classes; for such differences of structure as slowly arise in inorganic aggregates, are not accompanied by what we can fairly call differences of function.

Why in a body politic and in a living body, these unlike actions of unlike parts are properly regarded by us as functions, while we cannot so regard the unlike actions of unlike parts in an inorganic body, we shall perceive on turning to the next and the most distinctive common trait.

Evolution establishes in them both, not differences simply, but definitely-connected differences—differences such that each makes the others possible. The parts of an inorganic aggregate are so related that one may change greatly without appreciably affecting the rest. It is otherwise with the parts of an organic aggregate or of a social aggregate. In either of these the changes in the parts are mutually determined, and the changed actions of the parts are mutually dependent. In both, too, this mutuality increases as the evolution advances. The lowest type of animal is all stomach, all respiratory surface, all limb. Development of a type having appendages by which to move about or lay hold of food, can take place only if these appendages, losing power to absorb nutriment directly from surrounding bodies, are supplied with nutriment by parts which retain the power of absorption. A respiratory surface to which the circulating fluids are brought to be aerated, can be formed only on condition that the concomitant loss of ability to supply itself with materials for repair and growth, is made good by the development of a structure bringing these materials. So is it in a society. What we call with perfect propriety its organization, has a necessary implication of the same kind. . . .

Here let it once more be pointed out that there exist no analogies between the body politic and a living body, save those necessitated by that mutual dependence of parts which they display in common. Though, in foregoing chapters, comparisons of social structures and functions to structures and functions in the human body, have in many cases been made, they have been made only because structures and functions in the human body furnish the most familiar illustrations of structures and functions in general. The social organism, discrete instead of concrete, asymmetrical instead of symmetrcial, sensitive in all its units instead of having a single sensitive centre, is not comparable to any particular type of individual organism, animal or vegetal. All kinds of creatures are alike in so far as each shows us co-operation among its components for the benefit of the whole; and this trait, common to them, is a trait common also to communities. Further, among the many types of individual organisms, the degree of this co-operation measures the degree of evolution; and this general truth, too, is exhibited among social organisms. Once more, to effect increasing co-operation, creatures of every order show us increasingly-complex appliances for transfer and mutual influence; and to this general characteristic, societies of every order furnish a corresponding characteristic. Community in the fundamental principles of organization is thus the only community asserted.

But now let us drop this alleged parallelism between individual organizations and social organizations. I have used the analogies elaborated, but as a scaffolding to help in building up a coherent body of sociological inductions. Let us take away the scaffolding: the inductions will stand by themselves.

We saw that societies are aggregates which grow; that in various types of them there are great varieties in the degrees of growth reached; that types of successively larger sizes result from the aggregation and re-aggregation of those of smaller sizes; and that this increase by coalescence, joined with interstitial increase, is the process through which have been formed the vast civilized nations.

Along with increase of size in societies goes increase of structure. Primitive wandering hordes are without established unlikenesses of parts. With growth of them into tribes habitually come some differences; both in the powers and occupations of their members. Unions of tribes are followed by more differences, governmental and industrial—social grades running through the whole mass, and contrasts between the differently-occupied parts in different localities. Such differentiations multiply as the compounding progresses. They proceed from the general to the special: first the broad division between ruling and ruled; then within the ruling part divisions into political, religious, military, and within the ruled part divisions into food-producing classes and handi-craftsmen; then within each of these divisions minor ones, and so on.

Passing from the structural aspect to the functional aspect, we note that while all parts of a society have like natures and activities there is hardly any mutual dependence, and the aggregate scarcely forms a vital whole. As its parts assume different functions they become dependent on one another, so that injury to one hurts others; until in highly-evolved societies, general perturbation is caused by derangement of any portion. This contrast between undeveloped and developed societies, is due to the fact that, with increasing specialization of functions comes increasing inability in each part to perform the functions of other parts.

The organization of every society begins with a contrast between the division which carries on relations, habitually hostile, with environing societies, and the division which is devoted to procuring necessaries of life; and during the earlier stages of development these two divisions constitute the whole. Eventually there arises an intermediate division serving to transfer products and influences from part to part. And in all subsequent stages, evolution to the two earlier systems of structures depends on evolution of this additional system.

While the society as a whole has the character of its sustaining system determined by the general character of its environment, inorganic and organic, the respective parts of this system differentiate in adaptation to the circumstances of the localities; and, after primary industries have been thus localized and specialized, secondary industries dependent upon them arise in conformity with the same principle. Further, as fast as societies become compounded and recompounded and the distributing system develops, the parts devoted to each kind of industry, originally scattered, aggregate in the most favourable localities; and the localized industrial structures, unlike the governmental structures, grow regardless of the original lines of division.

Increase of size, resulting from the massing of groups, necessitates means of communication; both for achieving combined offensive and defensive actions, and for exchange of products. Scarcely traceable tracks, paths, rude roads, finished roads, successively arise; and as fast as intercourse is thus facilitated, there is a transition from direct barter to trading carried on by a separate class; out of which evolves, in course of time, a complex mercantile agency of wholesale and retail distributors. The movement of commodities effected by this agency, beginning as a slow flux to and reflux from certain places at long intervals, passes into rhythmical, regular, rapid currents; and materials for sustentation distributed hither and thither, from being few and crude become numerous and elaborated. Growing efficiency of transfer with greater variety of transferred products, increases the mutual dependence of parts at the same time that it enables each part to fulfil its function better.

Unlike the sustaining system, evolved by converse with the organic and inorganic environments, the regulating system is evolved by converse, offensive and defensive, with environing societies. In primitive headless groups temporary chieftainship results from temporary war; chronic hostilities generate permanent chieftainship; and gradually from the military control results the civil control. Habitual war, requiring prompt combination in the actions of parts, necessitates subordination. Societies in which there is little subordination disappear, and leave outstanding those in which subordination is great; and so there are established societies in which the habit fostered by war and surviving in peace, brings about permanent submission to a government. The centralized regulating system thus evolved is in early stages the sole regulating system. But in large societies that become predominantly industrial, there is added a decentralized regulating system for the industrial structures; and this, at first subject in every way to the original system, acquires at length substantial independence. Finally there arises for the distributing structures also, an independent controlling agency.

15

SOCIETAL TYPOLOGIES

A GLANCE at the respective antecedents of individual organisms and social organisms, shows why the last admit of no such definite classification as the first. Through a thousand generations a species of plant or animal leads substantially the same kind of life; and its successive members inherit the acquired adaptations. When changed conditions cause divergences of forms once alike, the accumulating differences arising in descendants only superficially disguise the original identity—do not prevent the grouping of the several species into a genus; nor do wider divergences that began earlier, prevent the grouping of genera into orders and orders into classes. It is otherwise with societies. Hordes of primitive men, dividing and subdividing, do, indeed, show us successions of small social aggregates leading like lives, inheriting such low structures as had resulted, and repeating those structures. But higher social aggregates propagate their respective types in much less decided ways. Though colonies tend to grow like their parents, yet the parent societies are so comparatively plastic, and the influences of new habitats on the derived societies are so great, that divergences of structure are inevitable. In the absence of definite organizations established during the similar lives of many societies descending one from another, there cannot be the precise distinctions implied by complete classification.

Two cardinal kinds of differences there are, however, of which

---

From *The Principles of Sociology* (London: Williams and Norgate, 1876), vol. 1, part 2, pp. 569–76.

we may avail ourselves for grouping societies in a natural manner. Primarily we may arrange them according to their degrees of composition, as simple, compound, doubly-compound, trebly-compound; and secondarily, though in a less specific way, we may divide them into the predominantly militant and the predominantly industrial—those in which the organization for offence and defence is most largely developed, and those in which the sustaining organization is most largely developed.

We have seen that social evolution begins with small simple aggregates; that it progresses by the clustering of these into larger aggregates; and that after consolidating, such clusters are united with others like themselves into still larger aggregates. Our classification, then, must begin with societies of the first or simplest order.

We cannot in all cases say with precision what constitutes a simple society; for, in common with products of evolution generally, societies present transitional stages which negative sharp divisions. As the multiplying members of a group spread and diverge gradually, it is not always easy to decide when the groups into which they fall become distinct. Here the descendants of common ancestors inhabiting a barren region, have to divide while yet the constituent families are near akin; and there, in a more fertile region, the group may hold together until clusters of families remotely akin are formed: clusters which, diffusing slowly, are held by a common bond that slowly weakens. By and by comes the complication arising from the presence of slaves not of the same ancestry, or of an ancestry but distantly allied; and these, though they may not be political units, must be recognized as units sociologically considered. Then there is the kindred complication arising where an invading tribe becomes a dominant class. Our only course is to regard as a simple society, one which forms a single working whole unsubjected to any other, and of which the parts cooperate, with or without a regulating centre, for certain public ends. Here is a table, presenting with as much definiteness as may be, the chief divisions and sub-divisions of such simple societies.

SIMPLE SOCIETIES	HEADLESS	*Nomadic:*—(hunting) Fuegians, some Australians, Wood-Veddahs, Bushmen, Chépángs and Kusúndas of Nepal.	
		Semi-settled:—most Esquimaux.	
		Settled:—Arafuras, Land Dyaks of Upper Sarawak River.	
	OCCASIONAL HEADSHIP	*Nomadic:*—(hunting) some Australians, Tasmanians.	
		Semi-settled:—some Caribs.	
		Settled:—Some Uaupés of the upper Rio Negro.	
	VAGUE AND UNSTABLE HEADSHIP	*Nomadic:*—(hunting) Andamanese, Abipones, Snakes, Chippewayans, (pastoral) some Bedouins.	
		Semi-settled:—some Esquimaux, Chinooks, Chippewas (at present), some Kamtschadales, Village Veddahs, Bodo and Dhimáls.	
		Settled:—Guiana tribes, Mandans, Coroados, New Guinea people, Tannese, Vateans, Dyaks, Todas, Nagas, Karens, Santals.	
	STABLE HEADSHIP	*Nomadic:*—	
		Semi-settled:—some Caribs, Patagonians, New Caledonians, Kaffirs.	
		Settled:—Guaranis, Pueblos.	

On contemplating these uncivilized societies which, though alike as being uncompounded, differ in their sizes and structures, certain generally-associated traits may be noted. Of the groups without political organization, or with but the vaguest traces of it, the lowest are those small wandering ones which live on the wild food sparsely distributed in forests, over barren tracts, or along sea-shores. Where small simple societies remain without chiefs though settled, it is where circumstances allow them to be habitually peaceful. Glancing down the table we find reason for inferring that the changes from the hunting life to the pastoral, and from the pastoral to the agricultural, favour increase of population, the development of political organizations, of industrial organization, and of the arts; though these causes do not of themselves produce these results.

COMPOUND SOCIETIES	OCCASIONAL HEADSHIP	*Nomadic:*—(pastoral) some Bedouins.
		Semi-settled:—Tannese.
		Settled:—
	UNSTABLE HEADSHIP	*Nomadic:*—(hunting) Dacotahs, (hunting and pastoral) Comanches, (pastoral) Kalmucks.
		Semi-settled:—Ostyaks, Beluchis, Kukis, Bhils, Congo-people, (passing into doubly compound), Teutons before 5th century.
		Settled:—Chippewas (in past times), Creeks, Mundrucus, Tupis, Khonds, some New Guinea people, Sumatrans, Malagasy (till recently), Coast Negroes, Inland Negroes, some Abyssinians, Homeric Greeks, Kingdoms of the Heptarchy, Teutons in 5th century, Fiefs of 10th century.
	STABLE HEADSHIP	*Nomadic:*—(pastoral) Kirghiz.
		Semi-settled:—Bechuanas, Zulus.
		Settled:—Uaupés, Fijians (when first visited), New Zealanders, Sandwich Islanders (in Cook's time), Javans, Hottentots, Dahomans, Ashantees, some Abyssinians, Ancient Yucatanese, New Granada people, Honduras people, Chibchas, some town Arabs.

The second table, given above on this page, contains societies which have passed to a slight extent, or considerably, or wholly, into a state in which the simple groups have their several governing heads subordinated to a general head. The stability or instability alleged of the headship in these cases, refers to the headship of the composite group, and not to the headships of the simple groups. As might be expected, stability of this compound headship becomes more marked as the original unsettled state passes into the completely settled state: the nomadic life obviously making it difficult to keep the heads of groups subordinate to a general head. Though not in all cases accompanied by considerable organization, this coalescence evidently conduces to organization. The completely-settled compound societies are mostly characterized by division into ranks, four, five, or six, clearly marked off; by established ecclesiastical arrangements; by industrial structures that show advancing division of labour, general and local; by buildings of some permanence clustered into places of some size; and by improved appliances of life generally.

In the succeeding table are placed societies formed by the re-compounding of these compound groups, or in which many governments of the types tabulated above have become subject to a still higher government. The first notable fact is that these doubly-compound societies are all completely settled. Along with their greater integration we see in many cases, though not uniformly, a more elaborate and stringent political organization. Where complete stability of political headship over these doubly-compound societies has been established, there is mostly, too, a developed ecclesiastical hierarchy. While becoming more complex by division of labour, the industrial organization has in many cases assumed a caste structure. To a greater or less extent, custom has passed into positive law; and religious observances have grown definite, rigid, and complex. Towns and roads have become general; and considerable progress in knowledge and the arts has taken place.

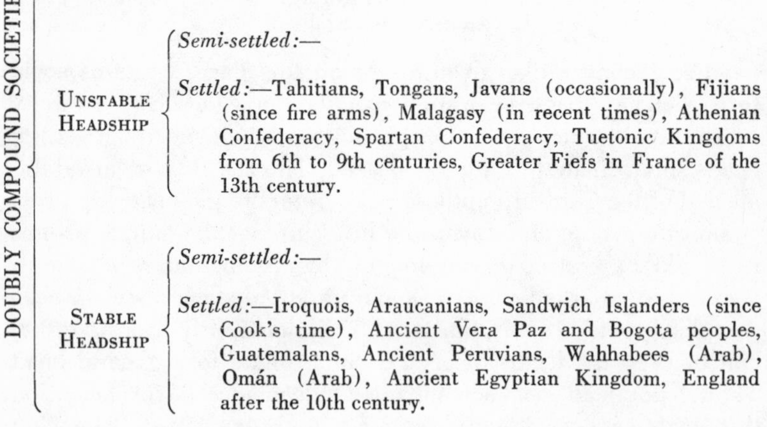

DOUBLY COMPOUND SOCIETIES		
Occasional Headship	*Semi-settled:*—	
	Settled:—Samoans	
Unstable Headship	*Semi-settled:*—	
	Settled:—Tahitians, Tongans, Javans (occasionally), Fijians (since fire arms), Malagasy (in recent times), Athenian Confederacy, Spartan Confederacy, Tuetonic Kingdoms from 6th to 9th centuries, Greater Fiefs in France of the 13th century.	
Stable Headship	*Semi-settled:*—	
	Settled:—Iroquois, Araucanians, Sandwich Islanders (since Cook's time), Ancient Vera Paz and Bogota peoples, Guatemalans, Ancient Peruvians, Wahhabees (Arab), Omán (Arab), Ancient Egyptian Kingdom, England after the 10th century.	

There remain to be added the great civilized nations which need no tabular form, since they mostly fall under one head—trebly compound. Ancient Mexico, the Assyrian Empire, the Egyptian Empire, The Roman Empire, Great Britain, France, Germany, Italy, Russia, may severally be regarded as having reached this stage of composition, or perhaps, in some cases, a still higher stage. Only in respect of the stabilities of their governments may they possibly require classing apart—not their political stabilities in the ordinary sense, but their stabilities in the sense of continuing to be the supreme centres of these great aggregates. So defining this trait, the ancient trebly-compound societies have mostly to be classed as unstable; and of the modern, the Kingdom of Italy and the German Empire have to be tested by time.

As already indicated, this classification must not be taken as more than a rough approximation to the truth. In some cases the data furnished by travellers and others are inadequate; in some cases their accounts are conflicting; in some cases the composition is so far transitional that it is difficult to say under which of two heads it should come. Here the gens or the phratry may be distinguished as a local community; and here these groups of near or remote kinsmen are so mingled with other such groups as practically to form parts of one community. Evidently the like combination of several such small communities, passing through stages of increasing cohesion, leaves it sometimes doubtful whether they are to be regarded as many or as one. And when, as with the larger social aggregates, there have been successive conquests, resulting unions, subsequent dissolutions, and re-unions otherwise composed, the original lines of structure become so confused or lost that it is difficult to class the ultimate product.

But there emerge certain generalizations which we may safely accept. The stages of compounding and re-compounding have to be passed through in succession. No tribe becomes a nation by simple growth; and no great society is formed by the direct union of the smallest societies. Above the simple group the first stage is a compound group inconsiderable in size. The mutual dependence of parts which constitutes it a working whole, cannot exist without some development of lines of intercourse and appliances for combined action; and this must be achieved over a narrow area before it can be achieved over a wide one. When a compound society has been consolidated by the co-operation of its component groups in war under a single head—when it has simultaneously differentiated somewhat its social ranks and industries, and proportionately developed its arts, which all of them conduce in some way to better co-operation, the compound society becomes practically a single one. Other societies of the same order, each having similarly reached a stage of organization alike required and made possible by this co-ordination of actions throughout a larger mass, now form bodies from which, by conquest or by federation in war, may be formed societies of the doubly-compound type. The consolidation of these has again an accompanying advance of organization distinctive of it—an organization for which it affords the scope and which makes it practicable—an organization having a higher complexity in its regulative, distributive, and industrial systems. And at later stages, by kindred steps, arise the still larger aggregates having still more complex structures. In this order has social evolution gone on, and only in this order does it appear to be possible. Whatever imperfections and incongruities the above classification has, do not hide these general facts—that there are societies of these different grades of composition; that those of the same grade have general resemblances in their structures; and that they arise in the order shown.

16

MILITANCY AND INDUSTRIALISM

WE PASS NOW to the classification based on unlikenesses between the kinds of social activity which predominate, and on the resulting unlikenesses of organization. The two social types thus essentially contrasted are the militant and the industrial.

It is doubtless true that no definite separation of these can be made. Excluding a few simple groups such as the Esquimaux, inhabiting places where they are safe from invasion, all societies, simple and compound, are occasionally or habitually in antagonism with other societies; and, as we have seen, tend to evolve structures for carrying on offensive and defensive actions. At the same time sustentation is necessary; and there is always an organization, slight or decided, for achieving it. But while the two systems in social organisms, as in individual organisms, co-exist in all but the rudimentary forms, they vary immensely in the ratios they bear to one another. In some cases the structures carrying on external actions are largely developed; the sustaining system exists solely for their benefit; and the activities are militant. In other cases there is predominance of the structures carrying on sustentation; offensive and defensive structures are maintained only to protect them; and the activities are industrial. At the one extreme we have those warlike tribes which, subsisting mainly by the chase, make the appliances for dealing with enemies serve also for procuring food, and have sustaining systems represented only by their women, who

From *The Principles of Sociology* (London: Williams and Norgate, 1876), vol. 1, part 2, pp. 576–96.

are their slave-classes; while, at the other extreme we have the type, as yet only partially evolved, in which the agricultural, manufacturing, and commercial organizations form the chief part of the society, and, in the absence of external enemies, the appliances for offence and defence are either rudimentary or absent. Transitional as are nearly all the societies we have to study, we may yet clearly distinguish the constitutional traits of these opposite types, characterized by predominance of the outer and inner systems respectively.

Having glanced at the two thus placed in contrast, it will be most convenient to contemplate each by itself.

As before pointed out, the militant type is one in which the army is the nation mobilized while the nation is the quiescent army, and which, therefore, acquires a structure common to army and nation. We shall most clearly understand its nature by observing in detail this parallelism between the military organization and the social organization at large.

Already we have had ample proof that centralized control is the primary trait acquired by every body of fighting men, be it horde of savages, group of brigands, or mass of soldiers. And this centralized control, necessitated during war, characterizes the government during peace. Among the uncivilized there is a marked tendency for the military chief to become also the political head (the medicine man being his only competitor); and in a conquering race of savages his political headship becomes fixed. Among semi-civilized the conquering commander and the despotic king are the same; and they remain the same among the civilized down to late times. The connexion is well shown where in the same race, we find a contrast in the habitual activities and in the forms of government. Thus the powers of the patriarchal chiefs of Kaffir tribes are not great; but the Zulus, who have become a conquering division of the Kaffirs, are under an absolute monarch. Of advanced savages the Fijians may be named as well showing this relation between habitual war and despotic rule: the persons and property of subjects are entirely at the king's or chief's disposal. We have seen that it is the same in the warlike African states, Dahomey and

Ashantee. The Ancient Mexicans, again, whose highest profession was that of arms, and whose eligible prince became king only by feats in war, had an autocratic government, which, according to Clavigero, became more stringent as the territory was enlarged by conquest. Similarly, the unmitigated despotism under which the Peruvians lived, had been established during the spread of the Ynca conquests. And that race is not the cause, we are shown by this recurrence in Ancient America of a relation so familiar in ancient states of the Old World.

The absoluteness of a commander-in-chief goes along with absolute control exercised by his generals over their subordinates, and by their subordinates over the men under them: all are slaves to those above and despots to those below. This structure repeats itself in the accompanying social arrangements. There are precise gradations of rank in the community and complete submission of each rank to the ranks above it. We see this in the society already instanced as showing among advanced savages the development of the militant type. In Fiji six classes are enumerated, from king down to slaves, as sharply marked off. Similarly in Madagascar, where despotism has been in late times established by war, there are several grades and castes. Among the Dahomans, given in so great a degree to bloodshed of all kinds, "the army, or, what is nearly synonymous, the nation," says Burton, "is divided, both male and female, into two wings"; and then, of the various ranks enumerated, all are characterized as legally slaves of the king. In Ashantee, too, where his officers are required to die when the king dies, we have a kindred condition. Of old, among the aggressive Persians, grades were strongly marked. So was it in warlike Ancient Mexico: besides three classes of nobility, and besides the mercantile classes, there were three agricultural classes down to the serfs—all in precise subordination. In Peru, also, below the Ynca, there were grades of nobility—lords over lords. Moreover, according to Garcilasso, in each town the inhabitants were registered in decades under a decurion, five of these under a superior, two such under a higher one, five of these centurions under a head, two of these under one who thus ruled a thousand men, and for every ten thousand there was a governor of Ynca race: the political rule being thus completely regimental. Till lately, another illustration was furnished by Japan. That there were kindred, if less elaborate, structures in ancient militant states of the Old World, scarcely needs saying; and that like structures were repeated in mediæval times, when a large nation like France had under the monarch several grades of feudal lords, vassals to those above and suzerains to those below, with serfs under the lowest, again shows us that everywhere the militant type has sharply-marked social gradations as it has sharply-marked military gradations.

Corresponding to this natural government there is a like form of supernatural government. I do not mean merely that in the ideal other-worlds of militant societies, the ranks and powers are conceived as like those of the real world around, though this also is to be noted; but I refer to the militant character of the religion. Ever in antagonism with other societies, the life is a life of enmity and the religion a religion of enmity. The duty of blood-revenge, most sacred of all with the savage, continues to be the dominant duty as the militant type of society evolves. The chief, baulked of his vengeance, dies enjoining his successors to avenge him; his ghost is propitiated by fulfilment of his commands; the slaying of his enemies becomes the highest action; trophies are brought to his grave in token of fulfilment; and, as tradition grows, he becomes the god worshipped with bloody sacrifices. Everywhere we find evidence. The Fijians offer the bodies of their victims killed in war to the gods before cooking them. In Dahomey, where the militant type is so far developed that women are warriors, men are almost daily sacrificed by the monarch to please his dead father; and the ghosts of old kings are invoked for aid in war by blood sprinkled on their tombs. The war-god of the Mexicans (originally a conqueror), the most revered of their gods, had his idol fed with human flesh: wars being undertaken to supply him with victims. And similarly in Peru, where there were habitual human sacrifices, men taken captive were immolated to the father of the Yncas, the Sun. How militant societies of old in the East similarly evolved deities who were similarly propitiated by bloody rites, needs merely indicating. Habitually their mythologies represent gods as conquerors; habitually their gods are named "the strong one," "the destroyer," "the avenger," "god of battles," "lord of hosts," "man of war," and so forth. As we read in Assyrian inscriptions, wars were commenced by their alleged will; and, as we read elsewhere, peoples were massacred wholesale in professed obedience to them. How its theological government, like its political government, is essentially military, we see even in late and qualified forms of the militant type; for down to the present time absolute subordination, like that of soldier to commander, is the supreme virtue, and disobedience the crime for which eternal torture is threatened.

Similarly with the accompanying ecclesiastical organization. Very generally where the militant type is highly developed, the political head and ecclesiastical head are identical—the king, chief descendant of his ancestor who has become a god, is also chief propitiator of him. It was so in Ancient Peru; and in Tezcuco and Tlacopan (Mexico) the high-priest was the king's second son. The Egyptian wall-paintings show us kings performing sacrifices; as do also the Assyrian. Babylonian records harmonize with Hebrew traditions in telling us of priest-kings. In Lydia it was the same: Crœsus was king and priest. In Sparta, too, the kings, while military chiefs, were also high priests; and a trace of the like original relation existed in Rome. A system of subordination essentially akin to the military, has habitually characterized the accompanying priesthoods. The Fijians have an hereditary priesthood forming a hierarchy. In Tahiti, where the high-priest was royal, there were grades of hereditary priests belonging to each social rank. In Ancient Mexico the priesthoods of different gods had different ranks, and there were three ranks within each priesthood; and in Ancient Peru, besides the royal chief priest, there were priests of the conquering race set over various classes of inferior priests. A like type of structure, with subjection of rank to rank, has characterized priesthoods in the ancient and modern belligerent societies of the Old World.

The like mode of government is traceable throughout the sustaining organization also, so long as the social type remains predominantly militant. Beginning with simple societies in which the slave-class furnishes the warrior-class with necessaries of life, we have already seen that during subsequent stages of evolution the industrial part of the society continues to be essentially a permanent commissariat, existing solely to supply the needs of the governmental-military structures, and having left over for itself only enough for bare maintenance. Hence the development of political regulation over its activities, has been in fact the extension throughout it of that military rule which, as a permanent commissariat, it naturally had. An extreme instance is furnished us by the Ancient Peruvians, whose political and industrial governments were identical—whose kinds and quantities of labour for every class in every locality, were prescribed by laws enforced by state officers—who had work legally dictated even for their young children, their blind, and their lame, and who were publicly chastised for idleness: regimental discipline being applied to industry just as our modern advocate of strong government would have it now. The late Japanese system, completely military in origin and nature, similarly permeated industry: great and small things—houses, ships, down even to mats—were prescribed in their structures. In the warlike monarchy of Madagascar the artizan classes are all in the employ of government, and no man can change his occupation or locality, under pain of death. Without multiplication of cases, these typical ones, reminding the reader of the extent to which even in modern fighting states industrial activities are officially regulated, will sufficiently show the principle.

Not industry only, but life at large, is, in militant societies, subject to kindred discipline. Before its recent collapse the government of Japan enforced sumptuary laws on each class, mercantile and other, up to the provincial governors, who must rise, dine, go out, give audience, and retire to rest at prescribed hours; and the native literature specifies regulations of a scarcely credible minuteness. In Ancient Peru, officers "minutely inspected the houses, to see that the man, as well as his wife, kept the household in proper order, and preserved a due state of discipline among their children"; and householders were rewarded or chastised accordingly. Among the Egyptians each person had, at fixed intervals, to report to a local officer his name, abode, and mode of living. Sparta, too, yields an example of a society specially organized for offence and defence, in which the private conduct of citizens in all its details was under public control enforced by spies and censors. Though regulations so stringent have not characterized the militant type in more recent ages, yet we need but recall the laws regulating food and dress, the restraints on locomotion, the prohibitions of some games and dictation of others, to indicate the parallelism of principle. Even now where the military organization has been kept in vigour by military activities, as in France, we are shown by the peremptory control of journals and suppression of meetings, by the regimental uniformity of education, by the official administration of the fine arts, the way in which its characteristic regulating system ramifies everywhere.

And then, lastly, is to be noted the theory concerning the relation between the State and the individual, with its accompanying sentiment. This structure which adapts a society for combined action against other societies, is associated with the belief that its members exist for the benefit of the whole and not the whole for the benefit of its members. As in an army the liberty of the soldier is denied and only his duty as a member of the mass insisted on; as in a permanently encamped army like the Spartan nation, the laws recognized no personal interests, but patriotic ones only; so in the militant type throughout, the claims of the unit are nothing and the claims of the aggregate everything. Absolute subjection of authority is the supreme virtue and resistance to it a crime. Other offences may be condoned, but disloyalty is an unpardonable offence. If we take the sentiments of the sanguinary Fijians, among whom loyalty is so intense that a man stands unbound to be knocked on the head, himself saying that what the king wills must be done; or those of the Dahomans, among whom the highest officials are the king's slaves, and on his decease his women sacrifice one another that they may all follow him; or those of the Ancient Peruvians, among whom with a dead Ynca, or great curaca, were buried alive his favourite attendants and wives that they might go to serve him in the other world; or those of the Ancient Persians, among whom a father, seeing his innocent son shot by the king in pure wantonness, "felicitated" the king "on the excellence of his archery," and among whom bastinadoed subjects "declared themselves delighted because his majesty had condescended to recollect them";

we are sufficiently shown that in this social type, the sentiment which prompts the assertion of personal rights in opposition to the ruling power, scarcely exists.

Thus the trait characterizing the militant structure throughout, is that its units are coerced into their various combined actions. As the soldier's will is so suspended that he becomes in everything the agent of his officer's will; so is the will of the citizen in all transactions, private and public, overruled by that of the government. The co-operation by which the life of the militant society is maintained, is a *compulsory* co-operation. The social structure adapted for dealing with surrounding hostile societies is under a centralized regulating system, to which all the parts are completely subject; just as in the individual organism the outer organs are completely subject to the chief nervous centre.

The traits of the industrial type have to be generalized from inadequate and entangled data. Antagonism more or less constant with other societies, having been almost everywhere and always the condition of each society, a social structure fitted for offence and defence exists in nearly all cases, and disguises the structure which social sustentation alone otherwise originates. Such conception as may be formed of it has to be formed from what we find in the few simple societies that have been habitually peaceful, and in the advanced compound societies which, though once habitually militant, have become gradually less so.

Already I have referred to the chiefless Arafuras, living in "peace and brotherly love with one another," of whom we are told that "they recognize the rights of property in the fullest sense of the word, without there being any authority among them than the decisions of their elders, according to the customs of their forefathers": that is, there has grown up a recognition of mutual claims and personal rights, with voluntary submission to a tacitly-elected representative government formed of the most experienced. Among the Todas who "lead a peaceful, tranquil life," disputes are "settled either by arbitration" or by "a council of five." The amiable Bodo and Dhimals, said to be wholly unmilitary, display an essentially-free social form. They have nothing but powerless head men, and are without slaves or servants; but they give mutual assistance in clearing ground and house-building: there is voluntary exchange of services—giving of equivalents of labour. The Mishmis again, described as quiet, inoffensive, not warlike, and only occasionally uniting in self-defence, have scarcely any political organization. Their village communities under merely nominal chiefs acknowledge no common chief of the tribe, and the rule is democratic: crimes are judged by an assembly.

Naturally few, if any, cases occur in which societies of this type have evolved into larger societies without passing into the militant type; for, as we have seen, the consolidation of simple aggregates into a compound aggregate habitually results from war, defensive or offensive, which, if continued, evolves a centralized authority with its coercive institutions. The Pueblos, however, industrious and peaceful agriculturists, who, building their unique villages, or compound houses containing 2,000 people, in such ways as to "wall out black barbarism," fight only when invaded, show us a democratic form of government: "the governor and his council are elected annually by the people." The case of Samoa, too, may be named as showing to some extent how, in one of these compound communities where the warlike activity is now not considerable, decline in the rigidity of political control has gone along with some evolution of the industrial type. Chiefs and minor heads, partly hereditary partly elective, are held responsible for the conduct of affairs; there are village-parliaments and district-parliaments. Along with this we find a considerably-developed sustaining organization separate from the political—masters who have apprentices, employ journeymen, and pay wages; and when payment for work is inadequate, there are even strikes upheld by a tacit trades-unionism.

Passing to more evolved societies it must be observed, first, that the distinctive traits of the industrial type do not become marked, even where the industrial activity is considerable, so long as the industrial government remains identified with the political. In Phœnicia, for example, "the foreign wholesale trade seems to have belonged mostly to the state, the kings, and the nobles. . . . Ezekiel describes the king of Tyrus as a prudent commercial prince, who finds out the precious metals in their hidden seats, enriches himself by getting them, and increases these riches by further traffic." Clearly, where the political and military heads have thus themselves become the heads of the industrial organization, the traits distinctive of it are prevented from showing themselves. Of ancient societies to be named in connexion with the relation between industrial activities and free institutions, Athens will be at once thought of; and, by contrast with other Greek states, it showed this relation as clearly as can be expected. Up to the time of Solon all these communities were under either oligarchs or despots. The rest of them, in which war continued to be the honoured occupation while industry was despised, retained this political type; but in Athens, where industry was regarded with comparative respect, where it was encouraged by Solon, and where immigrant artizans found a home, there commenced an industrial organization which, gradually growing, distinguished the Athenian society from adjacent societies, as it was distinguished from them by those democratic institutions that simultaneously developed.

Turning to later times, the relation between a social *régime* predominantly industrial and a less coercive form of rule, is shown us by the Hanse Towns, by the towns of the Low Countries out of which the Dutch Republic arose, and in high degrees by ourselves, by the United States, and by our colonies. Along with wars less frequent and these carried on at a distance; and along with an accompanying growth of agriculture, manufactures, and commerce, beyond that of continental states more military in habit; there has gone in England a development of free institutions. As further implying that the two are related as cause and consequence, there may be noted the fact that the regions whence changes towards greater political liberty have come, are the leading industrial regions; and that rural districts, less characterized by constant trading transactions, have retained longer the earlier type with its appropriate sentiments and ideas.

In the form of ecclesiastical government we see parallel changes. Where the industrial activities and structures evolve, this branch of the regulating system, no longer as in the militant type a rigid hierarchy, little by little loses strength, while there grows up one of a different kind: sentiments and institutions both relaxing. Right of private judgment in religious matters gradually establishes itself along with establishment of political rights. In place of a uniform belief imperatively enforced, there come multiform beliefs voluntarily accepted; and the ever-multiplying bodies espousing these beliefs, instead of being governed despotically, govern themselves after a manner more or less representative. Military conformity coercively maintained gives place to a varied non-conformity maintained by willing union.

The industrial organization itself, which thus as it becomes predominant affects all the rest, of course shows us in an especial degree this change of structure. From the primitive predatory condition under which the master maintains slaves to work for him, there is a transition through stages of increasing freedom to a condition like our own, in which all who work and employ, buy and sell, are entirely independent; and in which there is an unchecked power of forming associations that rule themselves on democratic principles. Combinations of workmen and counter-combinations of employers, no less than political societies and leagues for carrying on this or that agitation, show us the representative mode of government; which characterizes also every joint-stock company for mining, banking, railway-making, or other commercial enterprise.

Further we see that as in the predatory type the military mode of regulation ramifies into all minor departments of social activity, so here does the industrial mode of regulation. Multitudinous objects are achieved by spontaneously-evolved combinations of citizens governed representatively. The tendency to this kind of organization is so ingrained that for every proposed end the proposed means is a society ruled by an elected committee headed by an elected chairman—philanthropic associations of multitudinous kinds, literary institutions, libraries, clubs, bodies for fostering the various sciences and arts, etc., etc.

Along with all which traits there go sentiments and ideas concerning the relation between the citizen and the State, opposite to those accompanying the militant type. In place of the doctrine that the duty of obedience to the governing agent is unqualified, there arises the doctrine that the will of the citizens is supreme and the governing agent exists merely to carry out their will. Thus subordinated in authority, the regulating power is also restricted in range. Instead of having an authority extending over actions of all kinds, it is shut out from large classes of actions. Its control over ways of living in respect to food, clothing, amusements, is repudiated; it is not allowed to dictate modes of production nor to regulate trade.

Nor is this all. It becomes a duty to resist irresponsible government, and also to resist the excesses of responsible government. There arises a tendency in minorities to disobey even the legislature deputed by the majority, when it interferes in certain ways; and their oppositions to laws they condemn as inequitable, from time to time cause abolition of them. With which changes of political theory and accompanying sentiment, is joined a belief, implied or avowed, that the combined actions of the social aggregate have for their end to maintain the conditions under which individual lives may be satisfactorily carried on; in place of the old belief that individual lives have for their end the maintenance of this aggregate's combined actions.

These pervading traits in which the industrial type differs so widely from the militant type, originate in those relations of individuals implied by industrial activities, which are wholly unlike those implied by militant activities. All trading transactions, whether between masters and workmen, buyers and sellers of commodities, or professional men and those they aid, are effected by free exchange. For some benefit which A's occupation enables him to give, B willingly yields up an equivalent benefit: if not in the form of something he has produced, then in the form of money gained by his occupation. This relation, in which the mutual rendering of services is unforced and neither individual subordinated, becomes the predominant relation throughout society in proportion as the industrial activities predominate. Daily determining the thoughts and sentiments, daily disciplining all in asserting their own claims while forcing them to recognize the correlative claims of others, it produces social units whose mental structures and habits mould social arrangements into corresponding forms. There results this type characterized throughout by that same individual freedom which every commercial transaction implies. The co-operation by which the multiform activities of the society are carried on, becomes a *voluntary* co-operation. And while the developed sustaining system which gives to a social organism the industrial type, acquires for itself, like the developed sustaining system of an animal, a regulating apparatus of a diffused or uncentralized kind; it tends also to decentralize the primary regulating apparatus, by making it derive from more numerous classes its deputed powers.

Necessarily the essential traits of these two social types are in most cases obscured, both by the antecedents and by the co-existing circumstances. Every society has been at each past period, and is at present, conditioned in a way more or less unlike the ways in which others have been and are conditioned. Hence the production of structures characterizing one or other of these opposed types, is, in every instance, furthered, or hindered, or modified, in a special manner. Observe the several kinds of causes.

There is, first, the deeply-organized character of the particular race, coming down from those pre-historic times during which the diffusion of mankind and differentiation of the varieties of man, took place. Very difficult to change, this must in every case qualify differently the tendency towards assumption of either type.

There is, next, the effect due to the immediately-preceding mode of life and social type. Nearly always the society we have to study contains decayed institutions and habits belonging to an ancestral society otherwise circumstanced; and these pervert more or less the effects of circumstances then existing.

Again, there are the peculiarities of the habitat in respect of contour, soil, climate, flora, fauna, severally affecting in one mode or other the activities, whether militant or industrial; and severally hindering or aiding, in some special way, the development of either type.

Yet further, there are the complications caused by the particular organizations and practices of surrounding societies. For, supposing the amount of offensive or defensive action to be the same, the nature of it depends in each case on the nature of the antagonist action; and hence its reactive effects on structure vary with the character of the antagonist. Add to this that direct imitation of adjacent societies is a factor of some moment.

There remains to be named an element of complication more potent perhaps than any of these—one which of itself often goes far to determine the type as militant, and which in every case profondly modifies the social arrangements. I refer to the mixture of races caused by conquest or otherwise. We may properly treat of it separately under the head of social constitution—not, of course, constitution politically understood, but constitution understood as referring to the relative homogeneity or heterogeneity of the units constituting the social aggregate.

Inevitably as the nature of the aggregate, partially determined by environing conditions, is in other respects determined by the natures of its units, where its units are of diverse natures the degrees of contrast between the two or more kinds of them, and the degrees of union between them, must greatly affect the results. Are they of unallied races or of races near akin; and do they remain separate or do they mix?

If units of two kinds are joined in the same society, their respective tendencies to evolve structures more or less unlike in character, must modify the product. And the special modification will in every case further or hinder the evolution of one or the other social type. Clearly where it has happened that a conquering race, continuing to govern a subject race, has developed the militant regulating system throughout the whole social structure, and for ages habituated its units to compulsory co-operation—where it has also happened that the correlative ecclesiastical system with its appropriate cult, has given to absolute subordination the religious sanction—and especially where, as in China, each individual is moulded by the governing power and stamped with the appropriate ideas of duty which it is heresy to question; it becomes impossible for any considerable change to be wrought in the social structure by other influences. It is the law of all organization that as it becomes complete it becomes rigid. Only where incompleteness implies a remaining plasticity, is it possible for the type to develop from the original predatory form to the form which industrial activity generates.

Especially where the two races, contrasted in their natures, do not mix, social co-operation implies a compulsory regulating system: the military form of structure which the dominant impose, ramifies throughout. Ancient Peru furnished an extreme case; and the Ottoman empire may be instanced. Social constitutions of this kind, in which aptitudes for forming unlike structures co-exist, are manifestly in states of unstable equilibrium. Any considerable shock dissolves the organization; and in the absence of unity of tendency, re-establishment of it is difficult if not impossible.

In cases where the conquering and conquered, though widely unlike, intermarry extensively, a kindred effect is produced in another way. The conflicting tendencies towards different social types, instead of existing in separate individuals, now exist in the same individual. The half-caste, inheriting from one line of ancestry proclivities adapted to one set of institutions, and from the other line of ancestry proclivities adapted to another set of institutions, is not fitted for either. He is a unit whose nature has not been moulded by any social type, and therefore cannot, with others like himself, evolve any social type. Modern Mexico and the South American Republics, with their perpetual revolutions, show us the result.

It is observable, too, that where races of strongly-contrasted natures have mixed more or less, or, remaining but little mixed, occupy adjacent areas subject to the same government, the equilibrium maintained so long as that government keeps up the coercive form, shows itself to be unstable when the coercion relaxes. Spain with its diverse peoples, Basque, Celtic, Gothic, Moorish, Jewish, partially mingled and partially localized, shows us this result.

Small differences, however, seem advantageous. Sundry instances point to the conclusion that a society formed from nearly-allied peoples of which the conquering eventually mingles with the conquered, is relatively well fitted for progress. From their fusion results a community which, determined in its leading traits by the character common to the two, is prevented by their differences of character from being determined in its minor traits—is left capable of taking on new arrangements determined by new influences: medium plasticity allows those changes of structure constituting advance in heterogeneity. One example is furnished us by the Hebrews; who, notwithstanding their boasted purity of blood, resulted from a mixing of many Semitic varieties in the country east of the Nile, and who, both in their wanderings and after the conquest of Palestine, went on amalgamating kindred tribes. Another is supplied by the Athenians, whose progress had for antecedent the mingling of numerous immigrants from other Greek states with the Greeks of the locality. The fusion by conquest of the Romans with other Aryan tribes, Sabini, Sabelli, and Samnites, preceded the first ascending stage of the Roman civilization. And our own country, peopled by different divisions of the Aryan race, and mainly by varieties of Scandinavians, again illustrates this effect produced by the mixture of units sufficiently alike to co-operate in the same social system, but sufficiently unlike to prevent that social system from becoming forthwith definite in structure.

Admitting that the evidence where so many causes are in operation cannot be satisfactorily disentangled, and claiming only probability for these inductions respecting social constitutions, it remains to point out their analogy to certain inductions respecting the constitutions of individual living things. Between organisms widely unlike in kind, no progeny can arise: the physiological units contributed by them respectively to form a fertilized germ, cannot work together so as to produce a new organism. Evidently as, while multiplying, the two classes of units tend to build themselves into two different structures, their conflict prevents the formation of any structure. If the two organisms are less unlike in kind—belonging, say, to the same genus though to different species—the two structures which their two groups of physiological units tend to build up, being tolerably similar, they can, and do, co-operate in making an organism that is intermediate. But this, though it will work, is imperfect in its latest-evolved parts: there results a mule incapable of propagating. If, instead of different species, remote varieties are united, the intermediate organism is not infertile; but many facts suggest the conclusion that infertility results in subsequent generations: the incongruous working of the united structures, though longer in showing itself, comes out ultimately. And then, finally, if instead of remote varieties, varieties nearly allied are united, a permanently-fertile breed results; and while the slight differences of the two kinds of physiological units are not such as to prevent harmonious co-operation, they are such as conduce to plasticity and unusually vigorous growth.

Here, then, seems a parallel to the conclusion indicated above, that hybrid societies are imperfectly organizable—cannot grow into forms completely stable; while societies that have been evolved from mixtures of nearly-allied varieties of man, can assume stable structures, and have an advantageous modifiability. . . .

Were this the fit place, some pages might be added respecting a possible future social type, differing as much from the industrial as this does from the militant—a type which, having a sustaining system more fully developed than any we know at present, will use the products of industry neither for maintaining a militant organization nor exclusively for material aggrandizement; but will devote them to the carrying on of higher activities. As the contrast between the militant and the industrial types, is indicated by inverting the belief that individuals exist for the benefit of the State into the belief that the State exists for the benefit of individuals; so the contrast between the industrial type and the type likely to be evolved from it, is indicated by the inversion of the belief that life is for work into the belief that work is for life. But we are here concerned with inductions derived from societies that have been and are, and cannot enter upon speculations respecting societies that may be. Merely naming as a sign, the multiplication of institutions and appliances for intellectual and æsthetic culture and for kindred activities not of a directly life-sustaining kind, but of a kind having gratification for their immediate purpose, I can here say no more.

Returning from this parenthetical suggestion, there remains the remark that to the complications caused by the crossings of these two classifications, have to be added the complications caused by the unions of races widely unlike or little unlike; which here mix not at all, there partially, and in other cases wholly. Respecting these kinds of constitutions, we have considerable warrant for concluding that the hybrid kind, essentially unstable, admits of being organized only on the principle of compulsory co-operation; since units much opposed in their natures cannot work together spontaneously. While, conversely, the kind characterized by likeness in its units is relatively stable; and under fit conditions may evolve into the industrial type: especially if the likeness is qualified by slight differences.

17

STRUGGLE IN EVOLUTION

One of the facts difficult to reconcile with current theories of the Universe, is that high organizations throughout the animal kingdom habitually serve to aid destruction or to aid escape from destruction. If we hold to the ancient view, we must say that high organization has been deliberately devised for such purposes. If we accept the modern view, we must say that high organization has been evolved by the exercise of destructive activities during immeasurable periods of the past. Here we choose the latter alternative. To the never-ceasing efforts to catch and eat, and the never-ceasing endeavours to avoid being caught and eaten, is to be ascribed the development of the various senses and the various motor organs directed by them. The bird of prey with the keenest vision, has, other things equal, survived when members of its species that did not see so far, died from want of food; and by such survivals, keenness of vision has been made greater in course of generations. The fleetest members of a herbivorous herd, escaping when the slower fell victims to a carnivore, left posterity; among which, again, those with the most perfectly-adapted limbs survived: the carnivores themselves being at the same time similarly disciplined and their speed increased. So, too, with intelligence. Sagacity that detected a danger which stupidity did not perceive, lived and propagated; and the cunning which hit upon a new

---

From *The Study of Sociology* (London: Williams and Norgate, 1873), pp. 192–99; *Life and Letters of Herbert Spencer,* by D. Duncan (London: Williams and Norgate, 1908), p. 336.

deception, and so secured prey not otherwise to be caught, left posterity where a smaller endowment of cunning failed. This mutual perfecting of pursuer and pursued, acting upon their entire organizations, has been going on throughout all time; and human beings have been subject to it just as much as other beings. Warfare among men, like warfare among animals, has had a large share in raising their organizations to a higher stage. The following are some of the various ways in which it has worked.

In the first place, it has had the effect of continually extirpating races which, for some reason or other, were least fitted to cope with the conditions of existence they were subject to. The killing-off of relatively-feeble tribes, or tribes relatively wanting in edurance, or courage, or sagacity, or power of co-operation, must have tended ever to maintain, and occasionally to increase, the amounts of life-preserving powers possessed by men.

Beyond this average advance caused by destruction of the least-developed races and the least-developed individuals, there has been an average advance caused by inheritance of those further developments due to functional activity. Remember the skill of the Indian in following a trail, and remember that under kindred stimuli many of his perceptions and feelings and bodily powers have been habitually taxed to the uttermost, and it becomes clear that the struggle for existence between neighbouring tribes has had an important effect in cultivating faculties of various kinds. Just as, to take an illustration from among ourselves, the skill of the police cultivates cunning among burglars, which, again, leading to further precautions generates further devices to evade them; so, by the unceasing antagonisms between human societies, small and large, there has been a mutual culture of an adapted intelligence, a mutual culture of certain traits of character not to be undervalued, and a mutual culture of bodily powers.

A large effect, too, has been produced upon the development of the arts. In responding to the imperative demands of war, industry made important advances and gained much of its skill. Indeed, it may be questioned whether, in the absence of that exercise of manipulative faculty which the making of weapons originally gave, there would ever have been produced the tools required for developed industry. If we go back to the Stone-Age, we see that implements of the chase and implements of war are those showing most labour and dexterity. If we take still-existing human races which were without metals when we found them, we see in their skilfully-wrought stone clubs, as well as in their large war-canoes, that the needs of defence and attack were the chief stimuli to the cultivation of arts afterwards available for productive purposes. Passing over intermediate stages, we may note a comparatively-recent stages the same relation. Observe a coat of mail, or one of the more highly-finished suits of armour—compare it with articles of iron and steel of the same date; and there is evidence that these desires to kill enemies and escape being killed, more extreme than any other, have had great effects on those arts of working in metal to which most other arts owe their progress. The like relation is shown us in the uses made of gunpowder. At first a destructive agent, it has become an agent of immense service in quarrying, mining, railway-making, &c.

A no less important benefit bequeathed by war, has been the formation of large societies. By force alone were small nomadic hordes welded into large tribes; by force alone were large tribes welded into small nations; by force alone have small nations been welded into large nations. While the fighting of societies usually maintains separateness, or by conquest produces only temporary unions, it produces, from time to time, permanent unions; and as fast as there are formed permanent unions of small into large, and then of large into still larger, industrial progress is furthered in three ways. Hostilities, instead of being perpetual, are broken by intervals of peace. When they occur, hostilities do not so profoundly derange the industrial activities. And there arises the possibility of carrying out the division of labour much more effectually. War, in short, in the slow course of things, brings about a social aggregation which furthers that industrial state at variance with war; and yet nothing but war could bring about this social aggregation.

These truths, that without war large aggregates of men cannot be formed, and that without large aggregates of men there cannot be a developed industrial state, are illustrated in all places and times among existing uncivilized and semi-civilized races, we everywhere find that union of small societies by a conquering society is a step in civilization. The records of peoples now extinct show us this with equal clearness. On looking back into our own history, and into the histories of neighbouring nations, we similarly see that only by coercion were the smaller feudal governments so subordinated as to secure internal peace. And even lately, the long-desired consolidation of Germany, if not directly effected by "blood and iron," as Bismarck said it must be, has been indirectly effected by them.

The furtherance of industrial development by aggregation is no less manifest. If we compare a small society with a large one, we get clear proof that those processes of co-operation by which social life is made possible, assume high forms only when the numbers of the co-operating citizens are great. Ask of what use a cloth-factory, supposing they could have one, would be to the members of a small tribe, and it becomes manifest that, producing as it would in a single day a year's supply of cloth, the vast cost of making it and keeping it in order could never be compensated by the advantage gained. Ask what would happen were a shop like Shoolbred's, supplying all textile products, set up in a village, and you see that the absence of a sufficiently-extensive distributing function would negative its continuance. Ask what sphere a bank would have had in the Old-English period, when nearly all people grew their own food and spun their own wool, and it is at once seen that the various appliances for facilitating exchange can grow up only when a community becomes so large that the amount of exchange to be facilitated is great. Hence, unquestionably, that integration of societies effected by war, has been a needful preliminary to industrial development, and consequently to developments of other kinds—Science, the Fine Arts, &c.

Industrial habits too, and habits of subordination to social requirements, are indirectly brought about by the same cause. The truth that the power of working continuously, wanting in the aboriginal man, could be established only by that persistent coercion to which conquered and enslaved tribes are subject, has become trite. An allied truth is, that only by a discipline of submission, first to an owner, then to a personal governor, presently to government less personal, then to the embodied law proceeding from government, could there eventually be reached submission to that code of moral law by which the civilized man is more and more restrained in his dealings with his fellows.

Such being some of the important truths usually ignored by men too exclusively influenced by the religion of amity, let us now glance at the no less important truths to which men are blinded by the religion of enmity.

Though, during barbarism and the earlier stages of civilization, war has the effect of exterminating the weaker societies, and of weeding out the weaker members of the stronger societies, and thus in both ways furthering the development of those valuable powers, bodily and mental, which war brings into play; yet during the later stages of civilization, the second of these actions is reversed. So long as all adult males have to bear arms, the average result is that those of most strength and quickness survive, while the feebler and slower are slain; but when the industrial development has become such that only some of the adult males are drafted into the army, the tendency is to pick out and expose to slaughter the best-grown and healthiest: leaving behind the physically-inferior to propagate the race. The fact that among ourselves, though the number of soldiers raised is not relatively large, many recruits are rejected by the examining surgeons, shows that the process inevitably works towards deterioration. Where, as in France, conscriptions have gone on taking away the finest men, generation after generation, the needful lowering of the standard proves how disastrous is the effect on those animal qualities of a race which form a necessary basis for all higher qualities. If the depletion is indirect also—if there is such an overdraw on the energies of the industrial population that a large share of heavy labour is thrown on the women, whose systems are taxed simultaneously by hard work and child-bearing, a further cause of physical degeneracy comes into play: France again supplying an example. War, therefore, after a certain stage of progress, instead of furthering bodily development and the development of certain mental powers, becomes a cause of retrogression.

In like manner, though war, by bringing about social consolidations, indirectly favours industrial progress and all its civilizing consequences, yet the direct effect of war on industrial progress is repressive. It is repressive as necessitating the abstraction of men and materials that would otherwise go to industrial growth; it is repressive as deranging the complex inter-dependencies among the many productive and distributive agencies; it is repressive as drafting off much administrative and constructive ability, which would else have gone to improve the industrial arts and the industrial organization. And if we contrast the absolutely-military Spartans with the partially-military Athenians, in their respective attitudes towards culture of every kind, or call to mind the contempt shown for the pursuit of knowledge in purely-military times like those of feudalism; we cannot fail to see that persistent war is at variance not only with industrial development, but also with the higher intellectual developments that aid industry and are aided by it.

So, too, with the effects wrought on the moral nature. While war, by the discipline it gives soldiers, directly cultivates the habit of subordination, and does the like indirectly by establishing strong and permanent governments; and while in so far it cultivates attributes that are not only temporarily essential, but are steps towards attributes that are permanently essential; yet it does this at the cost of maintaining, and sometimes increasing, detrimental attributes—attributes intrinsically anti-social. The aggressions which selfishness prompts (aggressions which, in a society, have to be restrained by some power that is strong in proportion as the selfishness is intense) can diminish only as fast as selfishness is held in check by sympathy; and perpetual warlike activities repress sympathy: nay, they do worse—they cultivate aggressiveness to the extent of making it a pleasure to inflict injury. The citizen made callous by the killing and wounding of enemies, inevitably brings his callousness home with him. Fellow-feeling, habitually trampled down in military conflicts, cannot at the same time be active in the relations of civil life. In proportion as giving pain to others is made a habit during war, it will remain a habit during peace: inevitably producing in the behaviour of citizens to one another, antagonisms, crimes of violence, and multitudinous aggressions of minor kinds, tending towards a disorder that calls for coercive government. Nothing like a high type of social life is possible without a type of human character in which the promptings of egoism are duly restrained by regard for others. The necessities of war imply absolute self-regard, and absolute disregard of certain others. Inevitably, therefore, the civilizing discipline of social life is antagonized by the uncivilizing discipline of the life war involves. So that beyond the direct mortality and miseries entailed by war, it entails other mortality and miseries by maintaining anti-social sentiments in citizens.

Taking the most general view of the matter, we may say that only when the sacred duty of blood-revenge, constituting the religion of the savage, decreases in sacredness, does there come a possibility of emergence from the deepest barbarism. Only as fast as retaliation, which for a murder on one side inflicts a murder or murders on the other, becomes less imperative, is it possible for larger aggregates of men to hold together and civilization to commence. And so, too, out of lower stages of civilization higher ones can emerge, only as there diminishes this pursuit of international revenge and re-revenge, which the code we inherit from the savage insists upon. Such advantages, bodily and mental, as the race derives from the discipline of war, are exceeded by the disadvantages, bodily and mental, but especially mental, which result after a certain stage of progress is reached. Severe and bloody as the process is, the killing-off of inferior races and inferior individuals, leaves a balance of benefit to mankind during phases of progress in which the moral development is low, and there are no quick sympathies to be continually seared by the infliction of pain and death. But as there arise higher societies, implying individual characters fitted for closer co-operation, the destructive activities exercised by such higher societies have injurious re-active effects on the moral natures of their members—injurious effects which outweigh the benefits resulting from extirpation of inferior races. After this stage has been reached, the purifying process, continuing still an important one, remains to be carried on by industrial war—by a competition of societies during which the best, physically, emotionally, and intellectually, spread most, and leave the least capable to disappear gradually, from failing to leave a sufficiently-numerous posterity. . . .

[What follows is a letter at the time of T. H. Huxley's oblique attack on Spencer and "social Darwinism" in *Evolution and Ethics.*] I am glad to hear that you think of taking up Huxley's "Evolution and Ethics." . . . Practically his view is a surrender of the general doctrine of evolution in so far as its higher applications are concerned, and is pervaded by the ridiculous assumption that, in its application to the organic world, it is limited to the struggle for existence among individuals under its ferocious aspects, and has nothing to do with the development of social organization, or the modifications of the human mind that take place in the course of that organization. . . . The position he takes, that we have to struggle against or correct the cosmic process, involves the assumption that there exists something in us which is not a product of the cosmic process, and is practically a going back to the old theological notions, which put Man and Nature in antithesis. Any rational, comprehensive view of evolution involves that, in the course of social evolution, the human mind is disciplined into that form which itself puts a check upon that part of the cosmic process which consists in the unqualified struggle for existence.

V. The Analysis of Institutions

18

CEREMONIAL INSTITUTIONS

THAT CONTROL of conduct which we distinguish as ceremony, precedes the civil and ecclesiastical controls. It begins with sub-human types of creatures; it occurs among otherwise ungoverned savages; it often becomes highly developed where the other kinds of rule are little developed; it is ever being spontaneously generated afresh between individuals in all societies; and it envelops the more definite restraints which State and Church exercise. The primitiveness of ceremonial regulation is further shown by the fact that at first, political and religious regulations are little more than systems of ceremony, directed towards particular persons living and dead: the code of law joined with the one, and the moral code joined with the other, coming later. There is again the evidence derived from the possession of certain elements in common by the three controls, social, political, and religious; for the forms observable in social intercourse occur also in political and religious intercourse as forms of homage and forms of worship. More significant still is the circumstance that ceremonies may mostly be traced back to certain spontaneous acts which manifestly precede legislation, civil and ecclesiastical. Instead of arising by dictation or by agreement, which would imply the pre-established organization required for making and enforcing rules, they arise by modifications of acts performed for personal ends; and so prove themselves to grow out of individual conduct before social arrange-

From *The Principles of Sociology* (London: Williams and Norgate, 1876), vol. 2, part 4, pp. 34–35, 78–80, 102–3, 194–204.

ments exist to control it. Lastly we note that when there arises a political head, who, demanding subordination, is at first his own master of the ceremonies, and who presently collects round him attendants whose propitiatory acts are made definite and fixed by repetition, there arise ceremonial officials. Though, along with the growth of organizations which enforce civil laws and enunciate moral precepts, there has been such a decay of the ceremonial organization as to render it among ourselves inconspicuous; yet in early stages the body of officials who conduct propitiation of living rulers, supreme and subordinate, homologous with the body of officials who conduct propitiation of dead apothesized rulers, major and minor, is a considerable element of the social structure; and it dwindles only as fast as the structures, political and ecclesiastical, which exercise controls more definite and detailed, usurp its functions.

Carrying with us these general conceptions, let us now pass to the several components of ceremonial rule. We will deal with them under the heads—Trophies, Mutilations, Presents, Visits, Obeisances, Forms of Address, Titles, Badges and Costumes, Further Class Distinctions, Fashion, Past and Future of Ceremony. . . .

[Spencer has been considering the functions of bodily mutilation, especially circumcision.] That this interpretation applies to the custom as made known in the Bible, is clear. We have already seen that the ancient Hebrews, like the modern Abyssinians, practised the form of trophy-taking which necessitates this mutilation of the dead enemy; and as in the one case, so in the other, it follows that the vanquished enemy not slain but made prisoner, will by this mutilation be marked as a subject person. That circumcision was among the Hebrews the stamp of subjection, all the evidence proves. On learning that among existing Bedouins, the only conception of God is that of a powerful living ruler, the sealing by circumcision of the covenant between God and Abraham becomes a comprehensible ceremony. There is furnished an explanation of the fact that in consideration of a territory to be received, this mutilation, undergone by Abraham, implied that "the Lord" was "to be *a* god unto" him; as also of the fact that the mark was to be borne not by him and his descendants only, as favoured individuals, but also by slaves not of his blood. . . .

If, as we have seen, trophy-taking as a sequence of conquest enters as a factor into those governmental restraints which conquest initiates, it is to be inferred that the mutilations originated by trophy-taking will do the like. The evidence justifies this inference. Beginning as marks of personal slavery and becoming marks of political and religious subordination, they play a part like that of oaths of fealty and pious self-dedications. Moreover, being acknowledgments of submission to a ruler, visible or invisible, they enforce authority by making conspicuous the extent of his sway. And where they signify class-subjection, as well as where they show the subjugation of criminals, they further strengthen the regulative agency.

If mutilations originate as alleged, some connexion must exist between the extent to which they are carried and the social type. On grouping the facts as presented by fifty-two peoples, the connexion emerges with as much clearness as can be expected. In the first place, since mutilation originates with conquest and resulting aggregation, it is inferable that simple societies, however savage, will be less characterized by it than the larger savage societies compounded out of such, and less than even semi-civilized societies. This proves to be true. Of peoples who form simple societies that practice mutilation either not at all or in slight forms, I find eleven —Fuegians, Veddahs, Andamanese, Dyas, Todas, Gonds, Santals, Bodo and Dhimals, Mishmis, Kamstchadales, Snake Indians; and these are characterized throughout either by absence of chieftainship, or by chieftainship of an unsettled kind. Meanwhile, of peoples who mutilate little or not at all, I find but two in the class of uncivilized compound societies; of which one, the Kirghiz, is characterized by a wandering life that makes subordination difficult; and the other, the Iroquois, had a republican form of government. Of societies practising mutilations that are moderate, the simple bear a decreased ratio to the compound: of the one class there are ten—Tasmanians, Tannese, New Guinea people, Karens, Nagas,

Ostyaks, Esquimaux, Chinooks, Comanches, Chipewayans; while of the other class there are five—New Zealanders, East Africans, Khonds, Kukis, Kalmucks. And of these it is to be remarked, that in the one class the simple headship, and in the other class the compound headship, is unstable. On coming to the societies distinguished by severer mutilations, we find these relations reversed. Among the simple I can name but three—the New Caledonians (among whom, however, the severer mutilation is not general), the Bushmen (who are believed to have lapsed from a higher social state), and the Australians (who have, I believe, similarly lapsed); while, among the compound, twenty-one may be named—Fijians, Sandwich Islanders, Tahitians, Tongans, Samoans, Javans, Sumatrans, Malagasy, Hottentots, Damaras, Bechuanas, Kaffirs, Congo people, Coast Negroes, Inland Negroes, Dahomans, Ashantees, Fulahs, Abyssinians, Arabs, Dacotahs.

In the second place, social consolidation being habitually effected by conquest, and compound and doubly-compound societies being therefore, during early stages, militant in their activities and types of structure, it follows that the connexion of the custom of mutilation with the size of the society is indirect, while that with its type is direct. And this the facts show us. If we put side by side those societies which are most unlike in respect of the practice of mutilation, we find them to be those which are most unlike as being wholly unmilitant in organization, and wholly militant in organization. At the one extreme we have the Veddas, Todas, Bodo and Dhimals; while, at the other extreme, we have the Fijians, Abyssinians, and ancient Mexicans.

Derived from trophy-taking, and developing with the development of the militant type, mutilations must, by implication, decrease as fast as the societies consolidated by militancy become less militant, and must disappear as the industrial type of structure evolves. That they do so, European history at large may be assigned in proof. And it is significant that in our own society, now predominantly industrial, such slight mutilations as continue are connected with that regulative part of the organization which militancy has bequeathed: there survive only the now-meaningless tattooings of sailors, the branding of deserters, and the cropping of the heads of felons. . . .

Spontaneously made among primitive men to one whose goodwill is desired, the gift thus becomes, as society evolves, the originator of many things.

To the political head, as his power grows, presents are prompted partly by fear of him and partly by the wish for his aid; and such presents, at first propitiatory only in virtue of their intrinsic worth, grow to be propitiatory as expressions of loyalty: from the last of which comes present-giving as a ceremonial, and from the first of which comes present-giving as tribute, eventually changing into taxes. Simultaneously, the supplies of food &c., placed on the grave of the dead man to please his ghost, developing into larger and repeated offerings at the grave of the distinguished dead man, and becoming at length sacrifices on the altar of the god, differentiate in an analogous way: the present of meat, drink, or clothes, at first supposed to beget goodwill because actually useful, becomes, by implication, significant of allegiance. Hence, making the gift grows into an act of worship irrespective of the value of the thing given; while, as affording sustenance to the priest, the gift makes possible the agency by which the worship is conducted. From oblations originate Church revenues.

Thus we unexpectedly come upon further proof that the control of ceremony precedes the political and ecclesiastical controls; since it appears that from actions which the first initiates, eventually result the funds by which the others are maintained.

When we ask what relations present-giving has to different social types, we note, in the first place, that there is little of it in simple societies where chieftainship does not exist or is unstable. Conversely, it prevails in compound and doubly-compound societies; as throughout the semi-civilized states of Africa, those of Polynesia, those of ancient America, where the presence of stable headships, primary and secondary, gives both the opportunity and the motive. Recognizing this truth, we are led to recognize the deeper truth that present-making, while but indirectly related to the social type as simple or compound, is directly related to it as more or less militant in organization. The desire to propitiate is great in proportion as the person to be propitiated is feared; and therefore the conquering chief, and still more the king who has made himself by force of arms ruler over many chiefs, is one whose goodwill is most anxiously sought by acts which simultaneously gratify his avarice and express submission. Hence, then, the fact that the ceremony of making gifts to the ruler prevails most in societies that are either actually militant, or in which chronic militancy during past times has evolved the despotic government appropriate to it. Hence the fact that throughout the East where this social type exists everywhere, the making of presents to those in authority is everywhere imperative. Hence the fact that in early European ages, while the social activities were militant and the structures corresponded, loyal presents to kings from individuals and corporate bodies were universal; while donations from superiors to inferiors, also growing out of that state of complete dependence which accompanied militancy, were common. . . .

Other derivative class-distinctions are sequent upon differences of wealth; which themselves originally follow differences of power. From that earliest stage in which master and slave are literally captor and captive, abundance of means has been the natural concomitant of mastery, and poverty the concomitant of slavery. Hence where the militant type of organization predominates, being rich indirectly implies being victorious, or having the political supremacy gained by victory. It is true that some primitive societies furnish exceptions. . . . Naturally the honouring of wealth, beginning in these early stages, continues through subsequent stages; and signs of wealth hence become class-distinctions: so originating various ceremonial restrictions.

Carrying with us the two ruling ideas thus briefly exemplified, we shall readily trace the genesis of sundry curious observances. . . .

Of the various class-distinctions which imply superior rank by implying greater wealth, the most curious remain. I refer to certain inconvenient, and sometimes painful, traits, only to be acquired by those whose abundant means enable them to live without labour, or to indulge in some kind of sensual excess.

One group of these distinctions, slightly illustrated among ourselves by the pride taken in delicate hands, as indicating freedom from manual labour, is exhibited in marked forms in some societies that are comparatively little advanced. "The chiefs in the Society Islands value themselves on having long nails on all, or on some, of their fingers." "Fijian kings and priests wear the finger nails long," says Jackson; and in Sumatra, "persons of superior rank encourage the growth of their hand-nails, particularly those of the fore and little fingers, to an extraordinary length." Everyone knows that a like usage has a like origin in China; where, however, long nails have partially lost their meaning: upper servants being allowed to wear them. But of personal defects similarly origining, China furnishes a far more striking instance in the cramped feet of ladies. Obviously these have become signs of class-distinction, because of the implied inability to labour, and the implied possession of means sufficient to purchase attendance.

Then, again, as marking rank because implying riches, we have undue, and sometimes excessive, fatness; either of the superior person himself or of his belongings. The beginnings of this may be traced in quite early stages; as among some uncivilized American peoples. "An Indian is *respectable* in his own community, in proportion as his wife and children look fat and well fed: this being a proof of his prowess and success as a hunter, and his consequent riches." From this case, in which the relation between implied wealth and implied power is directly recognized, we pass in the course of social development to cases in which, instead of the normal fatness indicating sufficiency, there comes the abnormal fatness indicating superfluity, and, consequently, greater wealth. In China, great fatness is a source of pride in a mandarin. Ellis tells us that corpulence is a mark of distinction among Tahitian females. Throughout Africa there prevails an admiration for corpulence in women, which, in some places, rises to a great pitch; as in Karague where the king has "very fat wives"—where, according to Speke, the king's sister-in-law "was another of those wonders of obesity, unable to stand excepting on all fours," and where, "as fattening is the first duty of fashionable female life, it must be duly enforced by the rod if necessary."

Still stranger are the marks of dignity constituted by diseases resulting from those excessive gratifications of appetite which wealth makes possible. Even among ourselves may be traced an association of ideas which thus originates. The story about a gentleman of the old school, who, hearing that some man of inferior extraction was suffering from gout, exclaimed—"Damn the fellow; wasn't rheumatism good enough for him," illustrates the still-current idea that gout is a gentlemanly disease, because it results from that high living which presupposes the abundant means usually associated with superior position. Introduced by this instance, the instance which comes to us from Polynesia will seem not unnatural. "The habitual use of ava causes a whitish scurf on the skin, which among the heathen Tahitians was reckoned a badge of nobility; the common people not having the means of indulgence requisite to produce it." But of all marks of dignity arising in this way, or indeed in any way, the strangest is one which Ximenez tells us of as existing among the people of ancient Guatemala. The sign of a disorder, here best left unspecified, which the nobles were liable to, because of habits which wealth made possible, had become among the Guatemalans a sign "of greatness and majesty;" and its name was applied even to the deity!

How these further class-distinctions, though not, like preceding ones, directly traceable to militancy, are indirectly traceable to it, and how they fade as industrialism develops, need not be shown at length.

Foregoing instances make it clear that they are still maintained rigorously in societies characterized by that type of organization which continuous war establishes; and that they prevailed to considerable degrees during the past warlike times of more civilized societies. Conversely, they show that as, along with the rise of a wealth which does not imply rank, luxuries and costly modes of life have spread to those who do not form part of the regulative organization; the growth of industrialism tends to abolish these marks of class-distinction which militancy originates. No matter what form they take, all these supplementary rules debarring the inferior from usages and appliances characterizing the superior, belong to a social *régime* based on coercive co-operation; while that unchecked liberty which, among ourselves, the classes regulated have to imitate the regulating classes in habits and expenditure, belongs to the *régime* of voluntary co-operation.

19

POLITICAL INSTITUTIONS

THE MERE GATHERING of individuals into a group does not constitute them a society. A society, in the sociological sense, is formed only when, besides juxtaposition there is cooperation.So long as members of the group do not combine their energies to achieve some common end or ends, there is little to keep them together. They are prevented from separating only when the wants of each are better satisfied by uniting his efforts with those of others, than they would be if he acted alone.

Cooperation, then, is at once that which cannot exist without a society, and that for which a society exists. It may be a joining of many strengths to effect something which the strength of no single man can effect; or it may be an apportioning of different activities to different persons, who severally participate in the benefits of one another's activities. The motive for acting together, originally the dominant one, may be defence against enemies; or it may be the easier obtainment of food, by the chase or othewise; or it may be, and commonly is, both of these. In any case, however, the units pass from the state of perfect independence to the state of mutual dependence; and as fast as they do this they become united into a society rightly so called.

But cooperation implies organization. If acts are to be effectually combined, there must be arrangements under which they are adjusted in their times, amounts, and characters.

From *The Principles of Sociology* (London: Williams and Norgate, 1876), vol. 2, part 5, pp. 244–48, 659–92, 306–10, 253–60, 727–30.

This social organization, necessary as a means to concerted action, is of two kinds. Though these two kinds generally co-exist, and are more or less interfused, yet they are distinct in their origins and natures. There is a spontaneous cooperation which grows up without thought during the pursuit of private ends; and there is a cooperation which, consciously devised, implies distinct recognition of public ends. The ways in which the two are respectively established and carried on, present marked contrasts.

Whenever, in a primitive group, there begins that cooperation which is effected by exchange of services—whenever individuals find their wants better satisfied by giving certain products which they can make best, in return for other products they are less skilled in making, or not so well circumstanced for making, there is initiated a kind of organization which then, and throughout its higher stages, results from endeavours to meet personal needs. Division of labour, to the last as at first, grows by experience of mutual facilitations in living. Each new specialization of industry arises from the effort of one who commences it to get profit; and establishes itself by conducing in some way to the profit of others. So that there is a kind of concerted action, with an elaborate social organization developed by it, which does not originate in deliberate concert. Though within the small sub-divisions of this organization, we find everywhere repeated the relation of employer and employed, of whom the one directs the actions of the other; yet this relation, spontaneously formed in aid of private ends and contained only at will, is not formed with conscious reference to achievement of public ends: these are not thought of. And though, for regulating trading activities, there arise agencies serving to adjust the supplies of commodities to the demands; yet such agencies do this not by direct stimulations or restraints, but by communicating information which serves to stimulate or restrain; and, further, these agencies grow up not for the avowed purpose of thus regulating, but in the pursuit of gain by individuals. So unintentionally has there arisen the elaborate division of labour by which production and distribution are now carried on, that only in modern days has there come a recognition of the fact that it has all along been arising.

On the other hand, cooperation for a purpose immediately concerning the whole society, is a conscious cooperation; and is carried on by an organization of another kind, formed in a different way. When the primitive group has to defend itself against other groups, its members act together under further stimuli than those constituted by purely personal desires. Even at the outset, before any control by a chief exists, there is the control exercised by the group over its members; each of whom is obliged, by public opinion, to join in the general defence. Very soon the warrior of recognized superiority begins to exercise over each, during war, an influence additional to that exercised by the group; and when his authority becomes established, it greatly furthers combined action. From the beginning, therefore, this kind of social cooperation is a conscious cooperation, and a cooperation which is not wholly a matter of choice—is often at variance with private wishes. As the organization initiated by it develops, we see that, in the first place, the fighting division of the society displays in the highest degree these same traits: the grades and divisions constituting an army, cooperate more and more under the regulation, consciously established, of agencies which override individual volitions—or, to speak strictly, control individuals by motives which prevent them from acting as they would spontaneously act. In the second place, we see that throughout the society as a whole there spreads a kindred form of organization—kindred in so far that, for the purpose of maintaining the militant body and the government which directs it, there are established over citizens, agencies which force them to labour more or less largely for public ends instead of private ends. And, simultaneously, there develops a further organization, still akin in its fundamental principle, which restrains individual actions in such wise that social safety shall not be endangered by the disorder consequent on unchecked pursuit of personal ends. So that this kind of social organization is distinguished from the other, as arising through conscious pursuit of public ends; in furtherance of which individual wills are constrained, first by the joint wills of the entire group, and afterwards more definitely by the will of a regulative agency which the group evolves.

Most clearly shall we perceive the contrast between these two kinds of organization on observing that, while they are both instrumental to social welfare, they are instrumental in converse ways. That organization shown us by the division of labour for industrial purposes, exhibits combined action; but it is a combined action which directly seeks and subserves the welfares of individuals, and indirectly subserves the welfare of society as a whole by preserving individuals. Conversely, that organization evolved for governmental and defensive purposes, exhibits combined action; but it is a combined action which directly seeks and subserves the welfare of the society as a whole, and indirectly subserves the welfares of individuals by protecting the society. Efforts for self-preservation by the units originate the one form of organization; while efforts for self-preservation by the aggregate originate the other form of organization. In the first case there is conscious pursuit of private ends only; and the correlative organization resulting from this pursuit of private ends, growing up unconsciously, is without coercive power. In the second case there is conscious pursuit of public ends; and the correlative organization, consciously established, exercises coercion.

Of these two kinds of cooperation and the structures effecting them, we are here concerned only with one. Political organization is to be understood as that part of social organization which consciously carries on directive and restraining functions for public ends. It is true, as already hinted, and as we shall see presently, that the two kinds are mingled in various ways—that each ramifies through the other more or less according to their respective degrees of predominance. But they are essentially different in origin and nature; and for the present we must, so far as may be, limit our attention to the last. . . .

For preserving its corporate life, a society is impelled to corporate action; and the preservation of its corporate life is the more probable in proportion as its corporate action is the more complete. For purposes of offence and defence, the forces of individuals have to be combined; and where every individual contributes his force, the probability of success is greatest. Numbers, natures, and circumstances being equal, it is clear that of two tribes or two larger societies, one of which unites the actions of all its capable members while the other does not, the first will ordinarily be the victor. There must be an habitual survival of communities in which militant cooperation is universal.

This proposition is almost a truism. But it is needful here, as a preliminary, consciously to recognize the truth that the social structure evolved by chronic militancy, is one in which all men fit for fighting act in concert against other societies. Such further actions as they carry on they can carry on separately; but this action they must carry on jointly.

A society's power of self-preservation will be great in proportion as, besides the direct aid of all who can fight, there is given the indirect aid of all who cannot fight. Supposing them otherwise similar, those communities will survive in which the efforts of combatants are in the greatest degree seconded by those of non-combatants. In a purely militant society, therefore, individuals who do not bear arms have to spend their lives in furthering the maintenance of those who do. Whether, as happens at first, the non-combatants are exclusively the women; or whether, as happens later, the class includes enslaved captives; or whether, as happens later still, it includes serfs; the implication is the same. For if, of two societies equal in other respects, the first wholly subordinates its workers in this way, while the workers in the second are allowed to retain for themselves the produce of their labour, or more of it than is needful for maintaining them; then, in the second, the warriors, not otherwise supported, or supported less fully than they might else be, will have partially to support themselves, and will be so much the less available for war purposes. Hence in the struggle for existence between such societies, it must usually happen that the first will vanquish the second. The social type produced by survival of the fittest, will be one in which the fighting part includes all who can bear arms and be trusted with arms, while the remaining part serves simply as a permanent commissariat.

An obvious implication, of a significance to be hereafter pointed out, is that the non-combatant part, occupied in supporting the combatant part, cannot with advantage to the self-preserving power of the society increase beyond the limit at which it efficiently fulfils its purpose. For, otherwise, some who might be fighters are superfluous workers; and the fighting power of the society is made less than it might be. Hence, in the militant type, the tendency is for the body of warriors to bear the largest practicable ratio to the body of workers.

Given two societies of which the members are all either warriors or those who supply the needs of warriors, and, other things equal, supremacy will be gained by that in which the efforts of all are most effectually combined. In open warfare joint action triumphs over individual action. Military history is a history of the successes of men trained to move and fight in concert.

Not only must there be in the fighting part a combination such that the powers of its units may be concentrated, but there must be a combination of the subservient part with it. If the two are so separated that they can act independently, the needs of the fighting part will not be adequately met. If to be cut off from a temporary base of operations is dangerous, still more dangerous is it to be cut off from the permanent base of operations; namely, that constituted by the body of non-combatants. This has to be so connected with the body of combatants that its services may be fully available. Evidently, therefore, development of the militant type involves a close binding of the society into a whole. As the loose group of savages yields to the solid phalanx, so, other things equal, must the society of which the parts are but feebly held together, yield to one in which they are held together by strong bonds.

But in proportion as men are compelled to cooperate, their self-prompted actions are restrained. By as much as the unit becomes merged in the mass, by so much does he lose his individuality as a unit. And this leads us to note the several ways in which evolution of the militant type entails subordination of the citizen.

His life is not his own, but is at the disposal of his society. So long as he remains capable of bearing arms he has no alternative but to fight when called on; and, where militancy is extreme, he cannot return as a vanquished man under penalty of death.

Of course, with this there goes possession of such liberty only as military obligations allow. He is free to pursue his private ends only when the tribe or nation has no need of him; and when it has need of him, his actions from hour to hour must conform, not to his own will but to the public will.

So, too, with his property. Whether, as in many cases, what he holds as private he so holds by permission only, or whether private ownership is recognized, it remains true that in the last resort he is obliged to surrender whatever is demanded for the community's use.

Briefly, then, under the militant type the individual is owned by the State. While preservation of the society is the primary end, preservation of each member is a secondary end—an end cared for chiefly as subserving the primary end.

Fulfilment of these requirements, that there shall be complete corporate action, that to this end the non-combatant part shall be occupied in providing for the combatant part, that the entire aggregate shall be strongly bound together, and that the units composing it must have their individualities in life, liberty, and property, thereby subordinated, presupposes a coercive instrumentality. No such union for corporate action can be achieved without a powerful controlling agency. On remembering the fatal results caused by division of counsels in war, or by separation into factions in face of an enemy, we see that chronic militancy tends to develop a despotism; since, other things equal, those societies will habitually survive in which, by its aid, the corporate action is made complete.

And this involves a system of centralization. The trait made familiar to us by an army, in which under a commander-in-chief there are secondary commanders over large masses, and under these tertiary ones over smaller masses, and so on down to the ultimate divisions, must characterize the social organization at large. A militant society requires a regulative structure of this kind, since, otherwise, its corporate action cannot be made most effectual. Without such grades of governing centres diffused throughout the non-combatant part as well as the combatant part, the entire forces of the aggregate cannot be promptly put forth. Unless the workers are under a control akin to that which the fighters are under, their indirect aid cannot be insured in full amount and with due quickness.

And this is the form of a society characterized by *status*—a society, the members of which stand one towards another in successive grades of subordination. From the despot down to the slave, all are masters of those below and subjects of those above. The relation of the child to the father, of the father to some superior, and so on up to the absolute head, is one in which the individual of lower status is at the mercy of one of higher status.

Otherwise described, the process of militant organization is a process of regimentation, which, primarily taking place in the army, secondarily affects the whole community.

The first indication of this we trace in the fact everywhere visible, that the military head grows into a civil head—usually at once, and, in exceptional cases, at last, if militancy continues. Beginning as leader in war he becomes ruler in peace; and such regulative policy as he pursues in the one sphere, he pursues, so far as conditions permit, in the other. Being, as the non-combatant part is, a permanent commissariat, the principle of graduated subordination is extended to it. Its members come to be directed in a way like that in which the warriors are directed—not literally, since by dispersion of the one and concentration of the other exact parallelism is prevented; but, nevertheless, similarly in principle. Labour is carried on under coercion; and supervision spreads everywhere. . . .

On inspecting sundry societies, past and present, large and small, which are, or have been, characterized in high degrees by militancy, we are shown, *a posteriori*, that amid the differences due to race, to circumstances, and to degrees of development, there are fundamental similarities of the kinds above inferred *a priori*. Modern Dahomey and Russia, as well as ancient Peru, Egypt, and Sparta, exemplify that owning of the individual by the State in life, liberty, and goods, which is proper to a social system adapted for war. And that with changes further fitting a society for warlike activities, there spread throughout it an officialism, a dictation, and a superintendence, akin to those under which soldiers live, we are shown by imperial Rome, by imperial Germany, and by England since its late aggressive activities.

Lastly comes the evidence furnished by the adapted characters of the men who compose militant societies. Making success in war the highest glory, they are led to identify goodness with bravery and strength. Revenge becomes a sacred duty with them: and acting at home on the law of retaliation which they act on abroad, they similarly, at home as abroad, are ready to sacrifice others to self: their sympathies, continually deadened during war, cannot be active during peace. They must have a patriotism which regards the triumph of their society as the supreme end of action; they must possess the loyalty whence flows obedience to authority; and that they may be obedient they must have abundant faith. With faith in authority and consequent readiness to be directed, naturally goes relatively little power of initiation. The habit of seeing everything officially controlled fosters the belief that official control is everywhere needful; while a course of life which makes personal causation familiar and negatives experience of impersonal causation, produces an inability to conceive of any social processes as carried on under self-regulating arrangements. And these traits of individual nature, needful concomitants as we see of the militant type, are those which we observe in the members of actual militant societies. . . .

More effective still in weakening those primitive political divisions initiated by militancy, is increasing industrialism. This acts in two ways—firstly, by creating a class having power derived otherwise than from territorial possessions or official positions; and, secondly, by generating ideas and sentiments at variance with the ancient assumptions of class-superiority. As we have already seen, rank and wealth are at the outset habitually associated. Existing uncivilized peoples still show us this relation. . . . Indeed it is manifest that before the development of commerce, and while possession of land could alone give largeness of means, lordship and riches were directly connected; so that, as Sir Henry

Maine remarks, "the opposition commonly set up between birth and wealth, and particularly wealth other than landed property, is entirely modern." When, however, with the arrival of industry at that stage in which wholesale transactions bring large profits, there arise trades who vie with, and exceed, many of the landed nobility in wealth; and when by conferring obligations on kings and nobles, such traders gain social influence; there comes an occasional removal of the barrier between them and the titled classes. . . . In proportion as men are habituated to maintain their own claims while respecting the claims of others, which they do in every act of exchange, whether of goods for money or of services for pay, there is produced a mental attitude at variance with that which accompanies subjection; and, as fast as this happens, such political distinctions as imply subjection, lose more and more of that respect which gives them strength.

Class-distinctions, then, date back to the beginnings of social life. Omitting those small wandering assemblages which are so incoherent that their component parts are ever changing their relations to one another and to the environment, we see that wherever there is some coherence and some permanence of relation among the parts, there begin to arise political divisions. Relative superiority of power, first causing a differentiation at once domestic and social, between the activities of the sexes and the consequent positions of the sexes, presently begins to cause a differentiation among males, shown in the bondage of captives: a master-class and a slave-class are formed.

Where men continue the wandering life in pursuit of wild food for themselves or their cattle, the groups they form are debarred from doing more by war than appropriate one another's units individually; but where men have passed into the agricultural or settled state, it becomes possible for one community to take possession bodily of another community, along with the territory it occupies. When this happens there arise additional class-divisions. The conquered and tribute-paying community, besides having its headmen reduced to subjection, has its people reduced to a state such that, while they continue to live on their lands, they yield up, through the intermediation of their chiefs, part of the produce to the conquerors: so foreshadowing what eventually becomes a serf-class.

From the beginning the militant class, being by force of arms the dominant class, becomes the class which owns the source of food—the land. During the hunting and pastoral stages, the warriors of the group hold the land collectively. On passing into the settled state, their tenures become partly collective and partly individual in sundry ways, and eventually almost wholly individual. But throughout long stages of social evolution, landowning and militancy continue to be associated.

The class-differentiation of which militancy is the active cause, is furthered by the establishment of definite descent, and especially male descent, and by the transmission of position and property to the eldest son of the eldest continually. This conduces to inequalities of position and wealth between near kindred and remote kindred; and such inequalities once initiated, tend to increase; since it results from them that the superior get greater means of maintaining their power by accumulating appliances for offence and defence.

Such differentiation is augmented, at the same time that a new differentiation is set up, by the immigration of fugitives who attach themselves to the most powerful member of the group: now as dependents who work, and now as armed followers—armed followers who form a class bound to the dominant man and unconnected with the land. And since, in clusters of such groups, fugitives ordinarily flock most to the strongest group, and become adherents of its head, they are instrumental in furthering those subsequent integrations and differentiations which conquests bring about.

Inequalities of social position, bringing inequalities in the supplies and kinds of food, clothing, and shelter, tend to establish physical differences; to the further advantage of the rulers and disadvantage of the ruled. And beyond the physical differences, there are produced by the respective habits of life, mental differences, emotional and intellectual, strengthening the general contrast of nature.

When there come the conquests which produce compound

societies, and, again, doubly compound ones, there result superpositions of ranks. And the general effect is that, while the ranks of the conquering society become respectively higher than those which existed before, the ranks of the conquered society become respectively lower.

The class-divisions thus formed during the earlier stages of militancy, are traversed and obscured as fast as many small societies are consolidated into one large society. Ranks referring to local organization are gradually replaced by ranks referring to general organization. Instead of deputy and sub-deputy governing agents who are the militant owners of the sub-divisions they rule, there come governing agents who more or less clearly form strata running throughout the society as a whole—a concomitant of developed political administration.

Chiefly, however, we have to note that while the higher political evolution of large social aggregates, tends to break down the divisions of rank which grew up in the small component social aggregates, by substituting other divisions, these original divisions are still more broken down by growing industrialism. Generating a wealth that is not connected with rank, this initiates a competing power; and at the same time, by establishing the equal positions of citizens before the law in respect of trading transactions, it weakens those divisions which at the outset expressed inequalities of position before the law.

As verifying these interpretations, I may add that they harmonize with the interpretations of ceremonial institutions already given. When the conquered enemy is made a slave, and mutilated by taking a trophy from his body, we see simultaneously originating the deepest political distinction and the ceremony which marks it; and with the continued militancy that compounds and re-compounds social groups, there goes at once the development of political distinctions and the development of ceremonies marking them. And as we before saw that growing industrialism diminishes the rigour of ceremonial rule, so here we see that it tends to destroy those class-divisions which militancy originates, and to establish quite alien ones which indicate differences of position consequent on differences of aptitude for the various functions which an industrial society needs. . . .

The stones composing a house cannot be otherwise used until the house has been pulled down. If the stones are united by mortar, there must be extra trouble in destroying their present combination before they can be re-combined. And if the mortar has had centuries in which to consolidate, the breaking up of the masses formed is a matter of such difficulty, that building with new materials becomes more economical than rebuilding with the old.

I name these facts to illustrate the truth that any arrangement stands in the way of re-arrangement; and that this must be true of organization, which is one kind of arrangement. When, during the evolution of a living body, its component substance, at first relatively homogeneous, has been transformed into a combination of heterogeneous parts, there results an obstacle, always great and often insuperable, to any considerable further change: the more elaborate and definite the structure the greater being the resistance it opposes to alteration. And this, which is conspicuously true of an individual organism, is true, if less conspicuously, of a social organism. Though a society, formed of discrete units, and not having had its type fixed by inheritance from countless like societies, is much more plastic, yet the same principle holds. As fast as its parts are differentiated—as fast as there arise classes, bodies of functionaries, established administrations, these, becoming coherent within themselves and with one another, struggle against such forces as tend to modify them. The conservatism of every long-settled institution daily exemplifies this law. Be it in the antagonism of a church to legislation interfering with its discipline; be it in the opposition of an army to abolition of the purchase-system; be it in the disfavour with which the legal profession at large has regarded law-reform; we see that neither in their structures nor in their modes of action, are parts that have once been specialized easily changed.

As it is true of a living body that its various acts have as their common end self-preservation, so is it true of its component organs that they severally tend to preserve themselves in their integrity. And, similarly, as it is true of a society that maintenance of its existence is the aim of its combined actions, so it is true of its separate classes, its sets of officials, its other specialized parts, that the dominant aim of each is to maintain itself. Not the function to be performed, but the sustentation of those who perform the function, becomes the object in view: the result being that when the function is needless, or even detrimental, the structure still keeps itself intact as long as it can. In early days the history of the Knights Templars furnished an illustration of this tendency. Down to the present time we have before us the familiar instance of trade-guilds in London, which having ceased to perform their original duties, nevertheless jealously defend their possessions and privileges. The convention of Royal Burghs in Scotland, which once regulated the internal municipal laws, still meets annually though it has no longer any work to do. And the accounts given in *The Black Book* of the sinecures which survived up to recent times, yield multitudinous illustrations.

The extent to which an organization resists re-organization, we shall not fully appreciate until we observe that its resistance increases in a compound progression. For while each new part is an additional obstacle to change, the formation of it involves a deduction from the forces causing change. If, other things remaining the same, the political structures of a society are further developed —if existing institutions are extended or fresh ones set up—if for directing social activities in greater detail, extra staffs of officials are appointed; the simultaneous results are—an increase in the aggregate of those who form the regulating part, and a corresponding decrease in the aggregate of those who form the part regulated. In various ways all who compose the controlling and administrative organization, become united with one another and separated from the rest. Whatever be their particular duties, they are similarly related to the governing centres of their departments, and, through them, to the supreme governing centre; and are habituated to like sentiments and ideas respecting the set of institutions in which they are incorporated. Receiving their subsistence through the national revenue, they tend towards kindred views and feelings respecting the raising of such revenue. Whatever jealousies there may be between their divisions, are over-ridden by sympathy when any one division has its existence or privileges endangered; since the interference with one division may spread to others. Moreover, they all stand in similar relations to the rest of the community, whose actions are in one way or other superintended by them; and hence are led into allied beliefs respecting the need for such superintendence and the propriety of submitting to it. No matter what their previous political opinions may have been, men cannot become public agents of any kind without being biassed towards opinions congruous with their functions. So that, inevitably, each further growth of the instrumentalities which control, or administer, or inspect, or in any way direct social forces, increases the impediment to future modifications, both positively by strengthening that which has to be modified, and negatively, by weakening the remainder; until at length the rigidity becomes so great that change is impossible and the type becomes fixed.

Nor does each further development of political organization increase the obstacles to change, only by increasing the power of the regulators and decreasing the power of the regulated. For the ideas and sentiments of a community as a whole, adapt themselves to the *régime* familiar from childhood, in such wise that it comes to be looked upon as natural. In proportion as public agencies occupy a larger space in daily experience, leaving but a smaller space for other agencies, there comes a greater tendency to think of public control as everywhere needful, and a less ability to conceive of activities as otherwise controlled. At the same time the sentiments, adjusted by habit to the regulative machinery, become enlisted on its behalf, and adverse to the thought of a vacancy to be made by its absence. In brief, the general law that the social organism and its units act and re-act until congruity is reached, implies that every further extension of political organization increases the obstacle to re-organization, not only by adding to the strength of the regulative part, and taking from the strength of the part regulated, but also by producing in citizens thoughts and feelings in harmony with the resulting structure, and out of harmony with anything substantially different. Both France and Germany exemplify this truth. M. Comte, while looking forward to an industrial state, was so swayed by the conceptions and likings appropriate to the French form of society, that his scheme of organization for the ideal future, prescribes arrangements characteristic of the militant type, and utterly at variance with the industrial type. Indeed, he had a profound aversion to that individualism which is a product of industrial life and gives the character to industrial institutions. So, too, in Germany, we see that the socialist party, who are regarded and who regard themselves as wishing to re-organize society entirely, are so incapable of really thinking away from the social type under which they have been nurtured, that their proposed social system is in essence nothing else than a new form of the system they would destroy. It is a system under which life and labour are to be arranged and superintended by public instrumentalities, omnipresent like those which already exist and no less coercive: the individual having his life even more regulated for him than now.

While, then, the absence of settled arrangements negatives cooperation, yet cooperation of a higher kind is hindered by the arrangements which facilitate cooperation of a lower kind. Though without established connexions among parts, there can be no combined actions; yet the more extensive and elaborate such connexions grow, the more difficult does it become to make improved combinations of actions. There is an increase of the forces which tend to fix, and a decrease of the forces which tend to unfix; until the fully-structured social organism, like the fully-structured individual organism, becomes no longer adaptable.

In a living animal, formed as it is of aggregated units originally like in kind, the progress of organization implies, not only that the units composing each differentiated part severally maintain their positions, but also that their progeny succeed to those positions. . . .

In a society also, establishment of structure is favoured by the transmission of positions and functions through successive generations. The maintenance of those class-divisions which arise as political organization advances, implies the inheritance of a rank and a place in each class. The like happens with those sub-divisions of classes which, in some societies, constitute castes, and in other societies are exemplified by incorporated trades. Where custom or law compels the sons of each worker to follow their father's occupation, there result among the industrial structures obstacles to change analogous to those which result in the regulative structures from impassable divisions of ranks. India shows this in an extreme degree; and in a less degree it was shown by the craft-guilds of early days in England, which facilitated adoption of a craft by the children of those engaged in it, and hindered adoption of it by others. Thus we may call inheritance of position and function, the principle of fixity in social organization.

There is another way in which succession by inheritance, whether to class-position or to occupation, conduces to stability. It secures supremacy of the elder; and supremacy of the elder tends towards maintenance of the established order. A system under which a chief-ruler, sub-ruler, head of clan or house, official, or any person having the power given by rank or property, retains his place until at death it is filled by a descendant, in conformity with some accepted rule of succession, in a system under which, by implication, the young, and even the middle-aged, are excluded from the conduct of affairs. So, too, where an industrial system is such that the son, habitually brought up to his father's business, cannot hold a master's position till his father dies, it follows that the regulative power of the elder over the processes of production and distribution, is scarcely at all qualified by the power of the younger. Now it is truth daily exemplified, that increasing rigidity of organization, necessitated by the process of evolution, produces in age an increasing strength of habit and aversion to change. Hence it results that succession to place and function by inheritance, having as its necessary concomitant a monopoly of power by the eldest, involves a prevailing conservatism; and thus further insures maintenance of things as they are.

Conversely, social change is facile in proportion as men's places and functions are determinable by personal qualities. Members of one rank who establish themselves in another rank, in so far directly break the division between the ranks; and they indirectly weaken it by preserving their family relations with the first, and forming new ones with the second; while, further, the ideas and sentiments pervading the two ranks, previously more or less different, are made to qualify one another and to work changes of character. Similarly if, between sub-divisions of the producing and distributing classes, there are no barriers to migration, then, in proportion as migrations are numerous, influences physical and mental, following inter-fusion, alter the natures of their units; at the same time that they check the establishment of differences of nature caused by differences of occupation. Such transpositions of individuals between class and class, or group and group, must, on the average, however, depend on the fitnesses of the individuals for their new places and duties. Intrusions will ordinarily succeed only where the intruding citizens have more than usual aptitudes for the businesses they undertake. Those who desert their original functions, are at a disadvantage in the competition with those whose functions they assume; and they can overcome this disadvantage only by force of some superiority: must do the new thing better than those born to it, and so tend to improve the doing of it by their example. This leaving of men to have their careers determined by their efficiencies, we may therefore call the principle of change in social organization.

As we saw that succession by inheritance conduces in a secondary way to stability, by keeping authority in the hands of those who by age are made most averse to new practices, so here, conversely, we may see that succession by efficiency conduces in a secondary way to change. Both positively and negatively the possession of power by the young facilitates innovation. While the energies are overflowing, little fear is felt of those obstacles to improvement and evils it may bring, which, when energies are failing, look formidable; and at the same time the greater imaginativeness that goes along with higher vitality, joined with a smaller strength of habit, facilitates acceptance of fresh ideas and adoption of untried methods. Since, then, where the various social positions come to be respectively filled by those who are experimentally proved to be the fittest, the relatively young are permitted to exercise authority, it results that succession by efficiency furthers change in social organization, indirectly as well as directly.

Contrasting the two, we thus see that while the acquirement of function by inheritance conduces to rigidity of structure, the acquirement of function by efficiency conduces to plasticity of structure. Succession by descent favours the maintenance of that which exists. Succession by fitness favours transformation, and makes possible something better. . . .

As with the militant type then, so with the industrial type, three lines of evidence converge to show us its essential nature. Let us set down briefly the several results, that we may observe the correspondences among them.

On considering what must be the traits of a society organized exclusively for carrying on internal activities, so as most efficiently to subserve the lives of citizens, we find them to be these. A corporate action subordinating individual actions by uniting them in joint effort, is not longer requisite. Contrariwise, such corporate action as remains has for its end to guard individual actions against all interferences not necessarily entailed by mutual limitation: the type of society in which this function is best discharged, being that which must survive, since it is that of which the members will most prosper. Excluding, as the requirements of the industrial type do, a despotic controlling agency, they imply, as the only congruous agency for achieving such corporate action as is needed, one formed of representatives who serve to express the aggregate will. The function of this controlling agency, generally defined as that of administering justice, is more specially defined as that of seeing that each citizen gains neither more nor less of benefit than his activities normally bring; and there is thus excluded all public action involving any artificial distribution of benefits. The *régime* of status proper to militancy having disappeared, the *régime* of contract which replaces it has to be universally enforced; and this negatives interferences between efforts and results by arbitrary apportionment. Otherwise regarded, the industrial type is distinguished from the militant type as being not both positively regulative and negatively regulative, but as being negatively regulative only. With this restricted sphere for corporate action comes an increased sphere for individual action; and from that voluntary corporation which is the fundamental principle of the type, arise multitudinous private combinations, akin in their structures to the public combination of the society which includes them. Indirectly it results that a society of the industrial type is distinguished by plasticity; and also that it tends to lose its economic autonomy, and to coalesce with adjacent societies.

The question next considered was, whether these traits of the industrial type as arrived at by deduction are inductively verified;

and we found that in actual societies they are visible more or less clearly in proportion as industrialism is more or less developed. Glancing at those small groups of uncultured people who, wholly unwarlike, display the industrial type in its rudimentary form, we went on to compare the structures of European nations at large in early days of chronic militancy, with their structures in modern days characterized by progressing industrialism; and we saw the differences to be of the kind implied. We next compared two of these societies, France and England, which were once in kindred states, but of which the one has had its industrial life much more repressed by its militant life than the other; and it became manifest that the contrasts which, age after age, arose between their institutions, were such as answer to the hypothesis. Lastly, limiting ourselves to England itself, and first noting how recession from such traits of the industrial type as had shown themselves, occurred during a long war-period, we observed how, during the subsequent long period of peace beginning in 1815, there were numerous and decided approaches to that social structure which we concluded must accompany developed industrialism.

We then inquired what type of individual nature accompanies the industrial type of society; with the view of seeing whether, from the character of the unit as well as from the character of the aggregate, confirmation is to be derived. Certain uncultured peoples whose lives are passed in peaceful occupations, proved to be distinguished by independence, resistance to coercion, honesty, truthfulness, forgivingness, kindness. On contrasting the characters of our ancestors during more warlike periods with our own characters, we see that, with an increasing ratio of industrialism to militancy, have come a growing independence, a less-marked loyalty, a smaller faith in governments, and a more qualified patriotism; and while, by enterprising action, by diminished faith in authority, by resistance to irresponsible power, there has been shown a strengthening assertion of individuality, there has accompanied it a growing respect for the individualities of others, as is implied by the diminution of aggressions upon them and the multiplication of efforts for their welfare.

To prevent misapprehension it seems needful, before closing, to explain that these traits are to be regarded less as the immediate results of industrialism than as the remote results of non-militancy. It is not so much that a social life passed in peaceful occupations is positively moralizing, as that a social life passed in war is positively demoralizing. Sacrifice of others to self is in the one incidental only; while in the other it is necessary. Such aggressive egoism as accompanies the industrial life is extrinsic; whereas the aggressive egoism of the militant life is intrinsic. Though generally unsympathetic, the exchange of services under agreement is now, to a considerable extent, and may be wholly, carried on with a due regard to the claims of others—may be constantly accompanied by a sense of benefit given as well as benefit received; but the slaying of antagonists, the burning of their houses, the appropriation of their territory, cannot but be accompanied by vivid consciousness of injury done them, and a consequent brutalizing effect on the feelings—an effect wrought, not on soldiers only, but on those who employ them and contemplate their deeds with pleasure. The last form of social life, therefore, inevitably deadens the sympathies and generates a state of mind which prompts crimes to trespass; while the first form, allowing the sympathies free play if it does not directly exercise them, favours the growth of altruistic sentiments and the resulting virtues.

20

THE TRUTH OF RELIGION

[SPENCER has been extolling the virtues of not yielding to partial attitudes.] The general principle above illustrated must lead us to anticipate that the diverse forms of religious belief, which have existed and which still exist, have all a basis in some ultimate fact. Judging by analogy the implication is, not that any one of them is altogether right, but that in each there is something right more or less disguised by other things wrong. It may be that the soul of truth contained in erroneous creeds is extremely unlike most, if not all, of its several embodiments; and indeed if, as we have good reason to assume, it is much more abstract than any of them, its unlikeness necessarily follows. But some essential variety must be looked for. To suppose that these multiform conceptions should be one and all *absolutely* groundless, discredits too profoundly that average human intelligence from which all our individual intelligences are inherited.

To the presumption that a number of diverse beliefs of the same class have some common foundation in fact, must in this case be added a further presumption derived from the omnipresence of the beliefs. Religious ideas of one kind or other are almost universal. Grant that among all men who have passed a certain stage of intellectual development, there are found vague notions concerning the origin and hidden nature of surrounding things, and there arises

---

From *First Principles*, 6th ed. (London: Williams and Norgate [1862], 1904), pp. 9–11; *The Principles of Sociology* (London: Williams and Norgate, 1876), vol. 3, part 6, pp. 160–75.

the inference that such notions are necessary products of progressing intelligence. Their endless variety serves but to strengthen this conclusion: showing as it does a more or less independent genesis—showing how, in different places and times, like conditions have led to similar trains of thought, ending in analogous results. A candid examination of the evidence quite negatives the supposition that creeds are priestly inventions. Even as a mere question of probabilities it cannot rationally be concluded that in every society, savage and civilized, certain men have combined to delude the rest in ways so analogous. Moreover, the hypothesis of artificial origin fails to account for the facts. It does not explain why, under all changes of form, certain elements of religious belief remain constant. It does not show how it happens that while adverse criticism has from age to age gone on destroying particular theological dogmas, it has not destroyed the fundamental conception underlying those dogmas. Thus the universality of religious ideas, their independent evolution among different primitive races, and their great vitality, unite in showing that their source must be deep-seated. In other words, we are obliged to admit that if not supernaturally derived as the majority contend, they must be derived out of human experiences, slowly accumulated and organized.

Should it be asserted that religious ideas are products of the religious sentiment which, to satisfy itself, prompts imaginations that it afterwards projects into the external world, and by-and-by mistakes for realities, the problem is not solved, but only removed farther back. Whence comes the sentiment? . . .

Two suppositions only are open to us; the one that the feeling which responds to religious ideas resulted, along with all other human faculties, from an act of special creation; the other that it, in common with the rest, arose by a process of evolution. If we adopt the first of these alternatives, universally accepted by our ancestors and by the immense majority of our contemporaries, the matter is at once settled: man is directly endowed with the religious feeling by a creator; and to that creator it designedly responds. If we adopt the second alternative, then we are met by the questions—What are the circumstances to which the genesis of the religious feeling is due? and—What is its office? Considering, as we must on this supposition, all faculties to be results of accumulated modifications caused by the intercourse of the organism with its environment, we are obliged to admit that there exist in the environment certain phenomena or conditions which have determined the growth of the religious feeling; and so are obliged to admit that it is as normal as any other faculty. Add to which that as, on the hypothesis of a development of lower forms into higher, the end towards which the progressive changes tend, must be adaptation to the requirements of life, we are also forced to infer that this feeling is in some way conducive to human welfare. Thus both alternatives contain the same ultimate implication. We must conclude that the religious sentiment is either directly created or is developed by the slow action of natural causes, and whichever conclusion we adopt requires us to treat the religious sentiment with respect. . . .

Unlike the ordinary consciousness, the religious consciousness is concerned with that which lies beyond the sphere of sense. A brute thinks only of things which can be touched, seen, heard, tasted, etc.; and the like is true of the young child, the untaught deaf-mute, and the lowest savage. But the developing man has thoughts about existences which he regards as usually intangible, inaudible, invisible; and yet which he regards as operative upon him. What suggests this notion of agencies transcending perception? How do these ideas concerning the supernatural evolve out of ideas concerning the natural? The transition cannot be sudden; and an account of the genesis of religion must begin by describing the steps through which the transition takes place.

The ghost-theory exhibits these steps quite clearly. We are shown by it that the mental differentiation of invisible and intangible being from visible and tangible beings progresses slowly and unobtrusively. In the fact that the other-self, supposed to wander in dreams, is believed to have actually done and seen whatever was dreamed—in the fact that the other-self when going away at death, but expected presently to return, is conceived as a double equally material with the original; we see that the supernatural agent in its primitive form, diverges very little from the natural agent—is simply the original man with some added powers of going about secretly and doing good or evil. And the fact that when the double of the dead man ceases to be dreamed about by those who knew him, his non-appearance in dreams is held to imply that he is finally dead, shows that these earliest supernatural agents are conceived as having been temporary existences: the first tendencies to a permanent consciousness of the supernatural, prove abortive.

In many cases no higher degree of differentiation is reached. The ghost-population, recruited by deaths on the one side but on the other side losing its members as they cease to be recollected and dreamed about, does not increase; and no individuals included in it come to be recognized through successive generations as established supernatural powers. Thus the Unkulunkulu, or old-old one, of the Zulus, the father of the race, is regarded as finally or completely dead; and there is propitiation only of ghosts of more recent date. But where circumstances favour the continuance of sacrifices at graves, witnessed by members of each new generation who are told about the dead and transmit the tradition, there eventually arises the conception of a permanently-existing ghost or spirit. A more marked contrast in thought between supernatural beings and natural beings is thus established. There simultaneously results an increase in the number of these supposed supernatural beings, since the aggregate of them is now continually added to; and there is a strengthening tendency to think of them as everywhere around, and as causing all unusual occurrences.

Differences among the ascribed powers of ghosts soon arise. They naturally follow from observed differences among the powers of living individuals. Hence it results that while the propitiations of ordinary ghosts are made only by their descendants, it comes occasionally to be thought prudent to propitiate also the ghosts of the more dreaded individuals, even though they have no claims of blood. Quite early there thus begin those grades of supernatural beings which eventually become so strongly marked.

Habitual wars, which more than all other causes initiate these first differentiations, go on to initiate further and more decided ones. For with those compoundings of small societies into greater ones, and re-compounding of these into still greater, which war effects, there, of course, with the multiplying gradations of power among living men, arises the idea of multiplying gradations of power among their ghosts. Thus in course of time are formed the conceptions of the great ghosts or gods, the more numerous secondary ghosts or demi-gods, and so on downwards—a pantheon: there being still, however, no essential distinction of kind; as we see in the calling of ordinary ghosts *manes*-gods by the Romans and *elohim* by the Hebrews. Moreover, repeating as the other life in the other world does, the life in this world, in its needs, occupations, and social organization, there arises not only a differentiation of grades among supernatural beings in respect of their powers, but also in respect of their characters and kinds of activity. There come to be local gods, and gods reigning over this or that order of phenomena; there come to be good and evil spirits of various qualities; and where there has been by conquest a posing of one society upon another, each having its own system of ghost-derived beliefs, there results an involved combination of such beliefs, constituting a mythology.

Of course primitive ghosts being doubles like their originals in all things; and gods (when not the living members of a conquering race) being doubles of the more powerful men; it results that they are primarily conceived as no less human than other ghosts in their physical characters, their passions, and their intelligences. Like the doubles of the ordinary dead, they are supposed to consume the flesh, blood, bread, wine, given to them; at first literally, and later in a more spiritual way by consuming the essences of them. They not only appear as visible and tangible persons, but they enter into conflicts with men, are wounded, suffer pain: the sole distinction being that they have miraculous powers of healing and consequent immortality.

Here, indeed, there needs a qualification; for not only do various peoples hold that gods die a first death (as naturally happens where they are members of a conquering race, called gods because of their superiority), but, as in the case of Pan, it is supposed, even among the cultured, that there is a second and final death of a god, like that second and final death of a man supposed among existing savages. With advancing civilization the divergence of the supernatural being from the natural being becomes more decided. There is nothing to check the gradual de-materialization of the ghost and of the god; and this de-materialization is insensibly furthered in the effort to reach consistent ideas of supernatural action: the god ceases to be tangible, and later he ceases to be visible or audible.

Along with this differentiation of physical attributes from those of humanity, there goes on more slowly a differentiation of mental attributes. The god of the savage, represented as having intelligence scarcely if at all greater than that of the living man, is deluded with ease. Even the gods of the semi-civilized are deceived, make mistakes, repent of their plans; and only in case of time does there arise the conception of unlimited vision and universal knowledge. The emotional nature simultaneously undergoes a parallel transformation. The grosser passions, originally conspicuous and carefully ministered to by devotees, gradually fade, leaving only the passions less related to corporeal satisfactions; and eventually these, too, become partially de-humanized.

Ascribed characters of deities are continually adapted and readapted to the needs of the social state. During the militant phase of activity, the chief god is conceived as holding insubordination the greatest crime, as implacable in anger, as merciless in punishment; and any alleged attributes of milder kinds occupy but small space in the social consciousness. But where militancy declines and the harsh despotic form of government appropriate to it is gradually qualified by the form appropriate to industrialism, the foreground of the religious consciousness is increasingly filled with those ascribed traits of the divine nature which are congruous with the ethics of peace: divine love, divine forgiveness, divine mercy, and now the characteristics enlarged upon.

To perceive clearly the effects of mental progress and changing social life, thus stated in the abstract, we must glance at them in the concrete. If, without foregone conclusions, we contemplate the traditions, records, and monuments, of the Egyptians, we see that out of their primitive ideas of gods, brute or human, there were evolved spiritualized ideas of gods, and finally of a god; until the priesthoods of later times, repudiating the earlier ideas, described them as corruptions: being swayed by the universal tendency to regard the first state as the highest—a tendency traceable down to the theories of existing theologians and mythologists. Again, if, putting aside speculations, and not asking what historical value the *Iliad* may have, we take it simply as indicating the early Greek notion of Zeus, and compare this with the notion contained in the Platonic dialogues; we see that Greek civilization had greatly modified (in the better minds, at least) the purely anthropomorphic conception of him: the lower human attributes being dropped and the higher ones transfigured. Similarly, if we contrast the Hebrew God described in early traditions, man-like in appearance, appetites, and emotions, with the Hebrew God as characterized by the prophets, there is shown a widening range of power along with a nature increasingly remote from that of man. And on passing to the conceptions of him which are now entertained, we are made aware of an extreme transfiguration. By a convenient obliviousness, a deity who in early times is represented as hardening men's hearts so that they may commit punishable acts, and as employing a lying spirit to deceive them, comes to be mostly thought of as an embodiment of virtues transcending the highest we can imagine.

Thus, recognizing the fact that in the primitive human mind there exists neither religious idea nor religious sentiment, we find that in the course of social evolution and the evolution of intelligence accompanying it, there are generated both the ideas and sentiments which we distinguish as religious; and that through a process of causation clearly traceable, they traverse those stages which have brought them, among civilized races, to their present forms. . . .

Those who think that science is dissipating religious beliefs and sentiments, seem unaware that whatever of mystery is taken from the old interpretation is added to the new. Or rather, we may say that transference from the one to the other is accompanied by increase; since, for an explanation which has a seeming feasibility, science substitutes an explanation which, carrying us back only a certain distance, there leaves us in presence of the avowedly inexplicable.

Under one of its aspects scientific progress is a gradual transfiguration of Nature. Where ordinary perception saw perfect simplicity it reveals great complexity; where there seemed absolute inertness it discloses intense activity; and in what appears mere vacancy it finds a marvellous play of forces. Each generation of physicists discovers in so-called "brute matter," powers which but a few years before the most instructed physicists would have thought incredible; as instance the ability of a mere iron plate to take up the complicated aerial vibrations produced by articulate speech, which, translated into multitudinous and varied electric pulses, are re-translated a thousand miles off by another iron plate and again heard as articulate speech. When the explorer of Nature sees that quiescent as they appear, surrounding solid bodies are thus sensitive to forces which are infinitesimal in their amounts—when the spectroscope proves to him that molecules on the Earth pulsate in harmony with molecules in the stars—when there is forced on him the inference that every point in space thrills with an infinity of vibrations passing through it in all directions; the conception to which he tends is much less that of a Universe of dead matter than that of a Universe everywhere alive: alive if not in the restricted sense, still in a general sense.

This transfiguration which the inquiries of physicists continually increase, is aided by that other transfiguration resulting from metaphysical inquiries. Subjective analysis compels us to admit that our scientific interpretations of the phenomena which objects present, are expressed in terms of our own variously-combined sensations and ideas—are expressed, that is, in elements belonging to consciousness, which are but symbols of the something beyond consciousness. Though analysis afterwards reinstates our primitive beliefs, to the extent of showing that behind every group of phenomenal manifestations there is always a *nexus*, which is the reality that remains fixed amid appearances which are variable; yet we are shown that this *nexus* of reality is for ever inaccessible to consciousness. And when, once more, we remember that the activities constituting consciousness, being rigorously bounded, cannot bring in among themselves the activities beyond the bounds, which therefore seem unconscious, though production of either by the other seems to imply that they are of the same essential nature; this necessity we are under to think of the external energy in terms of the internal energy, gives rather a spiritualistic than a materialistic aspect to the Universe: further thought, however, obliging us to recognize the truth that a conception given in phenomenal manifestations of this ultimate energy can in no wise show us what it is.

While the beliefs to which analytic science thus leads, are such as do not destroy the object-matter of religion, but simply transfigure it, science under its concrete forms enlarges the sphere for religious sentiment. From the very beginning the progress of knowledge has been accompanied by an increasing capacity for wonder. Among savages, the lowest are the least surprised when shown remarkable products of civilized art: astonishing the traveller by their indifference. And so little of the marvellous do they perceive in the grandest phenomena of Nature, that any inquiries concerning them they regard as childish trifling. This contrast in mental attitude between the lowest human beings and the higher human beings around us, is paralleled by contrasts among the grades of these higher human beings themselves. It is not the rustic, nor the artizan, nor the trader, who sees something more than a mere matter of course in the hatching of a chick; but it is the biologist, who, pushing to the uttermost his analysis of vital phenomena, reaches his greatest perplexity when a speck of protoplasm under the microscope shows him life in its simplest form, and makes him feel that however he formulates its processes the actual play of forces remains unimaginable. Neither in the ordinary tourist nor in the deer-stalker climbing the mountains above him, does a highland glen rouse ideas beyond those of sport or of the picturesque; but it may, and often does, in the geologist. He, observing that the glacier-rounded rock he sits on has lost by weathering but half an inch of its surface since a time far more remote than the beginnings of human civilization, and then trying to conceive the slow denudation which has cut out the whole valley, has thoughts of time and of power to which they are strangers—thoughts which, already utterly inadequate to their objects, he feels to be still more futile on noting the contorted beds of gneiss around, which tell him of a time, immeasurably more remote, when far beneath the Earth's surface they were in a half-melted state, and again tell him of a time, immensely exceeding this in remoteness, when their components were sand and mud on the shores of an ancient sea. Nor is it in the primitive peoples who supposed that the heavens rested on the mountain tops, any more than in the modern inheritors of their cosmogony who repeat that "the heavens declare the glory of God," that we find the largest conceptions of the Universe or the greatest amount of wonder excited by contemplation of it. Rather, it is in the astronomer, who sees in the Sun a mass so vast that even into one of his spots our Earth might be plunged without touching its edges; and who by every finer telescope is shown an increased multitude of such suns, many of them far larger.

Hereafter as heretofore, higher faculty and deeper insight will raise rather than lower this sentiment. At present the most powerful and most instructed mind has neither the knowledge nor the capacity required for symbolizing in thought the totality of things. Occupied with one or other division of Nature, the man of science usually does not know enough of the other divisions even rudely to conceive the extent and complexity of their phenomena; and supposing him to have adequate knowledge of each, yet he is unable to think of them as a whole. Wider and stronger intellect may hereafter help him to form a vague consciousness of them in their totality. We may say that just as an undeveloped musical faculty, able only to appreciate a simple melody, cannot grasp the variously-entangled passages and harmonies of a symphony, which in the minds of composer and conductor are unified into involved musical effects awakening far greater feeling than is possible to the musically uncultured; so, by future more evolved intelligences, the course of things now apprehensible only in parts may be apprehensible all together, with an accompanying feeling as much beyond that of the present cultured man, as his feeling is beyond that of the savage.

And this feeling is not likely to be decreased but to be increased by that analysis of knowledge which, while forcing him to agnosticism, yet continually prompts him to imagine some solution of the Great Enigma which he knows cannot be solved. Especially must this be so when he remembers that the very notions, origin, cause and purpose, are relative notions belonging to human thought, which are probably irrelevant to the Ultimate Reality transcending human thought; and when, though suspecting that explanation is a word without meaning when applied to this Ultimate Reality, he yet feels compelled to think there must be an explanation.

But one truth must grow ever clearer—the truth that there is an Inscrutable Existence everywhere manifested, to which he can neither find nor conceive either beginning or end. Amid the mysteries which become the more mysterious the more they are thought about, there will remain the one absolute certainty, that he is ever in presence of an Infinite and Eternal Energy, from which all things proceed.

21

AN ECCLESIASTICAL SYSTEM AS A SOCIAL BOND

ONCE MORE WE must return to the religious idea and the religious sentiment in their rudimentary forms, to find an explanation of the part played by ecclesiastical systems in social development.

Though ancestor-worship has died out, there survive among us certain of the conceptions and feelings appropriate to it, and certain resulting observances, which enable us to understand its original effects, and the original effects of those cults immediately derived from it. I refer more especially to the behaviour of descendants after the death of a parent or grand-parent. Three traits, of which we shall presently see the significance, may be noted.

When a funeral takes place, natural affection and usage supporting it, prompt the assembling of the family or clan: of children especially, of other relations to a considerable extent, and in a measure of friends. All, by taking part in the ceremony, join in that expression of respect which constituted the original worship and still remains a qualified form of worship. The burial of a progenitor consequently becomes an occasion on which, more than on any other, there is a revival of the thoughts and feelings appropriate to relationship, and a strengthening of the bonds among kindred.

An incidental result which is still more significant, not unfrequently occurs. If antagonisms among members of the family exist,

---

From *The Principles of Sociology* (London: Williams and Norgate, 1876), vol. 3, part 6, pp, 95–106.

they are not allowed to show themselves. Being possessed by a common sentiment towards the dead, and in so far made to sympathize, those who have been at enmity have their animosities to some extent mitigated; and not uncommonly reconciliations are effected. So that beyond a strengthening of the family-group by the gathering together of its members, there is a strengthening of it caused by the healing of breaches.

One more co-operative influence exists. The injunctions of the deceased are made known; and when these have reference to family-differences, obedience to them furthers harmony. Though it is true that directions concerning the distribution of property often initiate new quarrels, yet in respect of pre-existing quarrels, the known wish of the dying man that they should be ended, is influential in causing compromise or forgiveness; and if there has been a desire on his part that some particular course or policy should be pursued after his death, this desire, even orally expressed, tends very much to become a law to his descendants, and so to produce unity of action among them.

If in our days these influences still have considerable power, they must have had great power in days when there was a vivid conception of ancestral ghosts as liable to be made angry by disregard of their wishes, and able to punish the disobedient. Evidently the family-cult in primitive times, must have greatly tended to maintain the family bond: alike by causing periodic assemblings for sacrifice, by repressing dissensions, and by producing conformity to the same injunctions.

Rising as we do from the ordinary father to the patriarch heading numerous families, propitiation of whose ghost is imperative on all of them, and thence to some head of kindred clans who, leading them to conquest, becomes after death a local chief god, above all others feared and obeyed; we may expect to find in the cults everywhere derived from ancestor-worship, the same influence which ancestor-worship in its simple original form shows us. We shall not be disappointed. Even concerning peoples so rude as the Ostyaks, we find the remark that "the use of the same consecrated spot, or the same priest, is also a bond of union;" and higher races yield still clearer evidence. Let us study it under the heads above indicated.

The original tribes of the Egyptians, inhabiting areas which eventually become the *nomes*, were severally held together by special worships. The central point in each "was always, in the first place, a temple, about which a city became formed." And since "some animals, sacred in one province, were held in abhorrence in another"—since, as we have seen, the animal-naming of ancestral chiefs, revered within the tribe but hated beyond it, naturally originated this; we have reason for concluding that each local bond of union was the worship of an original ancestor-god.

Early Greek civilization shows like influences at work. . . .

The like happened in Italy. Concerning the Etruscans, Mommsen says—"Each of these leagues consisted of twelve communities, which recognized a metropolis, especially for purposes of worship, and a federal head or rather a high-priest." It was thus with the Latins too. Alba was the chief place of the Latin League; and it was also the place at which the tribes forming the league assembled for their religious festivals: such union as existed among them was sanctified by a cult in which all joined. A kindred fact is alleged of ancient Rome. "The oldest constitution of Rome is religious throughout," says Seeley. "Institutions suggested by naked utility come in later, and those which they practically supersede are not abolished, but formally retained on account of their religious character."

Though generally in such cases the need for joint defence against external enemies is the chief prompter to federation; yet in each case the federation formed is determined by that community of sacred rites which from time to time brings the dispersed divisions of the same stock together, and keeps alive in them the idea of a common origin as well as the sentiment appropriate to it.

Though Christendom has not exemplified in any considerable degree a like consolidating effect—though its worship, being an adopted one, has not supplied that bond which results where the worship is of some great founder of the tribe or traditional god of the race; yet it can hardly be questioned that unity of creed and ceremony has to some extent served as an integrating principle. Though Christian brotherhood has not been much displayed among Christian peoples, still, it has not been absolutely a mere name. Indeed it is manifest that since similarity of thought and sympathy of feeling must further harmony by diminishing reasons for difference, agreement in religion necessarily favours union.

Still more clearly shown is the parallelism between suspension of family animosities at funerals, and temporary cessation of hostilities between clans on occasions of common religious festivals. Already I have pointed out that among some of the uncivilized, burial places of chiefs become sacred, to the extent that fighting in them is forbidden: one of the results being the initiation of sanctuaries. Naturally an interdict against quarrels at burial-places, or sacred places where sacrifices are to be made, tends to become an interdict against quarrels with those who are going there to sacrifice. The Tahitians would not molest an enemy who came to make offerings to the national idol; and among the Chibchas pilgrims to Iraca (Sogamoso) were protected by the religious character of the country even in time of war. These cases at once recall cases from ancient European history. . . .

And then beyond these various influences indirectly aiding consolidation, come the direct influences of judgments supposed to come from God through an inspired person—Delphian oracle or Catholic high-priest. "As men of a privileged spiritual endowment" the priests of Delphi were "possessed of the capacity and mission of becoming in the name of their god the teachers and counsellors, in all matters, of the children of the land"; and obviously, in so far as their judgments concerning inter-tribal questions were respected, they served to prevent wars. In like manner belief in the pope as a medium through whom the divine will was communicated, tended in those who held it to cause subordination to his decisions concerning international disputes, and in so far to diminish the dissolving effects of perpetual conflicts: instance the acceptance of his arbitration by Philip Augustus and Richard I. under threat of ecclesiastical punishment; instance the maintenance of peace between the king of Castile and Portugal by Innocent III. under penalty of excommunication; instance Eleanor's invocation—"has not God given you the power to govern nations;" instance the formal enunciation of the theory that the pope was supreme judge in disputes among princes.

No less clearly do the facts justify the analogy above pointed out between the recognized duty of fulfilling a deceased parent's wishes, and the imperative obligation of conforming to a divinely-ordained law.

Twice in six months within my own small circle of friends, I have seen exemplified the subordination of conduct to the imagined dictate of a deceased person: the first example being yielded by one who, after long hesitation, decided to alter a house built by his father, but only in such way as he thought his father would have approved; the second being yielded by one who, not himself objecting to play a game on Sunday, declined because he thought his late wife would not have liked it. If in such cases supposed wishes of the dead become transformed into rules of conduct, much more must expressed injunctions tend to do this. And since maintenance of family-union is an end which such expressed injunctions are always likely to have in view—since the commands of the dying patriarch, or the conquering chief, naturally aim at prosperity of the clan or tribe he governed; the rules or laws which ancestor-worship originates, will usually be of a kind which, while intrinsically furthering social cohesion, further it also by producing ideas of obligation common to all.

Already I have pointed out that, among primitive men, the customs which stand in place of laws, embody the ideas and feelings of past generations; and, religiously conformed to as they are, exhibit the rule of the dead over the living. From usages of the Veddahs, the Scandinavians, and the Hebrews, I there drew evidence that in some cases the ghosts of the dead are appealed to for guidance in special emergencies; and I gave proof that, more generally, apotheosized men or gods are asked for directions: instances being cited from accounts of Egyptians, Peruvians, Tahitians, Tongans, Samoans, Hebrews, and sundry Aryan peoples. Further, it was shown that from particular commands answering special invocations, there was a transition to general commands passing into permanent laws: there being in the bodies of laws so derived, a mingling of regulations of all kinds—sacred, secular, public, domestic, personal. . . .

Evidently bodies of laws regarded as supernaturally given by the traditional god of the race, originating in the way shown, habitually tend to restrain the anti-social actions of individuals towards one another, and to enforce concerted action in the dealings of the society with other societies: in both ways conducing to social cohesion.

The general influence of Ecclesiastical Institutions is conservative in a double sense. In several ways they maintain and strengthen social bonds, and so conserve the social aggregate; and they do this in large measure by conserving beliefs, sentiments, and usages which, evolved during earlier stages of the society, are shown by its survival to have had an approximate fitness to the requirements, and are likely still to have it in great measure. Elsewhere (*Study of Sociology*, Chap. V) I have, for another purpose, exemplified the extreme resistance to change offered by Ecclesiastical Institutions, and this more especially in respect of all things pertaining to the ecclesiastical organization itself. Here let me add a further series of illustrations. . . .

Of course while thus resisting changes of usage, ecclesiastical functionaries have resisted with equal or greater strenuousness, changes of beliefs; since any revolution in the inherited body of beliefs, tends in some measure to shake all parts of it, by diminishing the general authority of ancestral teaching. This familiar aspect of ecclesiastical conservatism, congruous with the aspects above exemplified, it is needless to illustrate.

Again, then, the ghost-theory yields us the needful clue. As, before, we found that all religious observances may be traced back to funeral observances; so here, we find these influences which ecclesiastical institutions exert, have their germs in the influences exerted by the feelings entertained towards the dead. The burial of a late parent is an occasion on which the members of the family gather together and become bound by a renewed sense of kinship; on which any antagonism among them is temporarily or permanently extinguished; and on which they are further united by being subject in common to the deceased man's wishes, and made, in so far, to act in concert. The sentiment of filial piety thus manifesting itself, enlarges in its sphere when the deceased man is the patriarch, or the founder of the tribe, or the hero of the race. But be it in worship of a god or funeral of a parent, we ever see the same three influences—strengthening of union, suspension of hostilities, reinforcement of transmitted commands. In both cases the process of integration is in several ways furthered.

Thus, looking at it generally, we may say that ecclesiasticism stands for the principle of social continuity. Above all other agencies it is that which conduces to cohesion; not only between the coexisting parts of a nation, but also between its present generation and its past generations. In both ways it helps to maintain the individuality of the society. Or, changing somewhat the point of view, we may say that ecclesiasticism, embodying in its primitive form the rule of the dead over the living, and sanctifying in its more advanced forms the authority of the past over the present, has for its function to preserve in force the organized product of earlier experiences *versus* the modifying effects of more recent experiences. Evidently this organized product of past experiences is not without credentials. The life of the society has, up to the time being, been maintained under it; and hence a perennial reason for resistance to deviation. If we consider that habitually the chief or ruler, propitiation of whose ghost originates a local cult, acquired his position through successes of one or other kind, we must infer that obedience to the commands emanating from him, and maintenance of the usages he initiated, is, on the average of cases, conducive to social prosperity so long as conditions remain the same; and that therefore this intense conservatism of ecclesiastical institutions is not without a justification.

Even irrespective of the relative fitness of the inherited cult to the inherited social circumstances, there is an advantage in, if not indeed a necessity for, acceptance of traditional beliefs, and consequent conformity to the resulting customs and rules. For before an assemblage of men can become organized, the men must be held together, and kept ever in presence of the conditions to which they have to become adapted; and that they may be thus held, the coercive influence of their traditional beliefs must be strong. So great are the obstacles which the anti-social traits of the savage offer to that social cohesion which is the first condition to social progress, that he can be kept within the needful bonds only by a sentiment prompting absolute submission—submission to secular rule reinforced by that sacred rule which is at first in unison with it. And hence, as I have before pointed out, the truth that in whatever place arising—Egypt, Assyria, Peru, Mexico, China—social evolution throughout all its earlier stages has been accompanied not only by extreme subordination to living kings, but also by elaborate worships of the deities originating from dead kings.

22

JOINT-STOCK COMPANIES

Early stages in the genesis of what is now called joint-stock enterprise, are instructive as showing, in several ways, how progress of each kind depends on several kinds of preceding progress; and as also showing how any industrial structure, specialized into the form now familiar to us, arose out of an indefinite germ in which it was mingled with other structures.

The creation of the accumulated fund we call capital, depends on certain usages and conditions. Among peoples who, besides burying with the dead man his valuables, sometimes even killed his animals and cut down his fruit trees, no considerable masses of property could be aggregated. The growth of such masses was also prevented by constant wars, which now absorbed them in meeting expenses and now caused the loss of them by capture. Yet a further prevention commonly resulted from appropriations by chiefs and kings. Their unrestrained greed either made saving futile, or by forcing men to hoard what they saved, rendered it useless for reproductive purposes.

Another obstacle existed. Going back, as the idea of capital does, to days when cattle and sheep mainly formed a rich man's movable property, and indicating, as the word does, the number of "heads" in his flocks and herds, it is clear that no fund of the kind which the word now connotes was possible. Cattle and sheep could

---

From *The Principles of Sociology* (London: Williams and Norgate, 1896), vol. 3, part 8, pp. 517–25; "Railway Morals and Railway Policy" (1854), reprinted in *Essays*, vol. 2 (1868), pp. 251–87.

not be disposed of at will. There was only an occasional market for large numbers; and the form of payment was ordinarily not such as rendered the amount easily available for commercial purposes. A money economy had to be well established; and even then, so long as money consisted exclusively of coin, large transactions were much restricted. Only along with the rise of a credit-currency of one or other kind, could individual capital or compound capital take any great developments.

Again, the form of partnership which joint-stock companies exhibit, had to be evolved out of simple partnerships, having their roots in family-organizations and gild-organizations. Fathers and sons, and then larger groups of relatives carrying on the same business, naturally, on emerging from the communal state, fell into one or other form of joint ownership and division of profits. And we may safely infer that the gild-organization afterwards evolved, which, considered in its general nature, was a partnership for purposes of defence and regulation, further educated men in the ideas and practices which the joint-stock system implies. Those who constantly combined their powers in pursuit of certain common interests, were led occasionally to combine their individual possessions for common interests—to form large partnerships.

A further needful remark is that these early companies were not wholly industrial but were partly militant. Already, when contemplating gilds, we have seen in them the spirit of antagonism common to all social structures in their days, when nobles fought against one another or joined against the king, when the people of towns had to defend themselves against feudal tyrannies, and when town was against town. Like the gilds, the early combinations of traders which foreshadowed companies, had defence and aggression within their functions. Even now industry is in a considerable measure militant, and it was then still more militant. . . .

The last stage in the development of these industrial associations which have compound capitals has still to be named. In modern forms of them we see the regulative policy, once so pronounced, reduced to its least degree. Both by the central government and by local governments, individuals were, in early days, greatly restricted in the carrying on of their occupations; and at the same time the combinations they formed for the protection and regulation of their industries, were formed by governmental authority, general or local, for which they paid. Of the various hindrances to combinations, originally for regulating industries but eventually for carrying on industries, the last was removed in 1855. Up to that time it had been held needful that the public should be safeguarded against wild and fraudulent schemes, by requiring that each shareholder should be liable to the whole amount of his property for the debts of any company he joined. But at length it was concluded that it would suffice if each shareholder was liable only to the amount of his shares; provided that his limited liability was duly notified to men at large.

Everyone knows the results. Under the limited-liability system many bubble-companies, analogous to those of old times, have arisen, and there has been much business under the winding-up Acts: the public has often proved itself an incompetent judge of the projects brought before it. But many useful undertakings have been proposed and carried out. One unanticipated result has been the changing of private trading concerns into limited-liability companies; whether with benefit may be questioned. But the measure has certainly yielded advantage by making it possible to raise capital for relatively small industries of speculative kinds. It has been beneficial, too, in making available for industrial purposes, numberless savings which otherwise would have been idle: absorption of them into the general mass of reproductive capital being furthered by the issue of shares of small denominations. So that now stagnant capital has almost disappeared.

Before leaving the topic it is proper to point out that in this case, as in other cases, coerciveness of regulation declines politically, ecclesiastically, and industrially at the same time. Many facts have shown us that while the individual man has acquired greater liberty as a citizen and greater religious liberty, he has also acquired greater liberty in respect of his occupations; and here we see that he has simultaneously acquired greater liberty of combination for industrial purposes. Indeed, in conformity with the universal law of rhythm, there has been a change from excess of restriction to deficiency of restriction. As is implied by legislation now pending, the facilities for forming companies and raising compound capitals have been too great. Of sundry examples here is one. Directors are allowed to issue prospectuses in which it is said that those who take shares will be understood to waive the right to know the contents of certain preliminary agreements, made with promoters—are allowed to ask the public to subscribe while not knowing fully the circumstances of the case. A rational interpretation of legal principles would have negatived this. In any proper contract the terms on both sides are distinctly specified. If they are not, one of the parties to the contract is bound completely while the other is bound incompletely—a result at variance with the very nature of contract. Where the transaction is one that demands definiteness on one side while leaving the other side indefinite, the law should ignore the contract as one that cannot be enforced. . . .

Believers in the intrinsic virtues of political forms, might draw an instructive lesson from the politics of our railways. If there needs a conclusive proof that the most carefully-framed constitutions are worthless, unless they be embodiments of the popular character—if there needs a conclusive proof, that governmental arrangements in advance of the time will inevitably lapse into congruity with the time; such proof may be found over and over again repeated in the current history of joint-stock enterprises.

As devised by Act of Parliament, the administrations of our public companies are almost purely democratic. The representative system is carried out in them with scarcely a check. Shareholders elect their directors, directors their chairman; there is an annual retirement of a certain proportion of the board, giving facilities for superseding them; and, by this means, the whole ruling body may be changed in periods varying from three to five years. Yet, not only are the characteristic vices of our political state reproduced in each of these mercantile corporations—some even in an intenser degree—but the very form of government, while remaining nominally democratic, is substantially so remodelled as to become a miniature of our national constitution. The direction, ceasing to fulfil its theory as a deliberative body whose members possess like powers, falls under the control of some one member of superior cunning, will, or wealth, to whom the majority become so subordinate, that the decision on every question depends on the course he takes. Proprietors, instead of constantly exercising their franchise, allow it to become on all ordinary occasions a dead letter: retiring directors are so habitually reëlected without opposition, and have so great a power of insuring their own election when opposed, that the board becomes practically a close body; and it is only when the misgovernment grows extreme enough to produce a revolutionary agitation among the shareholders, that any change can be effected.

Thus, a mixture of the monarchic, the aristocratic, and the democratic elements, is repeated with such modifications only as the circumstances involve. The modes of action, too, are substantially the same: save in this, that the copy outruns the original. Threats of resignation, which ministries hold out in extreme cases, are commonly made by railway-boards to stave off a disagreeable inquiry. By no means regarding themselves as servants of the shareholders, directors rebel against dictation from them; and frequently construe any amendment to their proposals into a vote of want of confidence. At half-yearly meetings, disagreeable criticism and objections are met by the chairman with the remark, that if the shareholders cannot trust his colleagues and himself, they had better choose others. With most, this assumption of offended dignity tells; and, under the fear that the company's interests may suffer from any disturbance, measures quite at variance with the wishes of the proprietary are allowed to be carried.

The parallel holds yet further. If it be true of national administrations, that those in office count on the support of all public *employés*; it is not less true of incorporated companies, that the directors are greatly aided by their officials in their struggles with shareholders. If, in times past, there have been ministries who spent public money to secure party ends; there are, in times present, railway-boards who use the funds of the shareholders to defeat the shareholders. Nay, even in detail, the similarity is maintained. Like their prototype, joint-stock companies have their expensive election contests, managed by election committees, employing election agents; they have their canvassing with its sundry illegitimate accompaniments; they have their occasional manufacture of fraudulent votes. And, as a general result, that class-legislation, which has been habitually changed against statesmen, is now habitually displayed in the proceedings of these trading associations: constituted though they are on purely representative principles. . . . [A long catalogue of abuses and corruptions, initiated by directors, against shareholders' interests, follows.]

Need we any longer wonder, then, at the persistence of Railway Companies in seemingly reckless competition and ruinous extensions? Is not this obstinate continuance of a policy that has year after year proved disastrous, sufficiently explicable on contemplating the many illegitimate influences at work? Is it not manifest that the small organized party always outmanœuvres the large unorganized one? Consider their respective characters and circumstances. Here are the shareholders diffused throughout the whole kingdom, in towns and country houses; knowing nothing of each other, and too remote to coöperate were they acquainted. Very few of them see a railway journal; not many a daily one; and scarcely any know much of railway politics. Necessarily a fluctuating body, only a small number are familiar with the Company's history—its acts, engagements, policy, management. A great proportion are incompetent to judge of the questions that come before them, and lack decision to act out such judgments as they may form—executors who do not like to take steps involving much responsibility; trustees fearful of interfering with the property under their care, lest possible loss should entail a lawsuit; widows who have never in their lives acted for themselves in any affair of moment; maiden ladies, alike nervous and innocent of all business knowledge; clergymen whose daily discipline has been little calculated to make them acute men of the world; retired tradesmen whose retail transactions have given them small ability for grasping large considerations; servants possessed of accumulated savings and cramped notions; with sundry others of like helpless character—all of them rendered more or less conservative by ignorance or timidity, and proportionately inclined to support those in authority. To these should be added the class of temporary shareholders, who, having bought stock on speculation, and knowing that a revolution in the Company is likely to depress prices for a time, have an interest in supporting the board irrespective of the goodness of its policy.

Turn now to those whose efforts are directed to railway expansion. Consider the constant pressure of local interests—of small towns, of rural districts, of landowners: all of them eager for branch accommodation; all of them with great and definite advantages in view; few of them conscious of the loss those advantages may entail on others. Remember the influence of legislators, prompted, some by their constituents, some by personal aims, and encouraged by the belief that additional railway facilities are in every case nationally beneficial; and then calculate the extent to which, as stated to Mr. Cardwell's committee, Parliament has "excited and urged forward" Companies into rivalry. Observe the temptations under which lawyers are placed—the vast profits accruing to them from every railway contest, whether ending in success or failure; and then imagine the magnitude and subtlety of their extension manœuvring. Conceive the urgency of the engineering profession; to the richer of whom more railway-making means more wealth; to the mass of whom more railway-making means daily bread. Estimate the capitalist-power of contractors; whose plant when employed brings great gain. Then recollect that to lawyers, engineers, and contractors the getting up and executing of new undertakings is a business—a business to which every energy is directed; in which long years of practice have given great skill; and to the facilitation of which, all means tolerated by men of the world are thought justifiable.

Finally, consider that the classes interested in carrying out new schemes, are in constant communication, and have every facility for combined action. . . . Is it any wonder then, that the widespread, ill-informed, unorganized body of shareholders, standing severally alone, and each preoccupied with his daily affairs, should be continually outgeneralled by the comparatively small but active, skilful, combined body opposed to them, whose very occupation is at stake in gaining the victory?

"But how about the directors?" it will perhaps be asked. "How can they be parties to those obviously unwise undertakings? They are themselves shareholders: they gain by what benefits the proprietary at large; they lose by what injures it. And if without their consent, or rather their agency, no new scheme can be adopted by the Company, the classes interested in fostering railway enterprise are powerless to do harm."

This belief in the identity of directional and proprietary interests, is the fatal error commonly made by shareholders. It is this which, in spite of many bitter experiences, leads them to be so careless and so trustful. "Their profit is our profit; their loss is our loss; they know more than we do; therefore let us leave the matter to them." Such is the argument which more or less definitely passes through the shareholding mind—an argument of which the premises are vicious, and the inference disastrous. Let us consider it in detail.

Not to dwell upon the disclosures that have in years past been made respecting the share-trafficking of boards, and the large profits realized by it—disclosures which alone suffice to disprove the assumed identity between the interests of directors and proprietary—and taking for granted that little, if any, of this now takes place; let us go on to notice the still-prevailing influences which render this apparent unity of purpose illusive. The immediate interest which directors have in the prosperity of the Company, is often much less than is supposed. Occasionally they possess only the bare qualification of £1,000 worth of stock. In some instances even this is partly nominal. Admitting, however, as we do frankly, that in the great majority of cases the full qualification, and much more than the qualification, is held; yet it must be borne in mind that the indirect advantages which a wealthy member of a board may gain from the prosecution of a new undertaking, will often far outweigh the direct injury it will inflict on him by the depreciation of his shares. A board usually consists, to a considerable extent, of gentlemen residing at different points throughout the tract of country traversed by the railway they control: some of them landowners; some merchants or manufacturers; some owners of mines or shipping. Almost always these are advantaged more or less by a new branch or feeder. Those in close proximity to it, gain either by enhanced value of their lands, or by increased facilities of transit for their commodities. Those at more remote parts of the main line, though less directly interested, are still frequently interested in some degree: for every extension opens up new markets either for produce or raw materials; and if it is one effecting a junction with some other system of railways, the greater mercantile conveniences afforded to directors thus circumstanced, become important.

Obviously, therefore, the indirect profits accruing to such from one of these new undertakings, may more than counterbalance the direct loss upon their railway investments; and though there are, doubtless, men far too honourable to let such considerations sway them, yet the generality can scarcely fail to be affected by temptations so strong. Then we have further to remember the influences brought to bear upon directors having seats in Parliament.

23

LABOUR IN INDUSTRIAL SOCIETY

For the revolution which gave to the Factory System its modern character, arose from the substitution of steam-power for water-power. One result was that, being no longer dependent on supply of water, the variations in which led to variations in activity of production, processes of manufacture were made continuous. Another result was that wide distribution of factories was no longer necessitated by wide distribution of water-power. Factories and the people working in them became clustered in large masses to which there was no limit; and there followed increased facilities both for bringing raw materials and taking away manufactured products. So that beyond the integration of many machines in one mill there came the integration of many mills in one town.

But now, from considering this evolution as a mechanical progress and as a progress in industrial organization, let us go on to consider it in relation to the lives of workers. Here its effects, in some respects beneficial, are in many respects detrimental. Though in his capacity of consumer the factory-hand, in common with the community, profits by the cheapening of goods of all kinds, including his own kind, yet in his capacity of producer he loses heavily—perhaps more heavily than he gains.

More and more of his powers, bodily and mental, are rendered superfluous. The successive improvements of the motor-agency

From *The Principles of Sociology* (London: Williams and Norgate, 1896), vol. 3, part 8, pp. 514–16, 526–27, 541–43, 559–63, 566–79.

itself show this effect. Originally the steam-engine required a boy to open and shut the steam valves at the proper moments. Presently the engine was made to open and shut its own valves, and human aid was to that extent superseded. For a time, however, it continued needful for regulating the general supply of steam. When the work the engine had to do was suddenly much increased or decreased, the opening through which the steam passed from the boiler had to be enlarged or diminished by an attendant. But for the attendant there was presently substituted an unintelligent apparatus—the governor. Then, after an interval, came a self-stoking apparatus, enabling the engine itself to supply fuel to its steam-generator. Now this replacing of muscular and mental processes by mechanical processes, has been going on not only in the motor but in the vast assemblages of machines which the motor works. From time to time each of them has been made to do for itself something which was previously done for it; so that now it stops itself, or part of itself, at the proper moment, or rings a bell when it has finished an appointed piece of work. To its attendant there remains only the task of taking away the work done and giving other work, or else of rectifying its shortcomings: tying a broken thread for instance.

Clearly these self-adjustments, continually decreasing the sphere for human agency, make the actions of the workman himself relatively automatic. At the same time the monotonous attention required, taxing special parts of the nervous system and leaving others inactive, entails positive as well as negative injury. And while the mental nature becomes to the implied extent deformed, the physical nature, too, undergoes degradations; caused by breathing vitiated air at a temperature now in excess now in defect, and by standing for many hours in a way which unduly taxes the vascular system. If we compare his life with the life of the cottage artisan he has replaced, who, a century ago, having a varied muscular action in working his loom, with breaks caused by the incidents of the work, was able to alternate his indoor activities with outdoor activities in garden or field, we cannot but admit that this industrial development has proved extremely detrimental to the operative.

In their social relations, too, there has been an entailed retrogression rather than a progression. The wage-earning factory-hand does, indeed, exemplify entirely free labour, in so far that, making contracts at will and able to break them after short notice, he is free to engage with whomsoever he pleases and where he pleases. But this liberty amounts in practice to little more than the ability to exchange one slavery for another; since, fit only for his particular occupation, he has rarely an opportunity of doing anything more than decide in what mill he will pass the greater part of his dreary days. The coercion of circumstances often bears more hardly on him than the coercion of a master does on one in bondage.

It seems that in the course of social progress, parts, more or less large, of each society, are sacrificed for the benefit of the society as a whole. In the earlier stages the sacrifice takes the form of mortality in the wars perpetually carried on during the struggle for existence between tribes and nations; and in later stages the sacrifice takes the form of mortality entailed by the commercial struggle, and the keen competition entailed by it. In either case men are used up for the benefit of posterity; and so long as they go on multiplying in excess of the means of subsistence, there appears no remedy. . . .

Trade Unions

Among those carrying on their lives under like conditions, whether in respect of place of living or mode of living, there arise in one way diversities of interests and in another way unities of interests. In respect of place of living this is seen in the fact that members of a tribe or nation have unity of interests in defending themselves against external enemies, while internally they have diversities of interests prompting constant quarrels. Similarly in respect of mode of living. Those who pursue like occupations, being competitors, commonly have differences, as is implied by the proverb "Two of a trade can never agree;" but in relation to bodies of men otherwise occupied, their interests are the same, and sameness of interests prompts joint actions for defence. In preceding chapters history has shown how this general law was illustrated in old times among traders. Now we have to observe how in modern times it is illustrated among their employés.

Union of artisans for maintenance of common advantages is traceable in small societies, even before master and worker are differentiated. . . . Apparently without formal combination there is thus a tacit agreement to maintain certain rates of payment. Something of kindred nature is found in parts of Africa. Reade says that a sort of trade-union exists on the Gaboon, and those who break its rules are ill-treated. The natives on the coast endeavour to keep all the trade with the white man in their own hands; and if one from any of the bush tribes is detected selling to the white man, it is thought a breach of law and custom. But the trade-union as we now know it, obviously implies an advanced social evolution. There is required in the first place a definite separation between the wage-earner and the wage-payer; and in the second place it is requisite that considerable numbers of wage-earners shall be gathered together; either as inhabitants of the same locality or as clustered migratory bodies, such as masons once formed. Of course fulfilment of these conditions was gradual, but when it had become pronounced, "The workmen formed their Trade-Unions against the aggressions of the then rising manufacturing lords, as in earlier times the old freemen formed their Frith-Gilds against the tyranny of mediæval magnates, and the free handicraftsmen their Craft-Gilds against the aggressions of the Old-burghers." Not that there was a lineal descent of trade-unions from craft-gilds. Evidence of this is lacking and evidence to the contrary abundant. Though very generally each later social institution may be affiliated upon some earlier one, yet it occasionally happens that social institutions of a kind like some which previously existed, arise *de novo* under similar conditions; and the trade-union furnishes one illustration. Akin in nature though not akin by descent, the trade-union is simply a gild of wage-earners. . . . [Spencer proceeds to evaluate their contemporary functions.]

Returning from this incidental criticism let us ask what are the effects of the trade-union policy, pecuniarily considered. After averaging the results over many trades in many years, do we find the wage-earner really benefited in his "Standard of Life"? . . . [He discusses first agricultural, then industrial workers, arguing that to artificially raise wages may force the industry to go elsewhere.]

One striking lesson furnished by English history should show trade-unionists that permanent rates of wages are determined by other causes than the wills of either employers or employed. When the Black Death had swept away a large part of the population (more than half it is said) so that the number of workers became insufficient for the work to be done, wages rose immensely, and maintained their high rate notwithstanding all efforts to keep them down by laws and punishments. Conversely, there have been numerous cases in which strikes have failed to prevent lowering of wages when trade was depressed. Where the demand for labour is great, wages cannot be kept down; and where it is small, they cannot be kept up.

What then are we to say of trade-unions? Under their original form as friendly societies—organizations for rendering mutual aid—they were of course extremely beneficial; and in so far as they subserve this purpose down to the present time, they can scarcely be too much lauded. Here, however, we are concerned not with the relations of their members to one another, but with their corporate relations to employers and the public. Must we say that though one set of artisans may succeed for a time in getting more pay for the same work, yet this advantage is eventually at the expense of the public (including the mass of wage-earners), and that when all other groups of artisans, following the example, have raised their wages, the result is a mutual cancelling of benefits? Must we say that while ultimately failing in their proposed ends, trade-unions do nothing else than inflict grave mischiefs in trying to achieve them?

This is too sweeping a conclusion. They seem natural to the passing phase of social evolution, and may have beneficial functions under existing conditions. Everywhere aggression begets resistance and counter-aggression; and in our present transitional state, semi-militant and semi-industrial, trespasses have to be kept in check by the fear of retaliatory trespasses.

Judging from their harsh and cruel conduct in the past, it is tolerably certain that employers are now prevented from doing unfair things which they would else do. Conscious that trade-unions are ever ready to act, they are more prompt to raise wages when trade is flourishing than they would otherwise be; and when there comes times of depression, they lower wages only when they cannot otherwise carry on their businesses.

Knowing the power which unions can exert, masters are led to treat the individual members of them with more respect than they would otherwise do: the *status* of the workman is almost necessarily raised. Moreover, having a strong motive for keeping on good terms with the union, a master is more likely than he would else be to study the general convenience of his men, and to carry on his works in ways conducive to their health. There is an ultimate gain in moral and physical treatment if there is no ultimate gain in wages.

Then in the third place must be named the discipline given by trade-union organization and action. Considered under its chief aspect, the progress of social life at large is a progress in fitness for living and working together; and all minor societies of men formed within a major society—a nation—subject their members to sets of incentives and restraints which increase their fitness. The induced habits of feeling and thought tend to make men more available than they would else be, for such higher forms of social organization as will probably hereafter arise. . . .

[Spencer then turns to evaluate the various forms of co-operative movement, which sought to provide a communitarian alternative to laissez-faire capitalism.] Apparently, however, there is more reason to accept the unfavourable interpretation of the evidence than the favourable interpretation; since both *a priori* and *a posteriori* it is manifest that destructive causes, hard to withstand, are ever at work. To secure business-management adequately intelligent and honest, is a chronic difficulty. Even supposing external transactions to be well and equitably conducted, adverse criticisms upon them are almost certain to be made by some of the members: perhaps leading to change of management. Then come the difficulties of preserving internal harmony. In cooperative workshops the members receive weekly wages at trade-union rates, and are ranked as higher or lower by the foreman. Officials are paid at better rates according to their values and responsibilities, and these rates are fixed by the committee. When the profits have been ascertained, they are divided among all in proportion to the amounts they have earned in wages or salaries. Causes of dissension are obvious. One who receives the lowest wages is dissatisfied—holds that he is as good a worker as one who gets higher wages, and resents the decision of the foreman: probably ascribing it to favouritism. Officials, too, are apt to disagree with one another, alike in respect of power and remuneration. Then among the hand-workers in general there is pretty certain to be jealousy of the brain-workers, whose values they under-estimate; and with their jealousies go reflections on the committee as unfair or as unwise. In these various ways the equilibrium of the body is frequently disturbed, and in course of time is very likely to be destroyed.

Must we then say that self-governing combinations of workers will never answer? The reply is that one class of the difficulties above set forth must ever continue to be great, though perhaps not insuperable, but that the other and more serious class may probably be evaded.

These members of industrial copartnerships, paying themselves trade-union wages, are mostly imbued with trade-union ideas and feelings. Among these is a prejudice against piece-work, quite naturally resulting from experience. Finding what a given piece of work ordinarily costs in day-wages, the employer offers to pay the workman for it at a certain lower rate; leaving him to get, by extra diligence, more work done and a larger payment. Immediately, the quantity executed is greatly increased, and the workman receives considerably more than he did in wages—so much more that the employer becomes dissatisfied, thinks he is giving too large a sum by the piece, and cuts down the rate. Action and reaction go on until, very generally, there is an approximation to the earnings by day-wages: the tendency, meanwhile, having been so to raise the employer's standard, that he expects to get more work out of the workman for the same sum.

But now, has not the resulting aversion to piece-work been unawares carried into another sphere, in which its effects must be quite different? Evils like these arising from antagonistic interests, cannot arise where there are no antagonistic interests. Each co-operator exists in a double capacity. He is a unit in an incorporated body standing in the place of employer; and he is a worker employed by this incorporated body. Manifestly, when, instead of an employing master, alien to the workers, there is an employing master compounded of the workers, the mischiefs ordinarily caused by piece-work can no longer be caused. Consider how the arrangement will work.

The incorporated body, acting through its deputed committee, gives to the individual members work at a settled rate for an assigned quantity—such rate being somewhat lower than that which, at the ordinary speed of production, would yield the ordinary wages. The individual members, severally put into their work such ability as they can and such energy as they please; and there comes from them an output, here of twenty, there of twenty-five, and occasionally of thirty per cent. greater than before. What are the pecuniary results? Each earns in a given time a greater sum, while the many-headed master has a larger quantity of goods to dispose of, which can be offered to buyers at somewhat lower prices than before; with the effect of obtaining a ready sale and increased returns. Presently comes one of the recurring occasions for division of profits. Through the managing body, the many-headed master gives to every worker a share which, while larger all round, is proportionate in each case to the sum earned. What now will happen in respect of the rate paid for piece-work? The composite master has no motive to cut down this rate: the interests of the incorporated members being identical with the interests of the members individually taken. But should there arise any reason for lowering the piece-work price, the result must be that what is lost to each in payment for labour, is regained by him in the shape of additional profit. Thus while each obtains exactly the remuneration due for his work, *minus* only the cost of administration, the productive power of the concern is greatly increased, with proportionate increase of returns to all: there is an equitable division of a larger sum.

Consider now the moral effects. Jealousies among the workers disappear. A cannot think his remuneration too low as compared with that of B, since each is now paid just as much as his work brings. Resentment against a foreman, who ranks some above others, no longer finds any place. Overlooking to check idleness becomes superfluous: the idling almost disappears, and another cause of dissension ceases. Not only do the irritations which superintendence excites decrease, but the cost of it decreases also; and the official element in the concern bears a reduced ratio to the other elements. The governing functions of the committee, too, and the relations of the workers to it, become fewer; thus removing other sources of internal discord: the chief remaining source being the inspection of work by the manager or committee, and refusal to pass that which is bad.

A further development may be named. Where the things produced are easily divisible and tolerably uniform in kind, work by the piece may be taken by single individuals; but where the things are so large, and perhaps complex (as in machinery), that an unaided man becomes incapable, work by the piece may be taken by groups of members. In such cases, too, in which the proper rate is difficult to assign, the price may be settled by an inverted Dutch auction, pursuing a method allied to that of the Cornish miners. Among them,

> an undertaking "is marked out, and examined by the workmen during some days, thus affording them an opportunity of judging as to its difficulty. Then it is put up to auction and bid for by different gangs of men, who undertake the work as co-operative piece-work, at so much per fathom": the lot being subsequently again bid for as a whole.

In the case now supposed, sundry pieces of work, after similar inspection, would be bid for on one of the recurring occasions appointed. Offering each in turn at some very low price, and meeting with no response, the manager would, step by step, raise the price, until presently one of the groups would accept. The pieces of work thus put up to auction, would be so arranged in number that towards the close, bidding would be stimulated by the thought of having no piece of work to undertake: the penalty being employment by one or other of the groups at day-wages. Now good bargains and now bad bargains, made by each group, would average one another; but always the good or bad bargain of any group would be a bad or good bargain for the entire body.

What would be the character of these arrangements considered as stages in industrial evolution? We have seen that, in common with political regulation and ecclesiastical regulation, the regulation of labour becomes less coercive as society assumes a higher type. Here we reach a form in which the coerciveness has diminished to the smallest degree consistent with combined action. Each member is his own master in respect of the work he does; and is subject only to such rules, established by majority of the members, as are needful for maintaining order. The transition from the compulsory cooperation of militancy to the voluntary cooperation of industrialism is completed. Under present arrangements it is incomplete. A wage-earner, while he voluntarily agrees to give so many hours work for so much pay, does not, during performance of his work, act in a purely voluntary way: he is coerced by the consciousness that discharge will follow if he idles, and is sometimes more manifestly coerced by an overlooker. But under the arrangement described, his activity becomes entirely voluntary.

Otherwise presenting the facts, and using Sir Henry Maine's terms, we see that the transition from *status* to contract reaches its limit. So long as the worker remains a wage-earner, the marks of *status* do not wholly disappear. For so many hours daily he makes over his faculties to a master, or to a cooperative group, for so much money, and is for the time owned by him or it. He is temporarily in the position of a slave, and his overlooker stands in the position of a slave-driver. Further, a remnant of the *régime of status* is seen in the fact that he and other workers are placed in ranks, receiving different rates of pay. But under such a mode of cooperation as that above contemplated, the system of contract becomes unqualified. Each member agrees with the body of members to perform certain work for a certain sum, and is free from dictation and authoritative classing. The entire organization is based on contract, and each transaction is based on contract. . . .

Socialism

Some socialists, though probably not many, know that their ideal modes of associated living are akin to modes which have prevailed widely during early stages of civilization, and prevail still among many of the uncivilized, as well as among some of the civilized who have lagged behind. In the chapter on "Communal Regulation" were given examples of communism as practised by tribes of Red men, by various Hindus, and by some unprogressive peoples in Eastern Europe. Further instances of each class will serve to exhibit at once the virtues of these methods of combined living and working and their vices. . . .

When with the fact that these Slavonic house-communities under modern conditions of comparative peace and commercial activity, are dissolving, we join the fact that they were formed during times of chronic war and remained coherent during such times; when we add that such communities are still coherent among the Montenegrins, whose active militancy continues; when we add, further, that maintenance of this combined living by American Indians has similarly gone along with perpetual intertribal conflicts; we are shown again, as before that in these small social unions, as in the larger social unions including them, the subordination of the individual to the group is great in proportion as the antagonism to other groups is great. Be it in the family, the cluster of relatives, the clan, or the nation, the need for joint action against alien families, clans, nations, &c., necessitates the merging of individual life in group-life.

Hence the socialist theory and practice are normal in the militant type of society, and cease to be normal as fast as the society becomes predominantly industrial in its type.

A state of universal brotherhood is so tempting an imagination, and the existing state of competitive strife is so full of miseries, that endeavours to escape from the last and enter into the first are quite natural—inevitable even. Prompted by consciousness of the grievous inequalities of condition around, those who suffer and those who sympathize with them, seek to found what they think an equitable social system. In the town, sight of a rich manufacturer who ignores the hands working in his mill, does not excite in them friendly feeling; and in the country, a ploughman looking over the hedge as a titled lady drives by, may not unnaturally be angered by the thought of his own hard work and poor fare in contrast with the easy lives and luxuries of those who own the fields he tills. After contemplating the useless being who now lounges in club-rooms and now rambles through game-preserves, the weary artisan may well curse a state of things in which pleasure varies inversely as desert; and may well be vehement in his demand for another form of society.

How numerous have been the efforts to set up such a form, and how numerous the failures, it is needless to show. Here it will suffice to give one of the most recent examples—that of the South Australian village-settlements. . . .

Of course this failure, like multitudinous such failures elsewhere, will be ascribed to mistake or mismanagement. Had this or that not been done everything would have gone well. That human beings as now constituted cannot work together efficiently and harmoniously in the proposed way, is not admitted; or, if by some admitted, then it is held that the mischiefs arising from defective natures may be prevented by a sufficiently powerful authority—that is, if for those separate groups one great organization centrally controlled is substituted. And it is assumed that such an organization, maintained by force, would be beneficial not for a time only but permanently. Let us look at the fundamental errors involved in this belief.

In an early division of this work, "Domestic Institutions," the general law of species-life was pointed out and emphasized—the law that during immature life benefit received must be great in proportion as worth is small, while during mature life benefit and worth must vary together. "Clearly with a society, as with a species, survival depends on conformity to both of these antagonist principles. Import into the family the law of the society, and let children from infancy upwards have life-sustaining supplies proportioned to their life-sustaining labours, and the society disappears forthwith by death of all its young. Import into the society the law of the family, and let the life-sustaining supplies be great in proportion as the life-sustaining labours are small, and the society decays from increase of its least worthy members and decrease of its most worthy members." Now, more or less fully, the doctrine of collectivists, socialists, and communists, ignores this distinction between the ethics of family-life and the ethics of life outside the family. Entirely under some forms, and in chief measure under others, it proposes to extend the *régime* of the family to the whole community. This is the conception set forth by Mr. Bellamy in *Looking Backwards*; and this is the conception formulated in the maxim—"From each according to his capacity, to each according to his needs."

In low grades of culture there is but vague consciousness of natural causation; and even in the highest grades of culture at present reached, such consciousness is very inadequate. Fructifying causation—the production of many effects each of which becomes the cause of many other effects—is not recognized. The socialist does not ask what must happen if, generation after generation, the material well-being of the inferior is raised at the cost of lowering that of the superior. Even when it is pointed out, he refuses to see that if the superior, persistently burdened by the inferior, are hindered in rearing their own better offspring, that the offspring of the inferior may be as efficiently cared for, a gradual deterioration of the race must follow. The hope of curing present evils so fills his consciousness that it cannot take in the thought of the still greater future evils his proposed system would produce.

Such mitigations of the miseries resulting from inferiority as the spontaneous sympathies of individuals for one another prompt, will bring an average of benefit; since, acting separately, the superior will not so far tax their own resources in taking care of their fellows, as to hinder themselves from giving their own offspring better rearing than is given to the offspring of the inferior. But people who, in their corporate capacity, abolish the natural relation between merits and benefits, will presently be abolished themselves. Either they will have to go through the miseries of a slow decay, consequent on the increase of those unfit for the business of life, or they will be overrun by some people who have not pursued the foolish policy of fostering the worst at the expense of the best.

At the same time that it is biologically fatal, the doctrine of the socialists is psychologically absurd. It implies an impossible mental structure.

A community which fulfils their ideal must be composed of men having sympathies so strong that those who, by their greater powers, achieve greater benefits, willingly surrender the excess to others. . . . The character of all is to be so noble that it causes continuous sacrifice of self to others, and so ignoble that it continuously lets others sacrifice to self. These traits are contradictory. The implied mental constitution is an impossible one.

Still more manifest does its impossibility become when we recognize a further factor in the problem—love of offspring. Within the family parental affection joins sympathy in prompting self-sacrifice, and makes it easy, and indeed pleasurable, to surrender to others a large part of the products of labour. But such surrender made to those within the family-group is at variance with a like surrender made to those outside the family-group. Hence the equalization of means prescribed by communistic arrangements, implies a moral nature such that the superior willingly stints his own progeny to aid the progeny of the inferior. He not only loves his neighbour as himself but he loves his neighbour's children as his own. The parental instinct disappears. One child is to him as good as another.

Of course the advanced socialist, otherwise communist, has his solution. Parental relations are to be superseded, and children are to be taken care of by the State. The method of Nature is to be replaced by a better method. From the lowest forms of life to the highest, Nature's method has been that of devolving the care of the young on the adults who produced them—a care at first shown feebly and unobtrusively, but becoming gradually more pronounced, until, as we approach the highest types of creatures, the lives of parents, prompted by feelings increasingly intense, are more and more devoted to the rearing of offspring. But just as, in the way above shown, socialists would suspend the natural relation between effort and benefit, so would they suspend the natural relation between the instinctive actions of parents and the welfare of progeny. The two great laws in the absence of either of which organic evolution would have been impossible, are both to be repealed! . . .

Reduced to its ultimate form, the general question at issue between socialists and anti-socialists, concerns the mode of regulating labour. Preceding chapters have dealt with this historically—treating of regulation that is paternal, patriarchal, communal, or by a gild—of regulation that has the form of slavery or serfdom—of regulation under arrangements partially free or wholly free. These chapters have illustrated in detail the truth, emphasized at the outset, that political, ecclesiastical, and industrial regulations simultaneously decrease in coerciveness as we ascend from lower to higher types of societies: the modern industrial system being one under which coerciveness approaches a minimum. Though now the worker is often mercilessly coerced by circumstances, and has nothing before him but hard terms, yet he is not coerced by a master into acceptance of these terms.

But while the evils which resulted from the old modes of regulating labour, not experienced by present or recent generations, have been forgotten, the evils accompanying the new mode are keenly felt, and have aroused the desire for a mode which is in reality a modified form of the old mode. There is to be a re-institution of *status*, not under individual masters but under the community as master. No longer possessing themselves and making the best of their powers, individuals are to be possessed by the State; which, while it supports them, is to direct their labours. Necessarily there is implied a vast and elaborate administrative body—regulators of small groups, subject to higher regulators, and so on through successively superior grades up to a central authority, which coordinates the multitudinous activities of the society in their kinds and amounts. Of course the members of this directive organization must be adequately paid by workers; and the tacit assumption is that the required payment will be, at first and always, much less than that which is taken by the members of the directive organization now existing—employers and their staffs; while submission to the orders of these State-officials will be more tolerable than submission to the orders of those who pay wages for work.

A complete parallelism exists between such a social structure and the structure of an army. It is simply a civil regimentation parallel to the military regimentation; and it establishes an industrial subordination parallel to the military subordination. In either case the rule is—Do your task and take your rations. In the working organization as in the fighting organization, obedience is requisite for maintenance of order, as well as for efficiency, and must be enforced with whatever rigour is found needful. Doubtless in the one case as in the other, multitudinous officers, grade over grade, having in their hands all authority and all means of coercion, would be able to curb that aggressive egoism illustrated above, which causes the failures of small socialistic bodies: idleness, quarrels, violence, would be prevented, and efficient work insisted upon. But when from regulation of the workers by the bureaucracy we turn to the bureaucracy itself, and ask how it is to be regulated, there is no such satisfactory answer. Owning, in trust for the community, all the land, the capital, the means of transit and communication, as well as whatever police and military force had to be maintained, this all-powerful official organization, composed of men characterized on the average by an aggressive egoism like that which the workers display, but not like them under any higher control, must inevitably advantage itself at the cost of the governed: the elective powers of the governed having soon failed to prevent it; since, as is perpetually shown, a large unorganized body cannot cope with a small organized one. Under such conditions there would be an increasing deduction from the aggregate produce by those new ruling classes, a widening separation of them from the ruled, and a growing assumption of superior rank. There must arise a new aristocracy for the support of which the masses would toil; and which, being consolidated, would wield a power far beyond that of any past aristocracy. Let any one contemplate the doings of the recent Trade Union Congress (September, 1896), whence delegates from societies that had tolerated non-unionists were expelled, whence reporters of papers having employés not belonging to printers unions were obliged to withdraw, and where wholesale nationalization of property (which necessarily implies confiscation) was approved by four to one; and then ask what scruples would restrain a bureaucracy pervaded by this temper.

Of course nothing will make socialists foresee any such results. Just as the zealous adherent of a religious creed, met by some fatal objection, feels certain that though he does not see the answer yet a good answer is to be found; or just as the lover to whom defects of his mistress are pointed out, cannot be made calmly to consider what will result from them in married life; so the socialist, in love with his scheme, will not entertain adverse criticisms, or gives no weight to them if he does. Illustrations like those above given, accumulated no matter to what extent, will not convince him that the forms of social organization are determined by men's natures, and that only as their natures improve can the forms become better. He will continue to hope that selfish men may be so manipulated that they will behave unselfishly—that the effects of goodness may be had without the goodness. He has unwavering faith in a social alchemy which out of ignoble natures will get noble actions.

VI. The End of the Century

24

ADVICE TO THE MODERNIZERS OF JAPAN

[SPENCER was much read and admired in Japan, whose leaders consulted him on matters of educational and general policy. He was approached by Mori Arinori, Japanese Minister in London. The following extracts are from letters written in 1892 to Kaneko Kentaro, Cabinet Minister. Compare Spencer's view of colonialism with that of Marx on the British in India, "actuated by the vilest self-interest" but "the unconscious tool of History."]

Since writing to you on Sunday it has recurred to me, in pursuance of my remarks about Japanese affairs and the miscarriage of your constitution, to make a suggestion giving in a definite form such a conservative policy as I thought should be taken.

My advice to Mr. Mori was that the proposed new institutions should be as much as possible *grafted* upon the existing institutions, so as to prevent breaking the continuity—that there should not be a *replacing* of old forms by new, but a modification of old forms to a gradually increasing extent. I did not at the time go into the matter so far as to suggest in what way this might be done, but it now occurs to me that there is a very feasible way of doing it.

You have, I believe, in Japan still surviving the ancient system of family organization. . . . Under this family or patriarchal organization it habitually happens that there exists in each group an eldest male ascendant, who is the ruling authority of the group—

From *Life and Letters of Herbert Spencer*, by D. Duncan (London: Williams and Norgate, 1908), pp. 319–23.

an authority who has in many cases a despotic power to which all descendants of the first and second generations unhesitatingly submit. This organization should be made use of in your new political form. These patriarchs or heads of groups should be made the sole electors of members of your representative body. . . . Several beneficial results would arise. In the first place, your electorate would be greatly reduced in number, and therefore more manageable. In the second place, the various extreme opinions held by the members of each group would be to a considerable extent mutually cancelled and made more moderate by having to find expression through the patriarch who would in a certain measure be influenced by the opinions of his descendants. And then, in the third place, and chiefly, these patriarchal electors, being all aged men, would have more conservative leanings than the younger members of their groups—would not be in favour of rash changes.

In pursuance of the principle for which I have contended, that free institutions, to which the Japanese have been utterly unaccustomed, are certain not to work well, and that there must be a gradual adaptation to them, I suggest that, for three of four generations, the assembly formed of representative men elected by these patriarchial heads of groups should be limited in their functions to making *statements* of *grievances*, or of evils or what they think evils, which they wish to have remedied—not having any authority either to take measures for remedying them, or authority even for suggesting measures, but having the function simply of saying what they regard as grievances. This would be a function completely on the lines of the function of our own representative body in its earliest stages. . . .

After three or four generations during which this representative assembly was powerless to do more than state what they thought were grievances, there might come three or four other generations in which they should have the further power of suggesting remedies—not the power of passing remedial laws, such as is possessed by developed representative bodies, but the power of considering in what way they thought the evils might be met, and then sending up their suggestions to the House of Peers and the Emperor.

And then, after this had been for generations the function of the representative body, there might eventually be given to it a full power of legislation, co-ordinate with that of the other two legislative authorities. Such an organization would make possible the long-continued discipline which is needful for use of political power, at the same time that it would at once do away with the possibilities of these quarrels from which you are now suffering.

Respecting the further questions you ask, let me, in the first place, answer generally that the Japanese policy should, I think, be that of *keeping Americans and Europeans as much as possible at arm's length.* In presence of the more powerful races your position is one of chronic danger, and you should take every precaution to give as little foothold as possible to foreigners.

It seems to me that the only forms of intercourse which you may with advantage permit are those which are indispensable for the exchange of commodities and exchange of ideas—importation and exportation of physical and mental products. No further privileges should be allowed to people of other races, and especially to people of the more powerful races, than is absolutely needful for the achievement of these ends. Apparently you are proposing by revision of the treaty powers with Europe and America "to open the whole Empire to foreigners and foreign capital." I regard this as a fatal policy. If you wish to see what is likely to happen, study the history of India. Once let one of the more powerful races gain a *point d'appui* and there will inevitably in course of time grow up an aggressive policy which will lead to collisions with the Japanese; these collisions will be represented as attacks by the Japanese which must be avenged; forces will be sent from America or Europe, as the case may be; a portion of territory will be seized and required to be made over as a foreign settlement; and from this there will grow eventually subjugation of the entire Japanese Empire. I believe that you will have great difficulty in avoiding this fate in any case, but you will make the process easy if you allow any privileges to foreigners beyond those which I have indicated.

In pursuance of the advice thus generally indicated, I should say, in answer to your first question, that there should be, not only a prohibition to foreign persons to hold property in land, but also a refusal to give them leases, and a permission only to reside as annual tenants.

To the second question I should say decidedly, prohibit to foreigners the working of the mines owned or worked by Government. Here there would be obviously liable to arise grounds of difference between the Europeans or Americans who worked them and the Government, and these grounds of difference would immediately become grounds of quarrel, and would be followed by invocations to the English or American Governments or other Powers to send forces to insist on whatever the European workers claimed, *for always the habit here and elsewhere among the civilized peoples is to believe what their agents or settlers abroad represent to them.*

In the third place, in pursuance of the policy I have indicated, you ought also to keep the coasting trade in your own hands and forbid foreigners to engage in it. This coasting trade is clearly not included in the requirement I have indicated as the sole one to be recognized—a requirement to facilitate exportation and importation of commodities. The distribution of commodities brought to Japan from other places may be properly left to the Japanese themselves, and should be denied to foreigners, for the reason that again the various transactions involved would become so many doors open to quarrels and resulting aggressions.

To your remaining question, respecting the inter-marriage of foreigners and Japanese, which you say is "now very much agitated among our scholars and politicians," and which you say is "one of the most difficult problems," my reply is that, as rationally answered, there is no difficulty at all. It should be positively forbidden. It is not at root a question of social philosophy. It is at root a question of biology. There is abundant proof, alike furnished by the inter-marriages of human races and by the inter-breeding of animals, that when the varieties mingled diverge beyond a certain slight degree *the result is invariably a bad one* in the long run. I have myself been in the habit of looking at the evidence bearing on this matter for many years past, and my conviction is based upon numerous facts derived from numerous sources. This conviction

I have within the last half hour verified, for I happen to be staying in the country with a gentleman who is well known as an authority on horses, cattle and sheep, and knows much respecting their interbreeding; and he has just, on inquiry, fully confirmed my belief that when, say of different varieties of sheep, there is an interbreeding of *those which are widely unlike*, the result, especially in the second generation, is a bad one—there arises an incalculable mixture of traits, and what may be called a chaotic constitution. And the same thing happens among human beings—the Eurasians in India, and the half-breeds in America, show this. The physiological basis of this experience appears to be that any one variety of creature in course of many generations acquires a certain constitutional adaptation to its particular form of life, and every other variety similarly acquires its own special adaptation. The consequence is that, if you mix the constitutions of two widely divergent varieties which have severally become adapted to widely divergent modes of life, you get a constitution which is adapted to the mode of life of neither—a constitution which will not work properly, because it is not fitted for any set of conditions whatever. By all means, therefore, peremptorily interdict marriages of Japanese with foreigners.

I have for the reasons indicated entirely approved of the regulations which have been established in America for restraining the Chinese immigration, and had I the power would restrict them to the smallest possible amount, my reasons for this decision being that one of two things must happen. If the Chinese are allowed to settle extensively in America, they must either, if they remain unmixed, form a subject race in the position, if not of slaves, yet of a class approaching to slaves; or if they mix they must form a bad hybrid. In either case, supposing the immigration to be large, immense social mischief must arise, and eventually social disorganization. The same thing will happen if there should be any considerable mixture of the European or American races with the Japanese.

You see, therefore, that my advice is strongly conservative in all directions, and I end by saying as I began—*keep other races at arm's length as much as possible.*

25

RETROSPECT AND PROSPECT

[FROM A LETTER to R. Buchanan, 1890.] Sanguine of human progress as I used to be in earlier days, I am now more and more persuaded that it cannot take place faster than human nature is itself modified; and the modification is a slow process, to be reached only through many, many generations. When I see the behaviour of these union men in the strikes we have had and are having; when I see their unscrupulous tyranny and utter want of any true conception of liberty, it seems to me unquestionable that any new *régime* constituted in their interests would soon lapse into a despotic organization of a merciless type.

[Letters to J. A. Skilton, 1895.] If, as it would seem, you think that I have got a scheme for the future of society in my head you are altogether mistaken. Your conception of applied sociology—a bringing to bear of evolutionary principles on social organization with a view to its improvement—is one which I do not entertain. The sole thing about which I feel confident is that no higher types of social organization can grow until international antagonisms and, consequently, wars cease. . . . You have faith in teaching, which I have not—you believe men are going to be changed in their conduct by being shown what line of conduct is rational. I believe no such thing. Men are not rational beings, as commonly

---

From *Life and Letters of Herbert Spencer*, by D. Duncan (London: Williams and Norgate, 1908), pp. 335, 366–67, 410; *The Principles of Sociology* (London: Williams and Norgate, 1896), vol. 3, part 8, pp. 598–601.

supposed. A man is a bundle of instincts, feelings, sentiments, which severally seek their gratification, and those which are in power get hold of the reason and use it to their own ends, and exclude all other sentiments and feelings from power. . . . There is no hope for the future save in the slow modification of human nature under social discipline. Not teaching, but action is the requisite cause. To have to lead generation after generation a life that is honest and sympathetic is the one indispensable thing. No adequate change of character can be produced in a year, or in a generation, or in a century. All which teaching can do—all which may, perhaps, be done by a wider diffusion of principles of sociology, is the checking of retrograde action. The analogy supplied by an individual life yields the true conception. You cannot in any considerable degree change the course of individual growth and organization—in any considerable degree antedate the stages of development. But you can, in considerable degree, by knowledge put a check upon those courses of conduct which lead to pathological states and accompanying degradations.

Any one who wishes to aid social advance should devote all his energies to showing, that no fundamental and permanent progress in social life can be made while warlike activities and the social organization appropriate to them continue. . . .

A true theory of social progress is not a *cause* of movement but is simply oil to the movement—serves simply to remove friction. The force producing the movement is the aggregate of men's instincts and sentiments, and these are not to be changed by a theory.

[Letter to M. D. Conway regarding a proposed international "supreme court of civilization," to prevent aggression; at the time of the Spanish-American War, 1898.] I sympathize in your feelings and your aims, but not in your hopes. . . . In people's present mood nothing can be done in that direction.

Now that the white savages of Europe are overrunning the dark savages everywhere—now that the European nations are vying with one another in political burglaries—now that we have entered upon an era of social cannibalism in which the strong nations are devouring the weaker—now that national interests, national prestige, pluck, and so forth are alone thought of, and equity has utterly dropped out of thought, while rectitude is scorned as "unctuous," it is useless to resist the wave of barbarism. There is a bad time coming, and civilized mankind will (morally) be uncivilized before civilization can again advance.

Such a body as that which you propose, even could its members agree, would be pooh-poohed as sentimental and visionary. The universal aggressiveness and universal culture of blood-thirst will bring back military despotism, out of which after many generations partial freedom may again emerge. . . .

[The concluding chapter of the *Principles of Sociology*. Note that Spencer closes with a quotation from *Social Statics*.] How long this phase of social life to which we are approaching will last, and in what way it will come to an end, are of course questions not to be answered. Probably the issue will be here of one kind and there of another. A sudden bursting of bonds which have become intolerable may in some cases happen: bringing on a military despotism. In other cases practical extinction may follow a gradual decay, arising from absolution of the normal relation between merit and benefit, by which alone the vigour of a race can be maintained. And in yet further cases may come conquest by peoples who have not yet emasculated by fostering their feebles—peoples before whom the socialistic organization will go down like a house of cards, as did that of the ancient Peruvians before a handful of Spaniards.

But if the process of evolution which, unceasing throughout past time, has brought life to its present height, continues throughout the future, as we cannot but anticipate, then, amid all the rhythmical changes in each society, amid all the lives and deaths of nations, amid all the supplantings of race by race, there will go on that adaptation of human nature to the social state which began when savages first gathered together into hordes for mutual defence—an adaptation finally complete. Many will think this a wild imagination. Though everywhere around them are creatures with structures and instincts which have been gradually so moulded as to subserve their own welfares and the welfares of their species, yet the immense majority ignore the implication that human beings, too, have been undergoing in the past, and will undergo in the future, progressive adjustments to the lives imposed on them by circumstances. But there are a few who think it rational to conclude that what has happened with all lower forms must happen with the highest form—a few who infer that among types of men those most fitted for making a well-working society will, hereafter as heretofore, from time to time emerge and spread at the expense of types less fitted, until a fully fitted type has arisen.

The view thus suggested must be accepted with qualifications. If we carry our thoughts as far forward as palæolithic implements carry them back, we are introduced, not to an absolute optimism but to a relative optimism. The cosmic process brings about retrogression as well as progression, where the conditions favour it. Only amid an infinity of modifications, adjusted to an infinity of changes of circumstances, do there now and then occur some which constitute an advance: other changes meanwhile caused in other organisms, usually not constituting forward steps in organization, and often constituting steps backwards. Evolution does not imply a latent tendency to improve, everywhere in operation. There is no uniform ascent from lower to higher, but only an occasional production of a form which, in virtue of greater fitness for more complex conditions, becomes capable of a longer life of a more varied kind. And while such higher type begins to dominate over lower types and to spread at their expense, the lower types survive in habitats or modes of life that are not usurped, or are thrust into inferior habitats or modes of life in which they retrogress.

What thus holds with organic types must hold also with types of societies. Social evolution throughout the future, like social evolution throughout the past, must, while producing step after step higher societies, leave outstanding many lower. Varieties of men adapted here to inclement regions, there to regions that are barren, and elsewhere to regions unfitted, by ruggedness of surface or insalubrity, for supporting large populations, will, in all probability, continue to form small communities of simple structures. Moreover, during future competitions among the higher races there will probably be left, in the less desirable regions, minor nations formed of men inferior to the highest; at the same time that the highest overspread all the great areas which are desirable in climate and fertility. But while the entire assemblage of societies thus fulfils the law of evolution by increase of heterogeneity,—while within each of them contrasts of structure, caused by differences of environment and entailed occupations, cause unlikenesses implying further heterogeneity; we may infer that the primary process of evolution—integration—which up to the present time has been displayed in the formation of larger and larger nations, will eventually reach a still higher stage and bring yet greater benefits. As, when small tribes were welded into great tribes, the head chief stopped inter-tribal warfare; as when small feudal governments became subject to a king, feudal wars were prevented by him; so, in time to come, a federation of the highest nations, exercising supreme authority (already foreshadowed by occasional arrangements among "the Powers"), may, by forbidding wars between any of its constituent nations, put an end to the re-barbarization which is continually undoing civilization.

When this peace-maintaining federation has been formed, there may be effectual progress towards that equilibrium between constitution and conditions—between inner faculties and outer requirements—implied by the final stage of human evolution. Adaptation to the social state, now perpetually hindered by anti-social conflicts, may then go on unhindered; and all the great societies, in other respects differing, may become similar in those cardinal traits which result from complete self-ownership of the unit and exercise over him of nothing more than passive influence by the aggregate. On the one hand, by continual repression of aggressive instincts and exercise of feelings which prompt ministration to public welfare, and on the other hand by the lapse of restraints, gradually becoming less necessary, there must be produced a kind of man so constituted that while fulfilling his own desires he fulfils also the social needs. Already, small groups of men, shielded by circumstances from external antagonisms, have been moulded into forms of moral nature so superior to our own, that, as said of the Let-htas, the account of their goodness "almost savours of romance"; and it is reasonable to infer that what has even now happened on a small scale, may, under kindred conditions, eventually happen on a large scale. Long studies, showing among other things the need for certain qualifications above indicated, but also revealing facts like that just named, have not caused me to recede from the belief expressed nearly fifty years ago that—"The ultimate man will be one whose private requirements coincide with public ones. He will be that manner of man who, in spontaneously fulfilling his own nature, incidentally performs the functions of a social unit; and yet is only enabled so to fulfil his own nature by all others doing the like."

Select Bibliography on Herbert Spencer

Abrams, P. *The Origins of British Sociology 1834–1914.* Heritage of Sociology. University of Chicago Press, 1968.

Bock, K. E. *The Acceptance of Histories: Towards a Perspective for Social Science.* Berkeley: University of California Press, 1956.

Brinton, C. "Spencer's Horrid Vision," *Foreign Affairs* 15 (1936–37).

Burrow, J. W. *Evolution and Society: a Study in Victorian Social Theory.* Cambridge University Press, 1966.

Carneiro, R. L. "Spencer, Herbert." *International Encyclopaedia of the Social Sciences,* 1968.

———. Introduction to Spencer's *The Principles of Sociology.* Classics in Anthropology. University of Chicago Press, 1969.

Duncan, D. *Life and Letters of Herbert Spencer.* London: Williams and Norgate, 1908.

Eisen, S. "Herbert Spencer and the Spectre of Comte." *Journal of British Studies* 7 (1967).

———. "Frederic Harrison and Herbert Spencer: Embattled Unbelievers." *Victorian Studies* 12 (1968).

Fine, S. *Laissez-Faire and the General Welfare State.* Ann Arbor: University of Michigan Press, 1956.

Gurvitch, G. *Trois chapitres de la sociologie: Comte, Marx et Spencer.* Paris: Centre de Documentation Universitaire, 1955.

Harris, M. *The Rise of Anthropological Theory.* London: Routledge and Kegan Paul, 1969.

Hearnshaw, F.J.C. *The Social and Political Ideas of Some Representative Thinkers of the Victorian Age.* London, 1933.

Hofstadter, R. *Social Darwinism in American Thought.* Boston: Beacon Press, 1955.

Kardiner, A., and Preble, E. *They Studied Man.* New York: Mentor Books, 1963.

MacRae, D. G. Introduction to Spencer's *The Man v. the State*. Harmondsworth: Penguin, 1970.

Nisbet, R. A. *Social Change and History: Aspects of the Western Theory of Development*. New York: Oxford University Press, 1969.

Peel, J.D.Y. "Spencer and the Neo-Evolutionists." *Sociology* 3 (1969).

———. *Herbert Spencer: The Evolution of a Sociologist*. London: Heinemann, 1971.

Rumney, J. *Herbert Spencer's Sociology*. New York: Atherton Press, 1934.

Russett, C. E. *The Concept of Equilibrium in American Social Thought*. Yale University Press, 1966.

Simon, W. H. "Herbert Spencer and the Social Organism." *Journal of the History of Ideas* 21 (1960).

Stark, W. "Herbert Spencer's Three Sociologies." *American Sociological Review* 26 (1961).

Stocking, G. W. *Race, Culture and Evolution*. New York: Free Press of Glencoe, 1968.

Taylor, A. J. "The Originality of Herbert Spencer." *Studies in English* 34 (1955).

Young, R. M. "Malthus and the Evolutionists." *Past and Present* 43 (1969).

———. *Mind, Brain and Adaptation in the Nineteenth Century*, Oxford: Clarendon Press, 1970.

There is a full bibliography of Spencer's own writings in Rumney, 1934.

Index